英语专业实用翻译教材系列

廖益清　主编

English-Chinese Simultaneous Interpreting

英汉同声传译

廖益清　高平　主编

中山大学出版社
SUN YAT-SEN UNIVERSITY PRESS
· 广州 ·

版权所有　翻印必究

图书在版编目（CIP）数据

英汉同声传译/廖益清，高平主编. —广州：中山大学出版社，2020.1
（英语专业实用翻译教材系列/廖益清主编）
ISBN 978-7-306-06674-9

Ⅰ.①英… Ⅱ.①廖… ②高… Ⅲ.①英语—同声翻译—高等学校—教材 Ⅳ.①H315.9

中国版本图书馆CIP数据核字（2019）第163043号

出 版 人：王天琪
策划编辑：熊锡源
责任编辑：熊锡源
封面设计：林绵华
责任校对：卢思敏
责任技编：何雅涛
出版发行：中山大学出版社
电　　话：编辑部 020 - 84111997，84110283，84110779
　　　　　发行部 020 - 84111998，84111981，84111160
地　　址：广州市新港西路135号
邮　　编：510275　　传　　真：020 - 84036565
网　　址：http://www.zsup.com.cn　E-mail：zdcbs@mail.sysu.edu.cn
印　　刷：佛山市浩文彩色印刷有限公司
规　　格：787mm×1092mm　1/16　14印张　290千字
版次印次：2020年1月第1版　2020年1月第1次印刷
定　　价：42.00元

如发现本书因印装质量影响阅读，请与出版社发行部联系调换

编写委员会

主　编：廖益清　高　平
副主编：朱雪娇　何　瑜　龙　娟
参　编：桂　灵　刘家妠　鲁凯伦　陈悦笛　罗彩虹
　　　　陈秋丽　梁昊文　黄越悦　姚　莹　肖岚心
　　　　周雪清

编写说明

随着中国经济持续、快速、健康发展，中国与世界各国在各个领域的交流也更加密切，对口译，尤其是同声传译的需求也越来越大。对于同声传译学习者而言，好的同声传译练习素材是提高口译能力的第一步。《英汉同声传译》借鉴了同类教材的优点，将口译理论与实践相结合，突出了自身同传素材的真实性、时代性的特点，旨在为广大同传学习者提供最好的同传模拟实战体验。

教材特点

1. 科学性。教材吸收了同传最新理论研究成果，以深入浅出的方式讲解理论知识，并将理论与典型的材料相结合，具有很强的针对性。题材多样，均为真实同传场景中的常见主题。

2. 真实性。当前市场上的英汉同传教材所使用的材料基本都是经过修改和重新编排的，本教材所使用的材料则是编者在同传实战中的原声同传材料，讲话中会出现口误、模糊、停顿等现象，实操性更强，更能锻炼学生临场应变能力，让学生在使用教材时有身临其境之感。

3. 口音多样化。所使用的音频为同传现场的演讲录音，很多演讲者发音并不标准，会有各种英语口音，这在一定程度上增加了同传的难度，同传材料的真实感和实操性更强。

4. 时代性。所使用的实战材料均来自于近年的同传实战，材料紧跟时代，如大数据和物联网都是当前热门话题，教材实用性较强。

章节介绍

本书共3部分、12单元。第一部分为同传概论，共2单元，每单元都包括同传概论、实战练习一和实战练习二。第二部分为同传技巧，共4单元，每单元都包括同传技巧、实战练习一和实战练习二。第三部分为同传实战，共6单元，每单元都包括实战练习一和实战练习二。所有的实战练习均为英译中，每篇演讲都由演讲背景、预习词汇、演讲文本3个部分组成。练习材料的主题涉及文化教育、观光旅游、酒店管理、金融服务、行业介绍、性别平等、研发合作、商事仲裁、时尚潮流、建筑和城市规划、知识产权和科学技术。值得一提的是，本书以段落形式将演讲原文和译文对应起来，方便同传学习者在同传练习之后进行参考。各章节简介如下：

第一单元对同传进行了简介，介绍了同传的几大特点。实战练习一为英国驻广州总领事馆总领事在一次交流会上的致辞。实战练习二为美国驻广州总领事馆总领事在"中美教育高峰论坛"上的致辞。

第二单元介绍了同传译员的职业操守，包括扎实的双语能力、丰富的百科知识、良好的心理素质、良好的团队合作精神以及优秀的职业操守。实战练习一为联合国妇女署中国国别主任在"2017 性别平等与企业社会责任：可持续发展之道"的"2017 性别平等与企业社会责任国际会议"上的致辞。实战练习二为"波兰独立之女性研讨会"上开展的讨论。

第三单元介绍了记忆训练，包括源语单语连续复述和影子训练。实战练习一为库克船长游轮公司代表在"2012 西澳大利亚州旅游局中国旅游洽谈会"上的演讲。实战练习二为尖峰旅行社的代表在"2012 西澳大利亚州旅游局中国旅游洽谈会"上的演讲。

第四单元介绍了顺句驱动原则。实战练习一为"亚洲酒店论坛集团高管会议"上嘉宾的小组讨论。实战练习二同样为"亚洲酒店论坛集团高管会议"上的小组讨论。

第五单元介绍了有稿同传，讲解了如何准备有稿同传和如何练习视译。实战练习一为英国驻广州总领事馆的代理总领事在"2016 英国—广东金融人才培训高峰论坛"上的致辞。实战练习二为英国贸易投资总署伦敦总部教育产业（中国）及金融专业培训副总监在"2016 英国—广东金融人才培训高峰论坛"上发表的主旨演讲。

第六单元介绍了同传中数字的处理，包括数字转换的基本方法、倍数、数字的趋势和数值以及模糊处理。实战练习一为全球前四大市场研究公司之一的 GfK 捷孚凯公司的家电部全球大客户副总裁在"2017 年广交会系列论坛——中国电子家电品牌与创新高峰论坛"上发表的题为"智能家居演变"的演讲。实战练习二为印度京德勒集团代表在"不锈钢产业发展大会"上发表的主旨演讲。

在第七单元中，实战练习一为斯科尔科沃园区驻华代表在"建设世界一流高科技园区国际会议"上发表的主旨演讲。实战练习二为美国律师 Jeffery 在"建设世界一流高科技园区国际会议"上发表的演讲。

在第八单元中，实战练习一为德和信律师事务所的律师在"国际仲裁峰会"上就"如何选择仲裁机构与仲裁员"发表的主旨演讲。实战练习二为德和信律师事务所的代表在"国际仲裁峰会"上发表的另一个主旨演讲。

在第九单元中，实战练习一为在线时尚潮流预测公司 Fashion Snoops 的亚太区总监在"广交会设计潮流趋势研讨会"上发表的有关于"叛逆少女"的演讲。实战练习二为在线时尚潮流预测公司 Fashion Snoops 的亚太区总监在"广交会设计潮流趋势研讨会"上发表的有关于"嘲弄艺术"的演讲。

在第十单元中，实战练习一为贝诺建筑事务所全球设计总监在"中英建筑论坛（珠海站）"上发表的主旨演讲。实战练习二为英国维尔金森·艾尔建筑事务所的亚太总监在"中英建筑论坛（珠海站）"上发表的主旨演讲。

在第十一单元中，实战练习一为美国联邦巡回上诉法院前首席法官、清华大学法学教授在深圳举行的"企业涉外知识产权讲座"中发表的演讲的第一部分内容。实战练习二为其在同一个活动中发表的演讲的第二部分内容。

在第十二单元中，实战练习一为被誉为"大数据之父"的牛津大学教授 Viktor Mayer Schonberger 在"美赛达汽车后市场新商业模式论坛"上发表的演讲。实战练习二为被誉为"物联网之父"的 Kevin Ashton 在"2015年腾讯智慧峰会"上的主旨发言。

使用对象

本书是本科英语专业或翻译专业学生的英汉同传教材，也可作为选修、辅修英语专业或翻译专业学生的英汉同传教材，同时可以作为有志于提高英汉同传实践能力爱好者的自学教材。

结语

本书在理论编写过程中，参考了同声传译的最新研究成果，且均已在教材最后标明出处。如有不当之处，敬请原谅。本书使用的实战练习均为国际会议材料，音频为会议现场录音，非常感谢演讲嘉宾和会议主办方的支持。

由于编写时间有限，本书难免存在一些纰漏，请各位专家和读者指正。

编　者

2019 年 8 月

MPR出版物链码使用说明

  本书中凡文字下方带有链码图标"——"的地方,均可通过"泛媒阅读"的"扫一扫"功能,扫描链码获得对应的多媒体内容。您可以通过扫描下方的二维码下载"泛媒阅读"APP。

目　　录

第一部分　同传概论 ·· 1

第一单元　文化教育 Culture and Education ·· 2
　　I. 同传简介 ·· 2
　　II. 实战练习一 ·· 2
　　III. 实战练习二 ··· 5

第二单元　性别平等 Gender Equality ·· 9
　　I. 职业操守 ·· 9
　　II. 实战练习一 ·· 10
　　III. 实战练习二 ··· 14

第二部分　同传技巧 ·· 27

第三单元　观光旅游 Tourism ·· 28
　　I. 记忆训练 ·· 28
　　II. 实战练习一 ·· 29
　　III. 实战练习二 ··· 35

第四单元　酒店管理 Hotel Management ·· 41
　　I. 顺句驱动 ·· 41
　　II. 实战练习一 ·· 43
　　III. 实战练习二 ··· 52

第五单元　金融服务 Financial Service ·· 65
　　I. 有稿同传 ·· 65
　　II. 实战练习一 ·· 66
　　III. 实战练习二 ··· 69

第六单元　行业介绍 Introduction to Industries ····································· 78
　　I. 数字处理 ·· 78
　　II. 实战练习一 ·· 80
　　III. 实战练习二 ··· 93

第三部分　同传实战 ·· 101

第七单元　研发合作 R&D Cooperation ·· 102
　　I. 实战练习一 ·· 102

  II. 实战练习二 ·········· 109

第八单元 商事仲裁 Commercial Arbitration ·········· 117
  I. 实战练习一 ·········· 117
  II. 实战练习二 ·········· 127

第九单元 时尚潮流 Fashion Trend ·········· 133
  I. 实战练习一 ·········· 133
  II. 实战练习二 ·········· 138

第十单元 建筑和城市规划 Building and Urban Planning ·········· 146
  I. 实战练习一 ·········· 146
  II. 实战练习二 ·········· 153

第十一单元 知识产权 Intellectual Property Rights ·········· 164
  I. 实战练习一 ·········· 164
  II. 实战练习二 ·········· 172

第十二单元 科学技术 Science and Technology ·········· 181
  I. 实战练习一 ·········· 181
  II. 实战练习二 ·········· 197

参考文献 ·········· 213

第一部分 同传概论

第一单元 文化教育
Culture and Education

I. 同传简介

口译按工作方式可分为交替传译和同声传译。同声传译又可称为同步传译,是指在发言人讲话的同时,译员以与发言人几乎相同的速度把讲话的内容用口头形式表达出来。同传可分为无稿同传、有稿同传、耳语传译和同声传读。大多数情况下,同传译员都会使用专门的同传设备进行口译。译员坐在同传箱中,通过耳机接收发言人讲话的内容,使用麦克风将口译的内容传递给听众;听众可以通过手里的无线电接收设备,选择所需要的语言频道。

同传通常都是以两至三人搭档的形式进行工作,每位译员一般口译20分钟,接着由另外一名译员接替进行口译,这样轮流完成任务。

与交传相比,同传具有以下几个特征:

(1) 在同声传译中,口译与发言几乎同时进行,发言和口译可以持续进行,无需间断,与交传相比,可以节省很多时间。

(2) 同传口译直接受到发言人讲话速度的影响。如果发言人讲话速度过快、信息密集,译员往往没有足够的时间接收和处理信息,口译中可能会大量遗漏信息。发言人语速过慢时,译员为了等待完整的信息,译出来的译文可能会出现大量停顿,表述不流畅。

(3) 与交传相比,同传译文质量要求相对低一些。在交传中,译员是先听一个部分的信息,再开口翻译,因此有一定的时间进行信息调整;而在同传中,发言者讲话和译员口译几乎同步进行,则没有时间像交传那样调整信息,流畅度也会打折扣。因此,一般同传译文的质量相对而言低于交传。

II. 实战练习一

1. 演讲背景

被誉为"英国首相的摇篮"的英国伊顿公学的下属伊顿英学团队 EtonX 来到深圳,与中山大学附属外国语实验中学等约 30 所中国国际中学的校长进行交流,探讨国际教育现代化的有效途径。下文为英国驻广州总领事馆总领事的开幕致辞。他

第一单元 文化教育 Culture and Education

在演讲中提到了英国政府对国际教育的重视,以及伊顿公学和伊顿英学采用了现代化的教育方法确保学生全面发挥潜能,走向成功。

2. 预习词汇

British Consulate-General in Guangzhou 英国驻广州总领事馆
EtonX Discussion Forum on Modern Approaches to International Education 伊顿英学创建国际教育的现代化途径研讨会
UK Trade & Investment 英国贸易投资总署
Eton College 伊顿公学
ethos 理念

3. 演讲文本

00:00—00:26

Distinguished guests, ladies and gentlemen, very good afternoon! On behalf of the British Consulate-General here in Guangzhou, here in Shenzhen today, welcome to this EtonX Discussion Forum on Modern Approaches to International Education. I am delighted to open today's international education event.

尊敬的各位来宾,女士们,先生们:大家下午好!我谨代表英国驻广州总领事馆,今天在深圳,欢迎在座各位参加伊顿英学创建国际教育的现代化途径研讨会。我很高兴能为今天的会议做开场致辞。

00:26—01:15

The international education sector is an important focus for British Consulate-General here in Southern China and for British Government throughout China. In 2015, the British Consulate-General and UK Trade & Investment have held a number of international schools' workshops in Beijing, in Shanghai. And all of them have been extremely well received by the industry. Just last month, I was in Changsha at a highly-successful seminar on international education, which took place with a wide range of British companies and investors involved. Today our purpose is to discuss best practice in this fast-growing sector.

国际教育是我们关注的重点领域,英国总领事馆在华南地区以及英国政府在整个中国都相当关注。2015年,英国驻广州总领事和英国贸易投资总署举办了一系列国际学校研讨会,分别在北京、上海举行,广受业内好评。上个月,我在长沙参加了一场十分成功的国际教育研讨会,(它)吸引了很多英国企业和投资者参加。今天,我们要探讨迅速发展的教育行业中的最佳实践。

01: 15—02: 30

Everyone here in one way or another is involved in ensuring the best educational outcomes for Chinese students, often with higher education overseas as the goal. When we think of Chinese students succeeding in accessing education overseas, it's very easy to focus solely on the academic aspects of that success. However, as our speakers from Eton College and from EtonX will show, the Eton ethos is much broader than a focus on pure academic achievement. I think they will demonstrate that a modern education, or a modern approach to international education can and should ensure that the student is allowed to develop to their fullest potential in all areas of their life. The goal of all educators and for their students is not just a successful academic life, but a successful life afterwards too, in whatever shape that may take.

在座各位都在以某种方式确保中国学生能获得最好的教学效果，通常以在海外接受高等教育为目标。一想到中国学生成功获得海外教育，我们很容易只关注他们的学业成绩。然而，伊顿公学和伊顿英学的演讲嘉宾将会告诉各位，伊顿的理念更为宽广，不仅仅是关注学生的学业成绩。我想他们会告诉大家，现代教育，或者国际教育的现代化途径，能够并且应该确保学生能充分发挥自己的潜能，全方位发挥。所有教育工作者对学生的目标并非只是学术拔尖，而是走出校门后能有成功的人生，无论他们日后从事什么职业。

02: 30—03: 45

Today we will hear how modern approaches are evolving, deploying educational technology and digital content to help teachers teach and students learn in new and different ways, but also hear how teaching itself can change to ensure that it's the student who is in control of their own learning, facilitated rather than directed by their teachers. This afternoon is designed to be a cultural exchange between Eton College, possibly the best-known school in the United Kingdom, and schools here in Shenzhen and from Guangdong. The masters are all here very much to learn from their counterparts here in China in the spirit of cultural cooperation through dialogue and ongoing learning. I hope very much that you enjoy the opportunity to learn from each other. So thank you very much for taking the time to listen to me this afternoon! I'll now hand over the floor back to Simon to carry on with today's proceedings. Thank you very much!

今天，我们将会听到教育现代化途径的发展进程，如何采用教育技术和数字内容帮助教师授课，帮助学生以全新的方式学习，还会听到上课方式本身是可以改变的，以确保学生能自己掌控学习进度，老师是引导而不是主导学生的学习。今天下午的会议是一场文化交流活动，伊顿公学——或许是全英国最著名的学校与深圳以及广东的学校之间开展交流。在座的英国专家学者能借此机会向各位中国同行学习,秉承文化合作交流和不断学习的精神。我热切期盼大家能把握这次机会相互学习。感谢大家抽空聆听我的演讲!现在有请西蒙继续主持今天的议程,谢谢大家!

III. 实战练习二

1. 演讲背景

2016年,美国驻广州总领事应邀参加以"一流教学:'双一流'大学建设的核心"为主题的"中美教育高峰论坛"并发表开幕致辞。他在致辞中强调了教育对于中美两国的重要性,也谈到了教育技术有助于提高学生的学习成果和效率。呼吁在座的嘉宾积极了解毕博信息技术公司的最新教育学习管理系统。最后还提到了美国大力支持教育技术创新,中国最有潜力使用这些新技术。

2. 预习词汇

diplomat 外交官
old-fashioned 老旧的
Tencent 腾讯
WeChat 微信
incumbent 义不容辞的
Blackboard 毕博信息技术公司
higher education 高等教育
Purdue University 普渡大学

3. 演讲文本

00:00—00:49

I am very excited to be here today. I think education is one of those issues where it doesn't matter where our countries are on other issues, whether we agree or disagree. One thing we all agree on is that education is so important for our children and for the future generations of young people in our countries. And I think for that reason, this event is very, very important. It is also a special event for me because in the former life before I was a diplomat, I was a teacher. When I was a teacher, we didn't have the technology that we have today. We were still writing on blackboards and doing things in a very old-fashioned way. I won't even tell you how long ago that was because it was a long time ago and I will give away my age I am afraid.

非常高兴能出席今天的活动。教育这个问题,无论我们两国能否在其他问题上达成共识,我们都赞同教育对于我们的孩子,我们两国的子孙后代都至关重要。出于这个原因，本次活动非常重要。这个活动对于我而言也很特别，因为我在成为一名外交官之前，是一名教师。那时候我们没有今天这样的技术。我们还在黑板上写字，用老旧的方式教学。我不会告诉大家那是什么时候的事情，因为实在是很久很久以前了，说了就会泄露我的年龄。

00：49—01：46

But it is exciting to be here today to learn more about these new technologies that are really helping young people learn better and learn more efficiently. Technology today is advancing at such a fast pace I think we can hardly keep up with it. Apple has introduced the iPhone 7. The other day, I went to Tencent to talk to the people at WeChat. Just amazing all of the technology that is evolving today. I think it is incumbent upon all of you as educators and administrators to try as best as you can to keep up with that technology. Because you know that the young people that you are teaching are going to be using that technology. So I think it is important for the teachers and the professors and the administrators to be able to use that technology also.

今天非常高兴来到这里，更多地了解新技术，这些技术帮助年轻人学得更好更高效。技术日新月异，我们很难跟上技术革新的步伐。苹果公司刚推出了iPhone 7。我前几天还去访问了腾讯公司，和微信部门的员工交谈。当今技术革新的速度让我惊叹不已。在座各位教育工作者、行政人员义不容辞，要竭尽全力跟上技术发展的步伐，因为你们教导的年轻人也要使用这些技术。关键是老师们、教授们和行政人员都能够使用这些技术。

01：46—02：20

The Internet has really transformed our world in many, many ways. And I think in education that is particularly so. We now, I think, use technology in an educational setting to help transform how people think and help them learn more efficiently and learn a broader range of topics and subjects. And I think that is really exciting for people in this room and for myself.

互联网改变了世界的方方面面。教育界尤其如此。我们在教育界使用技术改变人们的思维方式，提高学习效率，学习更多的主题和学科。这对于在座的各位以及我本人，都是非常激动人心的进步。

02：20—03：12

Blackboard, I understand, was founded in 1997. So it is not a new company. It has been around for a long time. Since 1997, Blackboard has been innovating and developing ways in which classrooms can be run more efficiently and in ways that can help instructors and teachers to teach young people. It is now I think the most well-known learning management system, educational learning management system in the world. And my colleague Catherine said that when she was in university, which was much more recently than I was, she used Blackboard. So you all know about this. I must admit I don't know very much about it. But I am glad to know that people who are in the room know more about this technology.

毕博信息技术公司,据我所知,成立于1997年。它并不是一家初创公司,已经有一段历史了。该公司自创立以来,一直致力于创新和研发,提高教学效率,帮助老师们更好地授课。我认为它是世界上最有名的教育学习管理系统。我的同事凯瑟琳说,她读大学的时候,她读大学比我晚多了,她说她就用毕博的系统。你们都了解毕博系统,我得承认我了解的不多,但我非常高兴得知在座的各位对这项技术有深入的了解。

03:12—03:48

In 2014, President Obama demonstrated his support for educational technology by allocating nearly half a billion, one half billion dollars to fund continued development and implementation of educational technological innovation. Even though there has been great support in this field, there is still much more that we can do, I think, both here in China and in the US to help give our students, give them a better and innovative educational experience.

2014年,奥巴马总统大力支持教育技术发展,拨款接近5亿美元,支持教育技术创新的持续开发和应用。尽管教育界已经获得了大力的支持,但我们还需要继续努力,中美两国都需要为我们的学生提供更好、更新的教育体验。

03:48—04:24

China, as we all know, has a tremendously large population. As China's economy develops, more and more people are looking to higher education. So I think China really does demonstrate or it is probably the one country in the world with so much potential to use these new technologies. Every day I hear of how much needs there is for more education, more higher education in China. What China is doing is to try to accommodate young people in China and to provide that kind of education.

中国是众所周知的人口大国。随着中国经济的发展,越来越多的人希望接受高等教育。中国的确展现了或者说它是世界上最有潜力使用这些新技术的国家。每天我都听说中国对教育、高等教育的需求很大。中国正努力满足年轻人的需求,为他们提供教育。

04:24—05:19

So I really hope that this meeting today, this forum will foster a better understanding of this kind of educational platforms and technologies. We have a lot of great speakers today. I have to say hello to my friend who I just met, Jason Fisch, from one of America's great universities, Purdue University, who I think will be speaking a little bit later today. I just want to again emphasize how important this kind of meetings are, because education, as I said at the outset, is really a bridge between our people. There are over 300,000 Chinese students studying in the US right now, and the number of American students studying in China grows and grows every year. So I think the numbers prove the point that education, what you are all involved in, is such an important part of our relationship, of our bilateral relationship between the United States and China.

希望今天的活动能够让大家更好地了解这些教育平台和技术。今天有很多杰出的演讲嘉宾。我得和我刚刚认识的朋友打招呼，他是杰森·菲什，来自美国著名高等学府普渡大学，我想他晚些时候会发表演讲。我还想再次强调这类会议的重要性，因为如我开场时所说，教育是连接中美两国人民的桥梁。超过30万中国学生在美国求学，在中国学习的美国学生数量逐年攀升。这些数字证明了教育，也正是大家所从事的行业，是中美双边关系的重要组成部分。

05:19—05:27

So thank you again and best of luck. I look forward to learning a little bit more about this amazing technology. Thanks!

再次感谢大家，祝大家好运！期待进一步了解这项先进的技术。谢谢！

第二单元　性别平等
Gender Equality

I. 职业操守

同声传译涉及至少两种语言之间的文化交流，是集脑力与体力于一体的高强度活动，因此对同传译员的综合素质要求很高。一般来讲，同传译员应具备以下素质：

1. 扎实的双语能力

首先，一名合格的译员必须双语基本功扎实，能够规范的使用两种语言并流畅的进行双语转换。其次，译员应具有非常熟练的听解能力，不仅能听解发音标准的演讲，还要能够听解具有浓重地方口音的演讲，比如来自南亚地区的人们讲的英语。此外，译员还要熟悉两种语言的文化背景知识。同传译员还要能紧跟发言者的讲话速度，一定要"牙齿伶俐"，做到吐字清晰、语言流畅利落。

2. 丰富的百科知识

在同传实战中，会议主题涉及面宽，如计算机、医学、生物、法律等，不可避免会碰到较为专业的知识。如果译员平时了解某些主题，掌握较多的相关知识，在口译活动中若碰到这一主题，翻译起来则会游刃有余。

3. 良好的心理素质

口译是极具挑战性的工作，因此许多口译学习者在练习口译或者在初次接触口译任务时，通常会紧张胆怯。口译学习者需要通过大量的口译训练、自我情绪控制和不断积累实践经验来克服怯场紧张情绪，做到镇定自若。

4. 良好的团队合作精神

同传译员一般是2～3人一组搭档完成口译任务，每人20分钟左右则需要休息，另一个人接过来继续翻译，这样互相配合，轮流工作。而轮休的译员除了放松调整，在必要的情况下还要帮助同伴记笔记、查找资料等。

5. 优秀的职业操守

译员应严格遵守《国际会议口译工作者协会关于职业道德准则的规定》。一名合格的口译员应认真负责，保持中立性；应能正确评价自己，不接超出自己能力的口译任务；一旦承接了口译任务，就要全力以赴，表现出良好的业务水准。

II. 实战练习一

1. 演讲背景

联合国妇女署中国国别主任应邀参加主题为"性别平等与企业社会责任：可持续发展之道"的"2017性别平等与企业社会责任国际会议"并发表开幕致辞。她在致辞中谈到了联合国妇女署主办本次活动的初衷，强调了性别平等的重要性，并分享了两种可以推动企业社会责任中性别平等的方法，以及女性在就业和领导力方面的平等权利需要得到进一步保障的原因。

2. 预习词汇

Deputy Secretary-General of the Shenzhen Municipal Government 深圳市政府副秘书长

Shenzhen Municipal Women's Federation 深圳市妇联

All-China Women's Federation 全国妇联

Guangdong Women's Federation 广东省妇联

special guest 特邀嘉宾

International Conference on Gender Equality and Corporate Social Responsibility 性别平等与企业社会责任国际会议

Shenzhen Women and Children's Development Foundation 深圳市妇女儿童发展基金会

UN Women 联合国妇女署

Gender Equality and CSR: A Path to Sustainability 性别平等与企业社会责任：可持续发展之道

2017 Global Gender Gap Report《2017年全球性别差距报告》

World Economic Forum 世界经济论坛

publicly traded company 上市公司

gender-sensitive CSR strategy 性别敏感的企业社会责任策略

stakeholder 利益攸关方

3. 演讲文本

00：00—01：13

因为我的英语比我的普通话好听，所以我用英语讲话。你们都有耳机，抱歉！

第二单元 性别平等 Gender Equality

Ms Liu Jiachen, Deputy Secretary-General of the Shenzhen Municipal Government, Madam Ma Hong, Chairwoman of the Shenzhen Municipal Women's Federation, Ms An Weiwei of the All China Women's Federation, Ms Liu Lanni, Deputy Chairwoman of the Guangdong Women's Federation, ladies and gentlemen, special guests, Guan Yue and Wang Shi, good morning. I am very, very honored to be here today. I would like to warmly welcome everyone to this year's International Conference on Gender Equality and Corporate Social Responsibility. I would also like to thank the Shenzhen Women and Children's Development Foundation for co-hosting this event with us, and thank the Shenzhen Municipal Women's Federation for its role as the guiding organization.

My English is better than my Chinese. So I am going to speak in English. Please listen to the simultaneous interpretation. Sorry. 深圳市政府副秘书长刘佳晨女士,深圳市妇联主席马宏女士,来自全国妇联的安薇薇女士,广东省妇联副主席刘兰妮女士,女士们先生们,特邀嘉宾关悦女士和王石先生:早上好!非常荣幸能够参与这次会议。热烈欢迎各位参加今年的"性别平等与企业社会责任国际会议"。感谢深圳市妇女儿童发展基金会与我们联合国妇女署共同承办此次会议。也要感谢深圳市妇女联合会对本次会议的指导。

01:14—02:52

This annual conference was initiated by UN Women in 2015 and now has been running for three years. The intention of this conference is to provide a platform for representatives of the government, private sector, academic institutions, and NGOs to share experiences and ideas on mainstreaming gender equality through sustainable Corporate Social Responsibility strategies. Every year we gather together to discuss and share insights on how to better facilitate gender equality within the private sector. This year, we are very happy to hold the conference in Shenzhen, the city which is renowned for its economic development and innovation, and which also has had many good experiences in promoting gender equality, both at the municipal level and within many private sector corporations. The theme of today's event is *Gender Equality and CSR: A Path to Sustainability*. Gender equality is a precondition of global development, as the benefits of half of the population must be considered in all aspects of our work. Considering the prominent role that the private sector plays in economic and social development, integrating gender equality into companies' policies is fundamental to achieving sustainability through corporate social responsibility.

这个一年一度的会议在2015年由联合国妇女署发起,到目前为止已经举办了三届。此次会议旨在提供一个平台给来自政府、私营组织、学术机构以及非政府组织的代表们,交流关于性别平等的主流化经验和看法,并采取可持续的企业社会责任策略。每一年我们都会共聚一堂，讨论和分享关于如何更好地促进私营企业内部的性别平等。今年我们非常高兴这个会议在深圳举办。深圳以其经济发展和创新理念著称，也有许多有益的经验去推动性别平等，在城市层面以及民营企业层面都有丰富的经验。今天会议的主题是"性别平等与企业社会责任：可持续发展之道"。性别平等是全球发展的前提条件，因为全球一半的人口是女性，她们的福祉是我们在各方面的工作中都必须要考虑的。鉴于私营部门在促进经济和社会发展中起到的重要作用，将性别平等融入到公司政策中是至关重要的，有利于维持企业社会责任的可持续发展。

02:53—04:05

There are two ways that companies can promote gender equality in CSR. On one hand, companies can implement external CSR programs that aim to promote gender equality and women's rights in society; on the other hand, corporations can integrate gender equality into their internal policies and regulations, so that they can create a gender equal workplace, and benefit both their female and male employees. Discrimination against women in the workplace goes well beyond overt acts of prejudice, and encompasses more subtle and invisible forms of discrimination such as restricted access to opportunities, and equal pay. *The 2017 Global Gender Gap Report* released by the World Economic Forum found that, despite having nearly equal levels of labor force participation, only 9.4% of publicly traded companies in China had women on their boards.

有两种方法可以推动企业社会责任中的性别平等。一方面，公司可以实施外部的 CSR 项目，这可以推动性别平等的发展，以及保障妇女在社会中的权利。另一方面，企业可以将性别平等纳入到企业内部的政策和规章当中，以此创造一个平等的职场环境，造福男性和女性员工。在职场环境中对女性的歧视远远不止公然的偏见，还包括了各种更加微妙、无形的歧视，比如说机会受限、同工不同酬。《2017年全球性别差距报告》是由世界经济论坛发布的，报告表明，尽管男女员工数量几乎相当，只有 9.4% 的中国上市公司的董事会中有女性成员。

04:06—05:21

While doing very similar jobs, women earn only 64% of what men earn. Also, on top of traditional working hours, a woman completes more than double the amount of unpaid work that a man does on a daily basis. All of these phenomena indicate that women's equal rights in employment and leadership need to be further promoted. Raising awareness for these issues demonstrates a positive step towards encouraging all members and sectors of society to actively participate in gender equality. The purpose of today is, of course, not only to enhance participants' understanding of the importance of gender equality, or how to integrate gender into companies' CSR strategies and policies, but also to consider the practicality and longevity of these programs and their impact on society. Despite the progress made within the private sector, more work still needs to be done to guarantee that employees are fully acknowledging their responsibilities to implement gender-sensitive CSR strategies.

尽管从事非常相似的工作,女性的薪酬只有男性的64%。除了传统的工作时间以外,女性还需要完成无偿工作,每天的工作量是男性的两倍。上述种种现象表明,女性在就业和领导力方面的平等权利需要得到进一步保障。提高对待这些问题的意识是一种积极的举措,鼓励社会各界人士以及各行各业积极地参与到性别平等的活动中来。今天会议的目的,当然不仅仅是为了提高与会者对于性别平等重要性的理解,或者说如何将性别平等融入企业社会责任的策略和政策中去,而且也是为了考虑这些项目的实用性和持续性以及它们对社会的影响。尽管在私营企业内部已取得一些进展,但是我们还需做更多的工作来保障雇员充分意识到他们有责任去落实性别敏感的企业社会责任策略。

05:22—06:16

In addition to this, more work needs to be done to guarantee that employees are fully supported by relevant stakeholders when implementing such strategies. This is why conferences like these are so important, so that key players can become more equipped to work together to make a positive change. Once again, many thanks to the Shenzhen Municipal Women's Federation and the Shenzhen Women and Children's Development Foundation for your efforts in putting together this event and many thanks to the speakers and participants for making this event possible today. I hope that everybody finds the discussions interesting and useful. And I am very excited to hear what the discussions will reveal. Thank you! 谢谢大家!

此外,我们还需做一些工作来保障雇员能够得到利益攸关方的大力支持,让我们可以顺利落实这些策略。因此,像今天这样的会议就显得十分重要,只有这样,利益攸关方才能提高能力,通力合作,带来积极的变化。我想再一次感谢深圳市妇女联合会和深圳市妇女儿童发展基金会为此次大会的成功举办所做的努力。我也十分感谢今天的演讲嘉宾和在座的各位来宾让今天的会议得以顺利召开。我希望所有人都能从有趣实用的讨论中受益良多。我也期待聆听大家的真知灼见。谢谢大家!Thank you!

III. 实战练习二

1. 演讲背景

下文摘自"波兰独立之女性研讨会"讨论环节的内容。四位波兰杰出女性代表与现场的观众积极互动,讨论女性职场平等、自愿婚育、兼顾工作家庭、饮食习惯改变等有趣的问题。

2. 预习词汇

general manager 总经理
deputy general manager 副总经理
deputy director general 副总裁
at a certain point 从某种意义上讲
black and white 黑白分明
stereotype 思维定势
from time to time 有时,偶尔
connoisseur 行家
vegan 严格素食主义者
chef 主厨;大厨

3. 演讲文本

00:00—01:06

Thank you for your invitation and thank you for your sharing. Well, shall I share my experience of relevant topic? As you know, I am the General Manager of a red wine company and I have two female deputies. That means all my senior management team members are female. So last year when I promoted the second deputy, Linda, my boss said, "no no no no no, how can your senior management team are all female?" This is the question within my expectation. So I answered, "Why the members of most of the companies are all males but not all female in my company?" Then my boss couldn't refuse my proposal. So what will be if this kind of situation occurs in your country?

感谢您的邀请,也谢谢您的分享。我可以分享与这话题相关的经历吗?你们知道,我是一家红酒公司的总经理,我有两位女性副总经理。也就是说,所有我的高管团队成员都是女性。去年,我提拔了其中一位副总经理 Linda。我的老板就说:"不不不,怎么能让自己的高管团队都是女性呢?"这种问题我早料到了。所以我这么回答:"为什么多数公司的成员可以全部是男性,而我的公司里不能全是女性

呢?"然后我的老板就无法拒绝我的提议。所以,如果同样的事情发生在波兰的话又会怎样呢?

01: 07—04: 38

Well, you know, I think it depends very much on the situation. Because, you are lucky to be great boss and to have wonderful employees that you could easily promote. So that's probably your managerial skills that makes this lady so confident and you know working in such a way that you wanted to work with them. I had an experience of leading a team of some 60 people. And at a certain point, I had three female deputies, all younger than me by two, three years. And many people complain, "Now I can see the pattern. You need to be a woman to be admitted to your team." It's rubbish. It is not true. They are just good enough, and very good and they want the job. And if I would have a male candidate, probably I would have a male deputy. But I have those three absolutely outstanding girls as my deputies. And then I move to another department of the ministry, again, to be the boss. And it turned out that, because it was a department, I was replacing someone who went for admission. And it allowed that I have two deputies, both male, much older than me. It was just like pure coincidence that I completely changed this working environment. But honestly speaking, judging after these two kinds of experience, I would say, well, those are absolutely wonderful. I mean, diversity is great. But you cannot force diversity, so if you have just better women or better men for that matter to work with you, you should not look for this kind of diversity in the forced way because then it will be harmful to the company. And I was not pushing to have female deputies in my second department, I was totally happy with these two men. So I think it depends and it should be just equal opportunities thing. If you have a male candidate who is good enough to apply, OK, you will be happy to work with him as much as you're working with your female deputies. But I would like to ask you one more question. Because you are absolutely outstanding. We work together for four years already. And you always come to my mind when I think about powerful women in business. You work in a huge company. You are China's wine company. So what is your experience with the female managers or the equality, you know, higher we go up the ladder, we see less and less women. Why is it so? Why do you think it is? On the level of regions, provinces, still there will be women, but you say, your boss is a man? When we look at the companies, usually women are deputies, deputy director general, the same is for the government. I have a lot of contacts with local governments here, municipal governments, and my counterparts are usually women being deputy director, deputy director general. Why is it so?

这么说吧，我觉得这得具体问题具体分析。很庆幸您是一个好老板，有一帮优秀的员工，您可以很容易提拔她们。也许是您出色的管理技巧，能让这位女士信心满满，或者说您员工的工作态度让您想和他们一起工作。我曾经带领一个约60人的团队。有一段时间，我有三个女副总经理，她们都比我年轻两三岁。很多人都抱怨说，"现在我看出来一种固定模式，只有女性才能加入您的团队。"简直一派胡言，这都不是真的。她们都很好，非常优秀，她们希望得到这份工作。如果我有一位男性候选人，可能我就会多一位男性副总经理。但是，我实际上有那三位非常出色的女孩子担任我的副总经理。然后我调到了另外一个部门，同样我又是老板。结果就是，我来到这个部门，我是取代另一个人，他也同样竞争这个职位。公司允许我有两名副总经理，都是男性，都比我年龄大很多。这纯粹就是巧合，因为我完全改变了这里的工作环境。但老实说，从这两段经历来看，我想说都十分精彩。我的意思是多样性是好事，但不能强求，如果有更符合的女性或男性人选担任那个职位，一起共事，就不应该硬性追求这种多样性，因为这会对公司不利。我没有非要两位女性副总经理在我第二个部门里帮我，我非常开心能和这两位男士一起工作。所以我觉得要视情况而定，机会应该平等。如果您有一位男性候选人，他非常优秀，足以胜任工作，那么您会很开心能和他一起共事，就像您和女员工一起工作时一样开心。但我想再问您一个问题。因为您特别出色，我们一起共事了四年，您给我的印象是商业女强人的感觉。您在一家大公司工作，那是一家中国的红酒公司。所以，您的经历是什么呢？关于和女性经理共事或平等方面，您有哪些经历呢？您知道，爬得越高，我们看到的女性会越来越少。这是为什么？为什么会发生这样的事？就不同区域和不同省份来看，仍然会有女性，但是您刚刚说，您的老板是男性，对吧？我们来看看公司的情况，通常女性是副总经理或副总裁，在政府里也是同样的情况。我和当地政府有很多来往，这里的市政府，我看到我的同行，通常都是女性担任副经理或副总裁。为什么会这样？

04：39—06：01

Thank you for your question. Well, I myself once being deputy for nine years and being general manager for six years. And your question is about, let me see…In my company, the situation is different because we have near 250 staff in my, at this company and most of them are female. So I can only choose from the majority. And I once count my, among my management team or managers, directors, half male, half men. Among the staff, I think most female are better, I only can say. Because the majority is female. So, we can choose better people from this majority. Thank you.

谢谢您的提问。我自己曾经当副总经理当了9年，当总经理6年了。您的问题是有关……我想想。在我的公司里，情况是非常不同的，因为我们有将近250名员工在这家公司，大多数都是女性。所以我只能从大多数人中挑选。曾经我数过，在我的管理团队或者经理和总监中，一半是女性，一半是男性。在员工中，我觉得大多数女性都更优秀。我只能这样说，是因为大多数员工都是女性。所以，我们可以从大多数员工中选出更优秀的人。谢谢。

06：02—07：33

I think that is the problem that we all face at a certain point with the recruitment. To what extent change? There are also of the recruitment I would like to ask you also about that. Because it happened to me a couple of times. I was recruiting for my team and I really wanted to make bigger diversity but well, because it is public administration, there is much more female candidate than male and they are usually better educated, better prepared and more like, you know, ready to jump onto it, more ideas about how to do it. For man, it was like the less bad choice, let's say so. But for women, it was very natural choice. Also because public administration seems to be quite a comfortable working environment for women, which is not always true but that is the stereotype. So I think that is the problem that we face. Shall we, you know, somehow change the criteria throughout the recruitment process? If we see that we don't have enough diversity or just say sorry, but this time female candidates are much better, maybe next time it will be about male candidate to be better. We shouldn't, I would say it again, we shouldn't force it, but I think that is the problem that we will face.

我觉得这个问题，从某种意义上讲，我们都会在招聘时遇到。这会对招聘产生多大的影响呢？我想问你这个问题，因为我遇到这个问题很多次了。我正在为我的团队招聘员工，我真的很想让我的团队更加多样化。但是，因为这是一个公共管理岗位，女性候选人比男性要多得多，她们通常有很好的教育背景，准备得更加充分，好像准备好立马上任似的，她们也有更多的创意来做好这份工作。对于男性，这个岗位好像是还算凑合。但对于女性而言，这是个非常自然的选择。也因为公共管理岗位似乎有相当舒服的工作环境，虽然不一定都是这样，但大家都这么认为。所以我觉得这是我们都面临的问题。我们可不可以稍微改变一下标准，改变招聘流程的标准？如果我们知道我们在男女比例上不够多样，或者说不好意思，这次女性求职者更合适，或许下次招聘会更倾向于男性求职者。我们不应该这样做。再说一次，我们无法硬性这样做，我觉得这是我们共同面临的问题。

07：34—08：14

We do because it is a choice. So you can choose this or the other way. I am a woman. But I am extremely black and white on these things. I will feel very bad if somebody would pick me for anything because I am a woman. Because this is really, you want to be picked because you are better. You do not want to be picked because you are a woman or because you are a man. So I believe in the style of diversity, and of course, that comes with gender, in many cases, I never pick because I want to have a quota on diversity, gender diversity. I always pick better.

我们这样做是因为这是个人选择。您可以选择这样做或用另外一种方式。我是女性,但对这些问题我是黑白分明的。让我特别难受的事情是有人选择我只因为我是女性。因为每个人都想别人选自己是因为自己更优秀,而不是因为自己的性别。所以我认为在方式多样化方面,当然,和性别相关,在很多情况下,我做选择不会因为多样性、性别多样性。我总是择优录取。

08:15—09:04

Well, I can only say only from my age point of view that people in my age are younger. They're just, they see now things very equally. I think it is really changed, all these manifestations, strikes, everything. All the social media tell a lot that we look at things super equally. So for me, I don't think even about it anymore if I have to choose somebody for my work. I don't, I just look for people who are good. So it does not really matter if it is a male, female, whatever. So I think it's changed, just the times.

我只能说,从我这个年龄来看,我的同龄人都很年轻,他们现在会非常平等地看待问题。我觉得这真的改变了所有这些外在现象、挫折等。社交媒体进行了大量报道,说我们非常平等地看待问题。所以对我来说,我根本不会考虑性别因素,如果我要选人为我工作的话。我不会这样,我只会挑选优秀的人,所以性别根本不重要。所以这就是变化,时代的变化。

09:05—09:17

Yes. Same in my company. Actually when I choose, when I want to promote my staff, I never have a gender problem. It does not matter.

是的。我的公司也一样。其实当我想提拔我的员工,我从来不会考虑性别问题。性别根本不重要。

09:18—09:25

Thank you very much. Do we have any more questions?
非常感谢。还有其他问题吗?

09:26—12:20

Thank you very much. I have a very common question. How to take a balance between family, I mean, for a woman? Or is it possible for a woman to take a balance between her family, and her job or her dream? For example, now my parents encourage me to continue my study of Polish in Poland, and they think that you'd better do that now, but not later. But I also want to continue my study in Poland of course, but I think maybe I can first work for two or three years, and then when I go back from Poland, no, and then when I finish my work or finish my job or finish working, and then I can go to Poland for study. But my mother thinks that if you will get married when you are working or and then maybe you'll have a child, then you should focus on your family, or you won't have so much energy to continue your study and so on. And one of my friends who also plans to continue her study in Germany, she also told me that her sister plans to continue her study but it costs a lot to study abroad for us. So she chose to work first, and then after two years, she got married and she had a child, and then she gave up continuing study. So my friend this time is very determined to continue study now because she and my mother, my parents think that now you are young, you don't need to worry about marriage, but after two or three years you will be older, and if a woman gets older, it will be hard for her to find a husband and so on. I know it is special in China, maybe in Poland or Europe, there is not such kind of problem. So, I wonder if, is it possible for a woman to get to take or to find a balance between her family and her dream? Because generally, or under most circumstances, a successful man can have a warm family at the same time, but a successful woman especially a business woman is always single, is sometimes single or under the most circumstances, is single. So yeah.

非常感谢您。我想问一个非常常见的问题,怎样兼顾家庭?女性怎么兼顾家庭?女性可以兼顾家庭、工作和梦想吗?比如,我爸妈鼓励我继续去波兰学习波兰语,他们觉得我最好现在就学,不能拖到以后。我也想继续去波兰深造,但是我觉得我可以先工作两三年,然后当我完成了我的工作,就可以去波兰学习。但我妈妈觉得如果我工作时结婚生子,那时就要专注于家庭,可能没有那么多精力继续学习。我有个朋友,计划去德国深造,她告诉我她姐姐也打算继续学习,但是去国外留学要花很多钱,所以她姐姐选择先去工作,两年后,结婚生子了,就放弃深造。所以我朋友这次非常坚定,现在就出国留学,因为她和我爸妈都觉得应该趁着现在还年轻,不需要操心婚姻,但是两三年后,年龄就大了。如果女人年龄大了,就很难找对象。我知道这只是中国的情况,或许在波兰、在欧洲,不存在这样的问题。所以,我想知道,女性是否可以兼顾家庭和梦想?因为总的来说,大多数情况下,成功的男性可以同时拥有幸福的家庭,但成功的女性,特别是商业女性,往往单身,大多数情况下是单身。这就是我的问题。

12:21—15:58

Thank you very much for this question. I think the situation is changing everywhere including China. And I hope that your generation will be the first to fight very vigorously. That is probably the only thing I really don't like about China. It is this perception of young women over 26, 27 years of age as the leftovers. I think it is the biggest insult that maybe address to a woman. That is what I think. Then the second thing, I think you said about that before because you partly answered your question already. Well. First, you don't need to marry, you don't need to have kids. Nobody can force you. If you want, go ahead, have a happy marriage and have kids. But it is not a pattern that you need to follow. So that would be my first reflection for your dilemma. But if you want, perfect, but why in two years after your studies? Women are having kids till their 40s. Medicine is advanced especially in China. Why do you think about getting married before even 25? I have hope in your generation. I wouldn't be surprised to listen to this kind of question of someone you know, already maybe 40s or 50s. But you should think about it that way if you want to be happy and to have your life fulfilled. You asked how to do that. Don't be forced to do anything against your will. If you want to go for studies now, go for studies now. If you want to go to work, go to work. It depends. It's up to you. If you have a supportive family and I understand you have, discuss with them. But going to work and starting work doesn't mean that you need to get married. And even if you get married, it doesn't mean that you need to have kids immediately. Maybe you should, if you are in love with someone, you want to get married, fine. But then you can continue your study because not the kind of question that you would ask any man if there would be men here sitting in the panel. Nobody will ask a question and how do you make balance in your life between your work and your private life, why don't we ask this question to men? Hello! If you would ask, if I will hear this question to be asked to men, I will think yes, equality is here. You know, so think first about yourself. Kasha, at the beginning of our discussion, said it is important to be a little bit selfish, a little bit egos. Because nobody will make you, help you, instead of you. It's up to you and don't feel pressed. Because now it is not 19th century. You don't need to fulfill someone's dreams. You need to fulfill your dreams. OK? Think about it in the first place. So maybe perspective from marriage with kids.

非常感谢您问了这个问题。我觉得情况正在发生变化,世界各地都在变化,包括中国。我希望你们能成为第一代积极抗争的人。也许我唯一不喜欢中国的地方就是,中国人普遍认为26、27岁以上的年轻女性就是剩女了。我觉得这是对女性最大的侮辱,这是我的看法。第二点,我觉得您之前自己也说过,其实您已经回答了一部分问题。首先,您不非得要结婚生子,没有人可以勉强您。如果您想结婚生子,那就去做,建立幸福的婚姻家庭。但这不是固定模式,不需要照做。所以这是我对您的处境的第一点思考。但如果您想结婚生子,很好啊,但为什么一定要毕业两年后就这样做?女性一直都可以生孩子,40岁之前都可以,医学在中国非常发达了。为什么您想在 25 岁之前结婚？我对你们这一代寄予希望。听到这类问题我已经见怪不怪，尤其是 40 多岁或 50 多岁人问这类问题。您应该想的是这样会不会让自己开心？能不能充实自己的生活？您问到该怎么做，不要强迫自己做不愿意做的事。如果您想现在去深造，那就现在去。如果您想去工作，那就去工作。这取决于您。如果您的家人支持您，我知道您的家人是支持您的，您可以和他们聊聊。但工作并不意味着要结婚。就算您结婚了，并不意味着要立刻生小孩。也许您会马上生小孩，因为您恋爱了，想结婚，没问题。您还是可以深造，因为这类问题您不会问男性，哪怕有男性朋友在这个讨论小组。没人会问男性这个问题，您怎么兼顾工作和私人生活？我们为什么不问男性这个问题？想想！如果您问这个问题，如果我听到这个问题是问男性朋友的，我觉得这就是平等。所以首先想想您自己。Kasha 在最开始的讨论中说道，人学会自私一点，要有一点自我很重要，因为没人能成就您，帮您，除了您自己，这取决于您。不要感觉有压力，因为现在不是 19 世纪，您不需要实现别人的梦想。您需要实现自己的梦想，好吗？要优先考虑这一点。也许可以从结婚生孩子这个角度思考。

15：59—17：20

You know what, I am working, as I have mentioned, 20 years. OK, and I learned that balance is a state of mind. It is an attitude. If you think about workplace balance in quantity, OK, there is no workplace balance because even if you say, OK, I work five hours and then I want to spend with my family ten hours. It will be a moment, when then you will say, no, I want actually 15 hours or maybe I want 10 hours. So it's a very difficult thing to really you know solve it when you think about quantity. When you switch your mind and start thinking about quality. Then you can influence. OK. Because every hour you spend at home, if it is a quality hour, it matters. And then you can really deliver your quality hours. So I have many friends who actually are spending hours at home. But you know what they do? They read books for themselves, they watch TV, they don't even talk to kids. I don't want this balance. OK. I want the balance which works for me, and the balance which works for me is very good at work, very good at home. So every hour I spend with my daughter is a quality hour. It makes me feel good. It is not the quantity balance. But it is a quality balance. So I think it can, you know, a little bit you know change the way how we are thinking about the balance.

您知道吗？我工作了 20 年，我刚刚已经说过。我明白了兼顾是一种心态，一种态度。如果您想兼顾工作数量，根本就没有兼顾可言，因为，就算您说我工作 5 小时，然后我想陪家人 10 小时。也会有那么一刻，您会说，不，我其实想要 15 小时，或者 10 小时。所以很难想出办法彻底解决这个问题，如果您考虑的是数量的话。当您转变心态，开始考虑质量，那么就能做到兼顾。因为您在家花的每个小时，如果都是有质量的话，才会变得重要。您才真正对得起您付出的时间。我有很多朋友，他们其实会在家呆很久，但是您知道他们在做什么吗？他们会自己看书、看电视，他们甚至不会和孩子们讲话。我不想这样来兼顾生活。我想要的方式必须对我有用，这种兼顾还对工作有利，对家庭也有利。我和我女儿一起度过的每个小时都是高品质时光，这让我感觉非常舒服。这不是数量上的兼顾，而是质量的兼顾。所以我觉得可以稍微改变一下，改变我们兼顾的方式。

17：21—17：59

I think I need to say that younger girls now in China, younger Chinese girls are, we know that we can choose to marry or not. We can choose to do what we want, but the older generation, the generation of our parents always have such kind of worries. So that, it is a kind of stereotype for me. I always, I also argue with my mother. I don't need to get married before, because they are old generation, according to my mother, you should get married before you are 30 years old.

中国现在的年轻女孩，我们知道可以选择结不结婚，可以选择做自己想做的事情，但老一辈的人，父母那一辈总是有这种担忧。所以，这对我来说是一种思维定势。我经常和我妈妈争论，我不需要在多少岁之前结婚。因为他们是老一辈的人，所以我妈妈会说，我应该在30岁之前结婚。

18：00—18：34

But we will always have this to our kids. My daughter is from time to time mentioning that maybe after high school, she will, just you know, stop for a year, she will not go to the university, and she will do the tour around the world. Honestly, I hate this idea. OK. And I will always share my point of view, but she will do what she will decide to do. I think you will do the same to your kids if you will decide to have any in the future. I think it's good to hear point of views; you don't have to agree. Again it is an attitude. It is your decision.

但我们经常会将自己的想法灌输给孩子。我女儿有时提到，高中毕业后，或许会迟一年上大学，她要去世界各地旅行。老实说，我并不赞同。我总是会告诉她我的想法，但是她会自己做决定。我觉得您也会这么对您的孩子，如果您日后打算要孩子的话。我觉得听听不同的看法是好事，您不一定要认同。这也是一种态度，由您决定。

18：35—18：37

You are not the only one, girl.

您不是唯一有这个困惑的孩子，姑娘。

18:38—18:41
I will insist my own idea, my own.
我会坚持自己的想法。

18:42—18:45
But they will always say this. I will always say what I think.
但他们会一直这样说,我也会一直说出我的想法。

18:46—18:55
Although my mother always says this, but every time she gave up and said OK, do what you want.
尽管我妈妈总是这样说,但是每次她都会投降,然后说,好,做你想做的事吧。

18:56—20:03
I think we've talked about everything already, but you just, you asked if it's possible to have a balance. I think everything is possible now. Everything is possible for us especially. We are living in a century where I think almost everything is possible if you want it. My parents were the same, my mom especially of course. Until 25, I was supposed be married with kids. Really. I felt the pressure and I see about my friends right now that they felt upon this pressure, because they are almost old, maybe not married, because now it's not really that necessary. But they have kids; they have families, most of my friends back in Poland. But I decided I am not the one, and I am running away. And I need to wait because I have to wait. And I am here and I am super happy. I am 31 years old. And I just decided to push it a little bit further because I can. And probably you can as well if you want. If you don't want then, that is fine, perfect. Just, even to choose whatever you want to do. That's my advice.

我觉得我们已经把该说的都说了,您刚刚问的是是否有可能兼顾。我觉得一切皆有可能。一切都是可能的,特别是对我们来说。我们所处的时代告诉我们,几乎一切都有可能,只要您想。我爸妈也一样,尤其是我妈妈。到了25岁,人人都希望我结婚生子。真的,我感受到了压力,看看我的朋友们,现在他们也感受到了压力,因为他们年纪不小了,或许还没结婚,因为现在真的不是非得结婚。但是他们有孩子,有家人。我很多波兰朋友都是这样。但我决定不要像他们一样,我逃了出来。我需要缓一缓,因为有这个必要。我来到了这里,也超级开心。我31岁了,我决定把结婚生子的事情再缓一缓,因为我可以做到。您也可以,只要您想。如果您不想这样,那也没问题。您只需要做您自己想做的事情。这就是我的建议。

20:04—21:44

So I have a question for Panny Joanna, because I have been part of some Polish food programs on and off and also becoming kind of Polish connoisseur is part of my inspiration. And I have seen like several years ago when I first started to get some contact with Polish food, it was very masculine. It was very masculine. From my impression, Polish food was very masculine when I was, for the first time to try Polish food like pasta is very strong and I have never heard of anyone who are vegetarian from Poland. But now I think I can see a lot of changes like people talk about how to be healthy, how to be like more vegetables and more sophisticated. Maybe it is part of the women's role that they try to reform how Polish people eat. Just like a lot of receptions now from Poland, we don't have vodka, maybe some of my male friends don't agree with this idea. But actually I think it is a very different stereotypes that I have seen that like, not in Russia that we can see lots of stereotypes like babushka or something like that. I think Polish women are very young and healthy and slim. So, is it part of the trend that's changing in terms of food and beverage?

我想问问Joanna，因为我参与了一些波兰食品项目，断断续续参加了一些，而且，成为波兰食品行家是我的一个梦想。几年前，那是我第一次开始接触波兰食物，非常粗犷。在我的印象中，波兰食物非常粗犷，那是我第一次尝试波兰食物，比如面食，味道很重，我之前从没听说过哪个素食主义者是从波兰来的。但现在，我觉得我看到了很多变化，比如人们会谈论怎样健康饮食、怎样多吃蔬菜、怎么吃得精致。也许一部分是因为女性，她们改变了波兰人的饮食习惯。就像很多波兰接待会，我们现在都看不到伏特加了，也许我有些男性朋友并不赞同。但其实，我觉得这是一种非常不同的思维定势，俄罗斯则不同，我们可以看到很多思维定势，比如俄罗斯头巾等等。我觉得波兰女性非常年轻、健康、苗条。所以，这是否是一种变化中的趋势，出现在餐饮领域呢？

21:45—23:01

Well, I think it is not only in Poland, everywhere in the world. We are changing. We are changing ourselves. We are changing our food habits. Everything is changing, fashion and, yeah, food as well. So it's not only in Poland but yes, it is changing a lot. I have to say we would like to follow our western neighbors. I think they are the first one usually to come up with different ideas like healthy eating, vegetarian. Vegans now is a big boon for vegans, right. Everything is vegan. We even all start to make vegan dumplings soon, 'cause people are coming to our place and asking. Polish people, Americans. Doesn't matter. From every place, they are asking about vegan dumplings. So we are gonna follow that idea and we will make one. That is how it's changing, people demand something more or they want to live healthier. They want to live differently. So there is no point to really stick to this Polish traditional food in our place. So we still have the traditional things but we are doing things differently, in a healthier way with looking just to the future.

我觉得这不仅发生在波兰,而是发生在世界各地。我们都在改变。我们正在改变自己,正在改变我们的饮食习惯。一切都在变化,包括时尚和食品。所以这不仅发生在波兰,波兰的确发生了很大的变化。不得不说,我们也想跟随我们的西方邻国。我觉得他们是最早开始有不同想法的人,比如健康饮食和素食主义。纯素食现在对严格素食主义者非常有利。一切都是纯素的。我们现在都开始做纯素饺子,因为人们来到我们这里就会问纯素饺子。不论是波兰人,还是美国人,都不重要。不管从哪个地方来,他们都会问纯素饺子。我们准备遵循这个想法,开始着手做。这就是改变的趋势,人们要求得更多,想活得更健康,想活得与众不同。所以没有必要坚持波兰传统食物,没有必要在我们这里恪守波兰食物传统。我们仍然有传统食物,只是我们做的方式发生了改变,采用更加健康的方式,这也是为了顺应未来的发展。

23:02—24:05

I would completely agree because now we also is the second most vegan friendly capital of the world after Berlin. It was officially voted by some vegan associations. And I was surprised coming back to Poland during my stay in China to see more and more vegan vegetarian places and the healthy food more and more available. And also, the pattern is changing very rapidly. But I think that also we can see more women in cuisine, so in professional cooking, most of the experts of Polish, well, good enough in traditions, maybe not all of them but many of them are Polish. We had one here a couple of months ago. But it's also changing that women who say well, I want to be a chef, a famous chef and I will open my own restaurant. That is a completely different picture from the one I remembered even five years ago. You are absolutely right.

我完全同意,因为现在我们也是世界第二大对严格素食主义者友好城市,仅次于柏林。这是一些严格素食主义协会正式投票的结果。让我非常惊讶的是,当我从中国回到波兰,我发现有越来越多倡导严格素食主义的地方,也有越来越多的健康食品。同时,这种模式变化得非常快。但我觉得,我们也看到了更多的女性投身烹饪,所以在专业烹饪领域,大部分专家都是波兰人,他们非常擅长传统菜肴,虽然不是所有人,但大多数都是波兰人。我们在这里遇到过一位,就在几个月前。正在发生变化的还有,女性会说:我想成为主厨,非常有名的主厨,我会开一家自己的餐厅。这是一个完全不同的景象,与我记忆中5年前的景象完全不同。您说得非常对。

第二部分 同传技巧

第三单元 观光旅游
Tourism

I. 记忆训练

同声传译员在口译时需要边听边译,工作强度较大。同传中,译员不可能完全词对词地译出字面意思,而是应当一个意义单位一个意义单位地听取信息,这就要求译员在翻译这个意义单位之前要将这个意义单位存储在短期记忆当中。此外,译员还要注意各个意义单位之间的连贯表达,这就要求译员在译出新的意义单位时还要短暂地记住前面的意义单位。因此同传学习者在训练初期一定要加强记忆技能的训练,训练的方法包括源语单语连续复述和影子训练。

1. 源语单语连续复述

源语单语连续复述指在播放一段源语之后,口译学习者在无笔记的情况下用源语将听到的信息复述出来,可以作为向同声传译记忆训练的过渡方法,在交替传译当中也会进行这一技能的训练。口译学习者在进行源语单语连续复述时不需要拘泥于原句的句式,应着重于意义的记忆和表达,可进行概括复述和细节复述。

2. 影子训练

即像影子一样追随发言人,再现发言人讲话的内容,因而被称为影子训练。影子训练可分为两个阶段。

第一阶段是以源语的形式几乎同步地复述源语,可以培养口译学习者对信息的高度注意力和边听边说的同步能力。其难度相对较小,适用于同传记忆训练初期。

第二阶段是以源语的形式进行延迟复述,可以说是影子训练的高级阶段。在一段时间的同步源语复述训练之后,口译学习者可以逐步加大难度,迟于源语半句甚至一句话的时间跟读,这样耳朵、嘴巴、大脑同时派上用场,强化了记忆和表达的训练。在跟读完一段五六分钟甚至更长的讲话之后,可尝试概括出讲话的主要内容,检测记忆训练效果。此外,在训练时还可以增加一些干扰,比如口译学习者在边听边复述的情况下,可动手在纸上写一些不相关的内容,比如数字,以分散注意力。

第三单元　观光旅游 Tourism

II. 实战练习一

1. 演讲背景

2012年，西澳大利亚州旅游局在广州举办"西澳大利亚州旅游局中国旅游洽谈会"，来自西澳大利亚州的20家当地旅游供应商和多家中国旅行社深入交流，积极探讨如何进一步展开合作，共同推广西澳大利亚州丰富的旅游资源。下文为库克船长游轮公司代表的演讲，他在演讲中介绍了天鹅河、弗里曼特尔和天鹅谷的美丽风光，也详细地推介了公司提供的游船服务类型，包括景观游船、午餐游船、红酒游船、晚餐游轮、定制游轮。

2. 预习词汇

Captain Cook Cruises 库克船长游轮
Perth 珀斯（澳大利亚西澳大利亚州首府）
Swan River 天鹅河（珀斯市内河流）
capacity 载客量
Fremantle 弗里曼特尔（澳大利亚西海岸城市）
Swan Valley 天鹅谷
winery 葡萄酒厂
Sydney Harbor 悉尼港
kayaking 独木舟，皮划艇
Pinnacles 尖峰石阵（澳大利亚旅游景点）
Wave Rock 波浪岩（西澳中部沙漠旅游景点）
Caversham Wildlife Park 凯维森野生动物园
Opera House （悉尼）歌剧院
Swan Bell Tower 天鹅钟塔
Cappuccino Strip 卡布奇诺咖啡大道
Sandalford winery 山度富酒庄
Houghton winery 霍顿酒庄
gourmet 美食；菜肴精美的
nougat 牛轧糖
spirits 烈酒
scenic cruise 景观游览船
yacht club 游艇俱乐部
Water Edge Estate 水边度假庄园

29

3. 演讲文本

00:00—00:16

OK, hello! Everybody! 你好! Everybody! And nice to see some familiar faces if you were with me before. I'm from Captain Cook Cruises. My name is Graeme Skeggs and I'm here to talk to you about the number one thing to do for anybody who comes to Perth.

大家好！你好！很高兴看到一些熟悉的面孔，也许之前我们也曾见过。我在库克船长游轮工作，我叫格雷姆·斯盖格，由我向各位介绍来珀斯的必做之事。

00:16—00:49

Captain Cook Cruises is obviously a cruise company. We operate cruises on the Swan River in Perth, which is the most beautiful natural asset you will find in Western Australia. As a company, we're the leading tour operator in Western Australia. We are the number one, the longest trading private company, and the largest number of visitors for any tour operator. We are family owned, still owned by the same original owners. So we are dedicated to our service and we're dedicated to providing a unique experience for all your passengers.

库克船长游轮，顾名思义，是经营游轮的公司。我们的经营范围在珀斯的天鹅河，这里有西澳大利亚最美的自然风光。我们公司是西澳大利亚领先的旅游公司，排名第一，历史最为悠久，旅客数量也最多。我们是家族企业，从未易主。所以我们专注于服务，为你们的旅客们提供最独特的旅行体验。

00:49—01:22

There is another company you may have heard of called Captain Cook Cruises in Sydney. They are a separate company on the different massive ownership. We are a private owned company in Captain Cook Cruises, Western Australia. We have seven vessels ranging from 50 capacity up to 350 capacity, and we only do day cruises on the Swan River. We have offices in Perth, the seaside town of Fremantle and the wine grown area of the Swan valley. And our motto is "Captain Cook Cruises, Not Just The Boat Trip".

大家也许听说过另一家公司，也叫库克船长游轮，在悉尼。那是另外一家公司，所有制和我们有很大不同。我们是私营企业，叫库克船长游轮，在西澳大利亚。公司拥有7艘游轮，载客量为50～350人，而且只在白天游览天鹅河。我们的办事处设在珀斯、海滨之城弗里曼特尔和葡萄酒产区天鹅谷。公司的口号是："库克船长游轮，不仅仅是坐船游览。"

第三单元　观光旅游 Tourism

01：25—01：48

Why us? Why choose to come with an operator such as ourselves? We operate on the Swan River, as I mentioned, which is the natural asset in Perth. And it is a cruise. We have cruises for all ages, from family, children, up to senior citizens. We are not just the cruise company, not just the boat trip. We also do operations that involve coach tours, tram tours and visit the zoos and wineries.

为何选择我们？为什么让我们带您出行？刚刚也提到，我们的业务在天鹅河一带，它是珀斯的自然风光，而且是坐游轮游览。公司有不同的游轮，适合各个年龄群体，家庭中从儿童到老年游客都可以选到合适的游轮。我们不仅仅是游轮公司，提供坐船旅行，还提供长途汽车旅行、电车旅行、游览动物园和酿酒坊。

01：48—02：23

We are ready for your markets. We are ready with pricing for the wholesale market, and also not quite as good as Phil did with his translation of being ready for the Chinese markets. But we are improving our cuisines to be more Asian-focused and I welcome, to be welcoming for the Chinese visitor. And as a loyal brand in Perth, you are going with one of the most trusted brands in Perth. We are on the recognized within the top 10 trusted brands within Perth. So you can be guaranteed to be go with a company with style. There are very friendly staff. We have a couple of mandarin speakers, but we are improving that every time.

我们时刻准备为您服务，已经制定好团购价格，而且有菲尔做翻译，我们也准备好服务中国游客。我们正在改进游轮，更侧重亚洲游客的需求，我真诚欢迎中国游客到访。我们长期在珀斯提供旅游服务，是当地最值得信赖的旅游公司之一，入选珀斯十大最可靠的品牌，因此公司可确保为您提供与时俱进的服务。我们的员工非常友善，虽然只有一部分会说普通话，但我们正在不断改进。

02：23—02：54

The Swan River is a natural asset. And it is bigger than the Sydney Harbor, and it is bigger than any other river in Australia. You will see things on the river that you won't see if you go on a coach tour or if you go on a private car tour. You will see the natural beauty and the lifestyle of people in Perth. We live on the river. We live around the river. And for those of you, not myself, who doesn't do swimming or kayaking, there is swimming, kayaking, fishing, and boating on the river. It links Perth with the port of Fremantle.

天鹅河是大自然的赠予，面积比悉尼港大，它也是澳大利亚最大的河流。您将看到独一无二的河流景观，长途汽车旅行或包车旅行时都看不到的景观。您能够享受自然风光,感受珀斯的生活方式。人们在河上和河边居住生活。对于各位来说,我除外,对于不常游泳或划皮划艇的游客来说,大家可以在河里游泳、划艇、钓鱼和乘船。天鹅河连接着珀斯和弗里曼特尔港。

02:54—03:18

And it is the absolute must-do experience before you go to the Pinnacles, before you go to Wave Rock, before you go to Caversham Wildlife Park, before you go anywhere outside of Perth, the one thing you must do is go on the Swan River. Well located just behind another magnificent sculpture, nearly as famous as the Opera House, which is the Swan Bell Tower.

还有一件必做之事,去尖峰石阵、波浪岩、凯维森野生动物园或离开珀斯之前,您一定要沿着天鹅河边游览一次。就在另一个宏伟的雕像后面,有一个几乎和悉尼歌剧院齐名的景点,那就是天鹅钟塔。

03:18—03:49

Fremantle. It is a historic port and it is just 11 kilometers by road or 18 kilometers by river, down to the water, sorry, to the sea. It is a port of maritime history and it's also a must-see destination in Perth. And you must see it by river. It is famous for its markets, the tourist attractions, for beer, wine, chocolate. We have a Cappuccino Strip. And for those of you who love your fish and chips, it is the must place go for fish and chips.

弗里曼特尔是一个历史悠久的港口,距珀斯市11公里,在天鹅河下游18公里,是天鹅河的出海口。这是一个承载着航海历史的港口,也是珀斯的必看景点之一。您一定要乘船在河上游览这个港口,这里的集市、旅游景点、啤酒、红酒和巧克力都非常有名,还有一条卡布奇诺咖啡大道。如果您喜欢吃炸鱼炸薯条,那您一定要来尝一尝这里的特色。

03:49—04:29

The Swan Valley. Some of you may have heard of the Swan Valley. It is the most famous wine growing area in Perth and it is the closest wine growing area to any capital city in Australia. It is a home to Sandalford wineries and Houghton wineries. And it is an area of natural beauty and outstanding nature. You will find gourmet produce there. You will find the cheese, wine, chocolate, beer and nougat, spirits. Anything you want you will find in the Swan Valley and it is only two hours by boat to go, by river, sorry, to go into the Swan Valley. It's where the locals spend their weekend and it is another must-see destination in Perth.

接下来是天鹅谷。有些人也许听说过这里，这是珀斯最有名的葡萄酒产区，也是距澳大利亚各州首府最近的葡萄酒产区。这里有山度富酒庄和霍顿酒庄，拥有无与伦比的自然景观和美味的菜肴，有奶酪、红酒、巧克力、啤酒、牛轧糖和烈酒。天鹅谷应有尽有，坐船只要两小时就能到达天鹅谷。当地人会在这儿过个周末，这也是珀斯的另一个必游之地。

04：30—04：58

Our most popular cruises are scenic cruises, which is 2 hours, 2 hours and 30 minutes in duration. And you get to see the rich people where they live along the river, wildlife, yacht clubs. You get a full commentary, which is literally in English. We do have a Mandarin translation. We also have wine tasting onboard from the local Swan Valley and also unlimited tea and coffee. And all our vessels are air-conditioned with huge, large sightseeing windows.

我们公司最受欢迎的游轮是景观游轮，有2小时和2.5小时两种行程。在船上您能看到很多富人，他们住在河边，还能看到野生动物和游艇俱乐部。全程配备解说，英语解说，我们还提供普通话译文。途中还有品酒环节，红酒都产自天鹅谷，并且无限量供应茶和咖啡。所有游轮都安装了空调和大幅观景窗。

04：58—05：31

Not only do we offer sightseeing cruises, we also do lunch cruises. We have cruises between Perth and Fremantle, with a buffet style menu onboard, which is being improved as we speak to include a few more Asian dishes meal and also rice dishes. We include a complimentary local beer, wine or soft drink, including in that package an afternoon tea and commentary throughout. And also we package together with the bus companies and tram companies to ensure a full experience for your guests.

我们不仅提供观景游轮，还有午餐游轮。在珀斯和弗里曼特尔之间，游轮上有自助午餐，正如之前提到，我们正在改善菜式，加入一些亚洲菜肴和米饭。船上还赠送当地啤酒、红酒或软饮料，包括下午茶以及所有解说。同时，我们还和汽车公司、电车公司推出旅游套餐服务，确保各位游客能有一份完整的旅行体验。

05：31—05：56

The wine cruises we operate into the Swan Valley, as I mentioned, and we have two, an all day and a half day, either with a buffet style meal or with a plated menu. All include premium wine and local produce from Western Australia, local cheeses, local olives and local wines. And we visit another famous winery, Water Edge Estate, one of the most famous wineries in Perth, and second only to Sandalford.

我们还有红酒游轮进入天鹅谷,刚刚我也提过,有两艘游艇,分别为全天和半天的行程,配有自助餐或点餐。所有餐式都配有优质红酒和西澳大利亚当地的农产品、奶酪、橄榄和红酒。我们还可以游览另一个著名酒庄,叫做水边度假庄园,也是珀斯最著名的酒庄之一,仅次于山度富酒庄。

05:56—06:25

Lastly we do dinner cruises. We are the only company to be operating dinner cruises. And this operates on the weekend and a perfect addition to any group itinerary for a farewell dinner or a gala dinner. We have one way, you stay onboard the boat or you can have one way you visit a winery and have it off the boat at a winery. All are inclusive, with all your beer, wine and soft drinks included throughout and also DJ or live entertainment.

我们还有晚餐游轮。我们是唯一一家运营晚餐游轮的公司。晚餐游轮在周末出港,可以进行团队旅行餐、告别晚宴或庆祝晚宴。您可以留在船上进餐,或者下船参观酒庄,在酒庄里吃饭。两种用餐形式都包含啤酒、红酒和软饮料,并有DJ或现场演出助兴。

06:25—06:58

Lastly we do do private charters. If you have a particular need, a particular theme, a particular menu that you would like, we can cater for between 200 and 250 passengers and any style you wish, whether it will be cocktail style, theater style, dinner style, breakfast, lunch, dinner or evening. No matter what you want we can tailor and make a charter to your requirements. We can also theme it to whatever you wish, whether it will be a wedding, an Arabian theme or just a plain cocktail we can do whatever you wish.

同时我们还提供定制游轮服务。如果您有特别的需求、主题或菜式,我们可以按您的要求为200~250人提供餐饮服务。任何形式的服务,无论是鸡尾酒会、剧院式聚会、晚餐会、早餐会、午餐或正餐,无论您有什么需求,我们都可以按您的要求定制。还可以为您定制主题,无论是婚礼、阿拉伯风情或普通的鸡尾酒会,我们都能满足您的需求。

06:58—07:20

And lastly to give you the geography, we have Perth in the middle. Right out towards the coast you have Fremantle, and near this towards us you have the Swan Valley. Thank you very much for your time! It has been a pleasure. Hope I have spoken not too quickly and enjoy the rest of your afternoon. Thank you!

最后向您介绍一下地理位置,珀斯在正中间。海岸右边是弗里曼特尔,在我们

第三单元　观光旅游 Tourism

不远的前面就是天鹅谷。感谢您的聆听！很荣幸向大家介绍这里。希望我的语速没有过快，也祝您度过一个美好的下午。谢谢大家！

III. 实战练习二

1. 演讲背景

下文同样摘自"2012西澳大利亚州旅游局中国旅游洽谈会"。演讲嘉宾是尖峰旅行社的代表，他在演讲中介绍了六条旅游路线，分别为尖峰四驱游、尖峰石阵冒险之旅、玛格丽特河全天之旅、玛格丽特河红酒之旅、四天西南之旅、蒙基米亚海滩之旅。

2. 预习词汇

Pinnacle Tours 尖峰旅行社
day touring 一日游
extended touring 长途旅游
Pinnacles 尖峰石阵
Margaret River 玛格丽特河
Monkey Mia 蒙基米亚海滩
Pinnacle Four-wheel Drive 尖峰四驱游
Caversham Wildlife Park 凯维森野生动物园
Lancelin 兰斯林
sand boarding 滑沙
New Norcia 新诺舍
wildflowers tour 野花之旅
Wave Rock 波浪岩
winery 葡萄酒厂
Perth 珀斯
Tree Top Walk 树顶栈道；树顶漫步
Albany 奥尔巴尼
Nature's Window 自然之窗
Monkey Mia Dolphin Resort 蒙基米亚海豚度假村
Adams 亚当斯
Broome 布鲁姆
FIT/Free Independent traveller 自助游；背包客
MICE/Meetings, Incentives, Conferences/Conventions, Exhibitions/Expositions/

35

Events 会展

3. 演讲文本

00:00—01:07

你好！Welcome back from afternoon tea. My name is Simon, from Australian Pinnacle Tours. We are the largest day touring and extended touring company in Western Australia. We go to all of those places. The most famous obviously is our name. We go to the Pinnacles. We go to Margaret River and the Southwest. And we go to Monkey Mia or Monkey Mia as you might call it. Now, as you have heard from all of my colleagues, Western Australia is very very very big. And as a result, we decided that in order to keep your bottoms very comfortable, we would spend a lot of money on our coaches, so we have built these very impressive vehicles and we spent a lot of money on them.

Hello！欢迎大家喝完下午茶回来。我叫西蒙，来自澳大利亚尖峰旅行社。我们是西澳最大的一日游和长途旅游公司。这些都是我们的旅游目的地。最有名的目的地当然是我们旅行社名字所指的尖峰石阵。我们还去玛格丽特河、西南地区、蒙基米亚海滩或者猴子米娅海滩。我的同事已经提过，西澳地域辽阔。所以，我们决定，为了让大家旅途坐得舒服点儿，我们会在长途客车上花很多钱。我们制造了这些令人赞叹的长途客车，花了很多钱。

01:08—01:58

And the reason we do that is because all of our tours are huge. They are very big, perfect surrounded by some beautiful icons. But it takes a while to get there so we thought why not make comfortable vehicles for you. Up the top there, you will see that is the custom-made four-wheel drive. It has 27 seats. That costs about 600,000 dollars to build. I don't know what that is in yuan. But they are very impressive. They have LCD TV screens and they actually have toilets on board as well. And again the reason we do that is because you have to drive a long way on our tours. And then the bottom is one of the coaches. We have some very impressive coaches as well.

这么做是因为我们的参观范围很大，包括一些美丽的地标。但到那儿去需要时间，所以我们想为什么不为大家提供舒适的长途客车呢？在PPT上面，您会看到定制的四驱车，有27个座位。造价约为60万澳元。我不知道换成人民币是多少。但它们真的很赞。车上有LCD电视屏，还有厕所。我们提供车是因为旅游的时候，你们要坐很远的车。PPT最下面是其中一种长途客车。我们也有一些令人赞叹的长途客车。

01: 59—02: 46

OK. As far as the selection of day tours, we do. There they are. The one at the top, the full day Pinnacle Tour is, by far, that sounds like popular. I think we carry about 60% of all of our passengers on that one tour. OK. And that whole list of tours from January next year will be available with mandarin-speaking guides. OK. You can book them. You just have to request it and you will be paying extra for it. To give you an idea [of what] it's gonna cost. We are going to, you all will be sent an email when we announce it. But it's going to cost around about 30 dollars Australian per person extra, on top of the tour, to get a mandarin-speaking guide.

说到一日游，我们可以提供给大家，都在那儿了。最上面那个全天尖峰之旅似乎是目前比较受欢迎的。我想我们的乘客有60%参加这条路线。好了，表上的所有路线从明年一月起都会配有讲普通话的导游，你们可以预订，只需要提出要求，付导游费即可。给大家一点概念，大概费用是多少。我们会给你们发邮件，告诉你们具体费用。不过，每人要额外付约30澳元，这是除了旅游费用之外，给普通话导游的费用。

02: 47—03: 33

OK. Just to run you through a few of the tours. As I said, the one at the top is the most popular by far. The Pinnacle Four-wheel Drive goes to... I think you already have David from Caversham Wildlife Park speak to you. We go to see some koalas and kangaroos at Caversham Wildlife Park. We obviously go to the Pinnacles as well. And then we do some, we have a bit of fun. It's a bit of an adventure tour. We go to Lancelin and we do some sand boarding and four-wheel driving in that impressive four-wheel drive we have got.

简单介绍一下其中的一些路线。我说过，最上面的那条是目前为止最受欢迎的。尖峰四驱游。我想凯维森野生动物园的戴维已经提过，我们会去动物园看考拉和袋鼠。当然，我们也去尖峰石阵。然后我们来点有意思的，去冒险。我们去兰斯林滑沙，坐四驱车，这条四驱车路线让人印象深刻。

03: 35—04: 03

OK. The second tour also goes to the Pinnacles. What we've done is we have made a Pinnacles tour that is an adventure tour. And then we have made a Pinnacles tour for older, more mature clients. They aren't as much fun as us. And that's called the Pinnacles tour at New Norcia and Wildflowers tour. And that one is much more comfortable, much more relaxed, and much more easier access for those people that may be a little bit older.

好。第二条路线也去尖峰石阵。我们让参观尖峰石阵变成一次冒险之旅。然后我们设计了一条尖峰石阵路线，为年长的客户而设。他们没有我们这么多乐子。那是新诺舍尖峰石阵之旅和野花之旅。这条路线更舒适、更轻松，对那些年纪稍大的人而言更合适。

04：05—04：31

The next two most popular tours is Wave Rock. Very surprisingly, Wave Rock is a rock that looks like a wave and it's crazy. And then the final tour is a seasonal tour that we run just between September. It's just finishing up now, just September to November, which is the wildflowers tour, which goes specifically to see wildflowers.

接下来两条最受欢迎的路线是波浪岩。非常令人惊讶，波浪岩是块石头，但看起来像波浪，很神奇。最后是一条季节性的路线，大概在9月份。刚刚才结束，只是9月到11月有，叫野花之旅，专门去看野花。

04：33—05：05

Next stop is our tours into the Margaret River region. You are going to hear a lot about the Southwest region later on. But very broadly, we have the full day Margaret River tour. That is the great tour if you don't have much time. But I have to be honest, it's huge. It's a really really big day tour. To give you an idea, to drive down to Margret River takes about 4 hours. That means you have to come back as well.

下一条路线去玛格丽特河流域。你们将会听到很多跟西南地区有关的介绍。总的来说，我们有玛格丽特河全天之旅。这条路线不错，如果您时间不多的话很适合。但实话实说，这个区域很大，真的很大。给你们一点概念，开车去玛格丽特河要四个小时，而您还得回来。

05：06—05：45

So what I would recommend for your clients if they can, would be to book, you see a bit further down the list, the two-and-three-day Margaret River wine experiences. They are much better. They are much more relaxed. You get to enjoy five wineries, chocolate factory and the cheese factory and you get to stay down there which is a beautiful place to stay. It's also, to be honest, a great way to avoid the first part of the week in Perth, which seems to be very busy in the hotels. You can get down into Margaret River.

因此，我推荐你们的客户，如果可以的话，订列表下面一点的两天及三天玛格丽特河红酒之旅。这个好得多，也轻松得多。参观五个酿酒坊、巧克力工厂和奶酪工厂，可以呆在这些美丽的地方。老实说，这也是一个好办法，这样的话前半个星期就不用呆在珀斯了，因为酒店这时候好像很忙。您可以到玛格丽特河去。

05:46—06:01

And then the last tour down there is the 4-day Southwest. That is more of a complete Southwest tour. It does the Tree Top Walk and Albany as well. And all of those tours are available with mandarin speaking guides from January.

那里的最后一条路线是四天西南之旅。这更像是一次完整的西南之旅。包括了树顶栈道和奥尔巴尼。这些路线都有普通话导游，从一月起就有。

06:02—06:39

Last but not least, it's the three-day tour to Monkey Mia. You might all have heard of Monkey Mia. It's certainly one of the most popular destinations with Chinese clients. And the reason is there is not many places in the world that you can hand feed dolphins at your feet in nature. It's very remote. As you can see, that's the place called Nature's Window. You get to feed the dolphins. And it's a three-day tour.

最后是为期三天的蒙基米亚海滩之旅。你们可能都听说过蒙基米亚海滩。它无疑是最受中国游客欢迎的目的地之一，因为，世上很少有地方可以让您亲手喂脚边的野生海豚。那个地方很偏远。你们看到的地方叫"自然之窗"，在那儿您可以喂海豚，这个旅程为期三天。

06:40—07:09

I should say all of our tours are accommodated. So we stay at hotels. Generally, we stay at the best hotels available in the region. Now as I am sure you have heard, Western Australia is very remote, so sometimes there is not so many options but the Monkey Mia Dolphin Resort is a good example of where we stay. It's a beautiful property and it's right on the beach, right where the dolphins are swimming.

我们的所有路线都包含住宿。我们住在酒店里。我们通常住该地区最好的酒店。我相信你们听说过，西澳很偏远，所以有时候并没有什么选择，而蒙基米亚海豚度假村就是我们住的酒店之一。酒店很美，就在海滩上，海豚就在那儿畅游。

07:10—08:14

Now the last thing I wanted to mention, which has only just occurred three days ago, to be honest. It's Pinnacle Tours has been sold. So it's being sold. For any of you that have been selling in Western Australia, you might have heard of this company. The company is called Adams. And they are the big charter groups coach line. I have bought Pinnacle Tours so now we have one company that is the one-stop shop for you, for everything that involves a bus. If you want to do golf charters, if you want to do ten-day charters up to Broome, if you have a conference on in Perth or if you are interested in doing small groups FIT, MICE, anything that involves any of the tours I was just telling you about, Pinnacle Tours in combination with Adams is now the place to go. Thank you.

  我想说的最后一件事,三天前才发生,实话实说。那就是尖峰旅行社被出售了。如果你们有人在西澳有旅游业务,你们可能听说过这家公司,它叫亚当斯,专营团体长途客车租赁。我已经买下了尖峰公司,所以现在我们的公司为您提供一站式服务,提供涉及长途客车的一切服务。如果您想租赁高尔夫球车,如果您想租车十天去布鲁姆,如果您在珀斯开会,或者您有兴趣做一小群人的自助游,办会展,或是任何涉及到我刚才给您介绍的旅游项目,建议您找尖峰旅行社和亚当斯。谢谢大家!

第四单元　酒店管理
Hotel Management

I. 顺句驱动

在笔译中，译员有充分的时间思考、查资料和翻译；在交替传译中，发言人讲完一段之后，译员开始翻译；在同声传译中，译员一般滞后于发言人几个词或者半句话的差距发言，二者讲话几乎是同步进行。口译与发言人之间的时间差越大，译员记忆负担就越大，记住的信息就越少，译出的信息也就越少。因此，为了减轻短期记忆负担、跟上发言人的节奏，译员要"按照自己听到原文的顺序，不停地把句子切成个别的意群或概念单位，再把这些单位比较自然地连接起来，翻译出整体的原意"（张维为，1999：41），这就是"顺句驱动"。实现顺句驱动的技巧包括转换、重复、增补等。

1. 断句

断句是同声传译技巧中最重要的一种，是指将英语或汉语句子按照适当的意义单位断开进行翻译，断句是实现顺句驱动的关键。

例1：Our outstanding achievement/is without doubt/the stability. /
译文：我们最大的成就/毫无疑问/就是稳定。/

例2：The election/which has led to your being chosen/to preside over this Assembly/——a very wise choice indeed/——is a tribute to your great country, /which has contributed to the world peace. /
译文：这次选举/选您/为本届大会的主席，/是极为明智的抉择，/是对贵国的敬意，/因为贵国推动了世界和平的发展。/

例1源语和目的语的语序是一致的，口译难度不大。例2句子比较复杂，如果在笔译中，为了使译文表达更贴切，可以进行较大的语序调整，但在同传中为了缩短译语和源语发言之间的时间差，需要尽量顺译，适当的断句就显得非常重要。

2. 转换

转换是指通过词性转换译出原文。在同传中，译员一般不想改变原文的语序，那么适当的词性转换可以使译文语句自然、通顺。

例3：The extension of China's Most Favored Nation status/by the U. S. /is conducive to/the advancement of sustained and stable bilateral trade relations. /

译文：延长中国最惠国待遇，/美国的这种做法/有助于/促进持续、稳定的双边贸易关系。/

例4：The international food shortage/had a direct impact on Kuwait/and other desert countries. /

译文：世界粮食短缺/直接影响到科威特/和其他沙漠国家。/

3. 重复

在顺句驱动原则下，使用重复的技巧有助于加强译文的衔接和连贯、弥合英汉表达的差异。

例5：He left for London/as soon as he received his boss' instruction. /
译文1：他出发去了伦敦，/一收到老板的指示。/
译文2：他出发去了伦敦，/收到老板的指示之后他就动身了。/
根据顺句驱动原则，这句话可在as处断开。如果处理成译文1，则显得零碎、不通顺。那么译员可以适当地重复源语中的部分内容，加强译文的衔接。译文2进行原意重复，并没有直接重复原词，使译文表达更生动。

4. 增补

增补也有助于更好地连接顺句驱动原则下被切分的意群。

例6：We are going to attend the meeting/at Red Forest Hotel/from 2 to 4 o'clock tomorrow afternoon. /
译文1：我们要去参加会议，/在红林酒店，/是明天下午的两点到四点。/
译文2：我们要去参加会议，/地点在红林酒店，/时间是明天下午的两点到四点。/
译文1总体上进行了顺译，但是断句之后中文表达不够顺畅。译文2通过在断句处增补地点和时间两个词语，将隐含的意思外显化，译文更通顺自然。

第四单元　酒店管理 Hotel Management

II. 实战练习一

1. 演讲背景

嘉佩乐酒店执行副总裁、丽晶酒店集团董事长、森塔拉酒店集团副总裁、洲际酒店集团首席发展官和美国州际酒店集团中国公司的代表应邀参加"亚洲酒店论坛集团高管会议",嘉宾们就"亚洲酒店核心竞争力"为题展开小组讨论。在进入讨论之前,每位嘉宾简要地介绍了自己所在的酒店集团,他们普遍认为,亚洲酒店的核心竞争力就在于亚洲人的热情好客、餐饮、水疗以及卓越的服务。

2. 预习词汇

Executive Vice President 执行副总裁
Capella Hotels 嘉佩乐酒店
Accor Hotel & Resorts 雅高酒店集团
Regent Hotels & Resorts 丽晶酒店集团
Chief Development Officer 首席发展官
InterContinental Hotels Group 洲际酒店集团
Centara Hotels & Resorts 森塔拉酒店集团
Capella Hotel Group 嘉佩乐酒店集团
third party operator 第三方运营商
food and beverage 餐饮
emerging market 新兴市场
hospitality 热情好客
Shangri-La 香格里拉酒店
Aman Resort 安缦度假村
Marriott 万豪酒店集团

3. 演讲文本

00:00—01:14

So we are about to switch channel to another channel. From this moment onward, we will be kicking off our discussion in English. So my panel is about core competencies of Asian hotels, as introduced by Mr. James Lv. So joining me this afternoon, we have five very distinguished members from the industry. So I would introduce them according to the first letter of their family name in the alphabetic order. So I will start with Mr. Masi, but I have just been informed that Mr. Masi just arrived. So he will be about to join us when he is ready. So I will have Mr. Moy Keen Choy, Mr. Moy. Let's give a big hand to welcome Mr. Moy. Mr. Moy is the Executive Vice President of Capella Hotels.

我们将进入下一个话题。从现在开始，我们将用英语进行讨论。我们小组讨论的是亚洲酒店的核心竞争力，正如 James Lv 先生介绍的那样。今天下午我们邀请了5位非常杰出的业内人士。我会按照姓氏的首字母的顺序来介绍他们。所以我应该先从 Masi 先生开始。但我得知 Masi 先生刚刚到这里。他会加入我们，等他准备好。因此，先请出 Moy Keen Choy 先生，让我们热烈欢迎 Moy 先生。Moy 先生是嘉佩乐酒店的执行副总裁。

01：15—01：47

Let's have a seat. Second one, I will have Mr. Steven Pan. Mr. Pan is... because we will not be having Mr. Raymond Tong with us from the Accor Hotels & Resorts. So instead I will have Mr. Steven Pan. Can I have Mr. Steven Pan?

请坐。接着我要请出 Steven Pan 先生。Pan 先生是……因为我们没能邀请到来自雅高酒店集团的 Raymond Tong 先生。因此，我将请出 Pan 先生。有请 Pan 先生。

01：48—02：29

Mr. Steven Pan, Steven Pan, sorry, I use the Cantonese surname. Mr. Steven Pan is the Chairman of Regent Hotels & Resorts. So he should be able to share with us a lot about what his brand is doing in the Regent. The third guest we are having is Mr. Kent Sun. Kent Sun. Mr. Kent Sun is the Chief Development Officer from InterContinental Hotels Group.

Steven Pan 先生，对不起，我用的是广东话。Steven Pan 先生是丽晶酒店集团的董事长。所以他能和我们分享很多关于他如何打造丽晶酒店这个品牌的。我们的第三位嘉宾是 Kent Sun 先生。Kent Sun 先生是洲际酒店集团的首席发展官。

02：30—02：53

And we will have, this is a difficult name for me. Mr. Suparat Uahwatanasakul, something like that. Yes. Thank you! Suparat [is] Vice President from Centara Hotels & Resorts.

我们还将邀请，这位嘉宾的名字好难读，Suparat Uahwatanasakul 先生，差不多是这样读的，是的。谢谢你们！Suparat 先生是森塔拉酒店集团的副总裁。

02：54—03：25

So while we are waiting for Mr. Joe Masi from the Interstate, we will kick off our

第四单元　酒店管理 Hotel Management

discussion now. And maybe I will just give each one of you, starting from Mr. Moy, 30 seconds for each of you to introduce yourself and introduce your brand a little bit. Can I start with Mr. Moy?

我们一边等来自州际酒店的 Joe Masi 先生，边开始我们的讨论。我会给你们每个人，从 Moy 先生开始，每人 30 秒介绍一下自己和各自的品牌。可以从 Moy 先生开始吗？

03：26—04：00

Good afternoon, everyone. My name is KC, KC Moy. I mean the initials. Everyone address me as KC. I am the Executive Vice President of Capella Hotel Group Asia based in Singapore. Our company manages luxury and ultra luxury hotels under the brands of Capella and Schulze. Currently our projects in China are under, we just have one shop opening in China, and then the rest are all still under development. Thank you!

下午好，各位。我的名字是 KC，KC Moy。我的意思是我名字首字母是 KC。每个人都叫我 KC，我是嘉佩乐酒店集团的执行副总裁，我们总部位于新加坡。我们公司管理豪华和超豪华酒店，旗下品牌为嘉佩乐和舒尔茨。目前我们在中国的项目正在进行中，我们在中国只有一家店，其余的都还在开发中。谢谢大家！

04：01—04：57

I am Steven Pan and I represent the Regent Hotels & Resorts. And Regents was started by Mr. Burns with the Regent Hong Kong in 1980. And our company, of course, we're original owner of Regent hotel assets. And our company acquired Regent Hotels & Resorts in 2010, with Mr. Burns, again. And currently we have hotels and resorts in Beijing, Taipei, Singapore, and Bhuket, Bali, Turks and Caicos and Berlin. And we have ten more resorts and hotel projects underway around the world. Thank you!

我是 Steven Pan，我代表丽晶酒店集团。丽晶酒店集团由 Burns 先生与香港丽晶共同创办于 1980 年。我们公司，当然，是丽晶酒店资产的原始所有者。我们公司收购了丽晶酒店集团，当时是 2010 年，我们再次与 Burns 先生合作。目前，我们的酒店和度假村位于北京、台北、新加坡、布吉、巴厘岛、特克斯和凯科斯群岛和柏林，我们还有 10 多个度假村和酒店项目正在世界各地开展。谢谢大家！

04：58—05：02

Before we pass on to Mr. Kent Sun, we will just have Mr. Joe Masi joining us.
在 Kent Sun 先生做自我介绍前，我们先请 Joe Masi 先生上台加入我们。

45

05:03—05:16

So just grab a seat. So maybe we also give a big hand to Mr. Joe Masi from Interstate Hotels & Resorts.

请坐。我们先热烈欢迎 Joe Masi 先生，他来自州际酒店集团。

05:17—06:14

OK. I am Kent, Kent Sun from IHG, InterContinental Hotels Group. I need to be very careful because they are quite confusing: Interstate and InterContinental Hotels Group. My role [is] called the Chief Development Officer in charge of the IHG's all the brands development in Greater China. So this is a quite challenging topic for me talking about the Asian hotels. For some of you, you know that IHG was initiated to make our Greater China business to stand alone. So we don't have any Asia Pacific Region anymore. Then the good news, you know, we do have a lot of Chinese customers visit other part of the world, including, particularly in Asia. So I think this also may be quite relevant. Another challenge to me, compared to my fellow panels, other panels, I am the purely local 土鳖. So it is quite challenging to me to answer some of the questions. Sunny, please help me.

好的。我是 Kent, Kent Sun，我来自洲际酒店集团。我需要非常小心，因为它们很让人困惑：州际和洲际酒店集团。我的职务是首席发展官，负责洲际酒店集团所有品牌在大中华区的发展。所以这对我来说是一个很有挑战性的讨论，谈论亚洲酒店很有挑战性。对你们中的一些人来说，你们知道洲际酒店集团把我们在大中华区的业务独立出来。所以我们没有亚太区这一说法。好消息是，我们确实有很多中国客户去到世界其他地区，特别是在亚洲。所以我认为我的工作与这个讨论是非常相关的。另一个挑战对我来说，与我的同行相比，与其他嘉宾相比，我纯粹是土鳖。所以回答一些问题对我来说很有挑战性。Sunny，请您帮帮我。

06:15—06:20

It would be very gentle. We'll take care of you. Mr. Suparat.

我的问题会非常友善的。我们会照顾您的。现在有请 Suparat 先生。

06:21—06:50

My name is Suparat Uahwatanasakul. I come from Centara Hotels & Resorts of Thailand. This company is about 30 years old. And we have 61 properties now in eight countries. We started to come, our strategy come to China about a year ago. And now we have right now four properties in China, looking for more opportunities here. Thank you.

第四单元 酒店管理 Hotel Management

我叫 Suparat Uahwatanasakul,来自泰国森塔拉酒店集团。我们公司大约有 30 年的发展历史。有 61 家酒店和度假村,分布在 8 个国家。我们开始,我们的战略大约在一年前进入中国。现在我们有四家酒店在中国,我们在这里寻找更多的机会。谢谢!

06:51—07:06

What about you, Mr. Masi? You came late, so I will also, after your introduction, I will give you the first question. In your understanding, what are the core competency [competencies] of Asian hotels? So you can start.

您呢,Masi 先生?您来晚了,我会在您自我介绍之后,问您第一个问题。您认为亚洲酒店的核心竞争力是什么?请讲。

07:07—08:21

OK. So I can introduce myself first? First of all, my apologies for being late, the joys of travelling, certainly some place away was coming out of Shanghai. But my name is Joe Masi. I am with the Interstate Hotels & Resorts China. And for those of you who don't know Interstate Hotels & Resorts, our headquarters is in Washington D. C. in the USA. And unlike my colleagues, we are a third party operator. Our core business is managing hotels. We are not a brand. And we have offices throughout the globe. And recently, we opened our office in Shanghai about two and a half years ago. So we are very very excited to be in Asia, where certainly a fair amount of the growth is. And we have been pretty successful thus far. We operate four hotels throughout China. We have another eight signed deals and another ten in the pipeline. So the response to our services has been pretty good and our Senior VP of Development Albert Chen is here and he will be able to talk to many of you later that have interest.

好的。所以,我可以先自我介绍一下?首先,很抱歉,我迟到了。旅行的乐趣,我是从上海过来的。我是 Joe Masi,来自美国州际酒店集团中国公司。向那些不了解我们公司的嘉宾解释一下,我们的总部就在美国的华盛顿哥伦比亚特区。和其他嘉宾的公司不同的是,我们是第三方运营商。我们的核心业务是酒店管理。我们不是一个品牌。我们在全球各地都有办事处。最近,我们开设了上海办事处,大约是两年半前。因此,我们非常高兴能来到亚洲,亚洲的增长相当可观。到目前为止,我们已经取得了很大的成功。我们在中国经营着四家酒店,有 8 个签约交易,还有 10 个正在筹备中。所以客户对我们的服务反馈相当不错,我们的高级发展副总裁 Albert Chen 先生也在这里,他会和你们很多人聊聊,如果你们有兴趣的话。

08:22—08:29

And how do you understand the terms or the title of the discussion today, the core competencies of Asian hotels?

您如何理解今天讨论的话题——亚洲酒店的核心竞争力？

08:30—10:10

You know, I have really given that some thoughts. And frankly, you know, I think, one of the reasons why I came to Asia was, you know, there was the romance, and I guess the mysterious nature of Asian hospitality. And I haven't been here now for eight years. I will tell you that, you know, there is no place else on earth like Asian hospitality. And Asia has the largest [larger] share of luxury hotels than anywhere else. A lot of new products coming [come] on board and all [are of] very high quality. Hardwares are very good. A lot of emphases go into the software, the people's skills. So, you know, I think Asia is really continuing to define itself by, you know why, really continuing to evolve and re-evolve to stay at the top of hospitality. You know. Certainly, food and beverage also plays a very very large role, I think, and in the core of the Asian hotel business. And there is [are] probably more hotels than not that your revenues are at least 50%, food and beverage. And many hotels, the food and beverage revenue outdoes the room revenue. So you know food and beverage in Asia really is a place where people can count on going to have a good meal or a good experience. And I think that is also a very key competency in hotels revenue.

我对此进行了一些思考。坦率地说，我认为，我来亚洲的原因之一是因为浪漫，是亚洲人好客的神秘本质。我已经8年没来过这里了。我要告诉你们，地球上没有其他地方像亚洲人那样好客。而且，亚洲的豪华酒店比其他任何地方都要多。很多新产品上市，质量都很好。硬件很不错。很多人都把重点放在了软件，人们的技能上。因此，我认为亚洲确实在不断自我定义，在继续演进和重新进化，以保持在酒店业的领先地位。当然，我认为，餐饮在亚洲酒店的核心业务中也在发挥着重要作用。而且，通常很多酒店的收入中至少50%来自餐饮。许多酒店，其餐饮收入超过了客房收入。所以，亚洲的餐饮业确实能让人们享受一顿美餐或拥有一次美好的体验。我认为这也是影响酒店收入的一个非常关键的竞争力。

10:11—10:24

What about Suparat? We have just, I have just seen this 15.7% up, you know, for Thailand. So what have you got to share regarding the core competenies? Not about Thailand, about Asia.

Suparat先生觉得呢？我们刚刚看到，增长了15.7%，这是泰国的增长率。那么，您在核心竞争力方面有什么想说的呢？不是关于泰国，而是关于亚洲。

10：25—11：39

If you look around today, OK, you see that, actually, there is more and more Asian traveller travel [travelling] around the world. I think the world is a little bit different than a couple years before. Now the Western world is a little bit struggling and Asia starts to come up. And we have a new emerging market that, you know, the people in the country start to make a travelling. So for me, you know, I think it is the same that, you know when Western people travel anywhere, and they want to stay in the Western hotels. You know, for Asian people, when they travel, sometimes they want to look at, to stay in the Asian hotels, too. You know. And Asians, we have a specific set of values, you know, being, you know, nice people. You know, service comes from the heart. Very flexible. You know. Try to serve people. I think all these things is [are] called competences for the Asian hotels. You know, everywhere around the world, not just, you know, Thailand or China, everywhere.

如果您放眼全球，会发现事实上，越来越多的亚洲游客在世界各地旅行。我认为这个世界和几年前有点不同。现在西方世界陷入困境，亚洲开始崛起。我们有了一个新的新兴市场，这个国家的人们开始旅行。所以对我来说，我认为这是一样的，西方人去任何地方旅行，他们想要住在西方的酒店里。对于亚洲人来说，他们旅行的时候，有时他们也想住亚洲的酒店。亚洲人有一套特定的价值观，那就是待人友善。服务是发自内心的，非常灵活，尽力服务他人。我认为所有这些都是亚洲酒店的能力。世界各地，不仅仅是泰国或中国，到处都是这样。

11：40—11：45

But I will come back with a question to you later. Now Kent Sun, Mr. Kent Sun to answer.

我稍后会向您提一个问题。现在请 Kent Sun 先生回答。

11：46—13：09

Thank you. To me, I think, for Asian hotels, the core competency [competencies] will be, no doubt, hospitality, service, people. Really the people make the difference. One is a nature of the human being in Asia. So we are very kind to each other, also very kind to our people. Again, if I use Chinese as an example, 热情好客. So basically, even we don't have…we always try to show our best thing to our guest, always try to treat our visitors, treat our guest with warm welcome, give them best treatment. Sometimes, in old days, for my parents' generation, even they don't have enough food to eat, they don't have the good conditions, but whenever there is a guest to come to our home, we always treated them very well. So similar philosophy for hotel industry. Basically, any guest come [who comes] to our hotel, naturally, our people offer them very best service. So this is to make Asian hotels different to the other part of the world. So if you can ask me to name one of the good examples, great example, it will be Shangri-La. So Shangri-La probably that will represent Asian hospitality. Thank you.

谢谢！对我来说，我认为对于亚洲酒店而言，其核心竞争力无疑是热情好客、服务和员工。说实在的，是员工让我们的酒店与众不同。一个是亚洲人的本性，所以我们对彼此都很友好，对我们的客人也很友好。如果我拿中国举例子，热情好客。所以，基本上，即使我们没有……我们总是尽量把最好的展示给客人，总是试着去招待客人，热情欢迎客人，给他们最好的待遇。有时，在过去，对于我父母那一代人来说，即使他们饭不够吃，条件也不好，但是每当有客人来我们家的时候，我们总是很好地招待客人。这类似于酒店行业的理念。基本上，有客人来我们酒店，自然我们的员工会为他们提供最好的服务。这就是亚洲的酒店区别于世界其他地方酒店的方面。所以如果要我举一个具体的例子，好的例子，那就是香格里拉。香格里拉能代表亚洲人的热情好客。谢谢！

13：10—13：18

So it is a willingness to serve, the service standard is something, you know, you'll define as the core competence, one of the key elements. (Yes.) What about you, Mr. Pan?

所以这是一种服务的意愿，服务标准是，您将其定义为核心竞争力，一个关键要素。(是的)。您觉得呢，Pan 先生？

13：19—15：19

I totally agree with what Kent, and what Joe and everybody said. It's because Regent started in Regent Hong Kong, so [it is] an Asian brand that has gone global. And the most important thing is the really innate gracious hospitality, the hospitality coming from the heart and that transcends, you know, styles or service. That is different from the rest of the world. And another part is food and beverage. Because food and beverage in a lot of Asian countries, especially Chinese dominated countries, often account [accounts] for more than half of the hotel revenue. This is not the same for the rest of the world. So the emphasis on food and beverage is very very important. And I would also like to add that in Asia, because there is a huge expat community in a lot of Asian countries, so there is a very unique Asian hospitality. That is a fusion of local innate graciousness with a western style of look. And it has an air in itself. And I guess you can see it in Aman Resort. And that is really a new Asian style in terms of design. And I would also like to add that, with that, the spa is also a concept that's usually related to the Asian hospitality competence. And lastly, I would also like to add that because in Asia, people value real estate a lot more. So I would say that the combination of hotels and residentials are also a very very strong component of Asian hospitality companies.

完全同意 Kent, Joe 和其他每个人的观点。这是因为丽晶酒店集团起步于香港丽晶,是一个已经走向全球的亚洲品牌。最重要的是真正与生俱来的热情好客,这种热情发自内心,超越酒店的风格或服务,这不同于世界其他地方。另一部分是餐饮。由于许多亚洲国家的餐饮,尤其是以华人为主的国家,其餐饮收入往往占酒店收入的一半以上。这就不同于世界其他地区。因此,重视餐饮非常重要。我还想补充一点,在亚洲,因为许多亚洲国家都有庞大的外籍人群,因此亚洲的好客非常独特,融合了当地与生俱来的亲切与酒店外观的西方风格,有自身的特点。我想你们可以从安缦度假村看到这一点。这确实是一种新的亚洲风格,就设计方面而言。我还想补充一点,在这一点上,水疗也是一个通常与亚洲酒店竞争力相关的概念。最后,我还想补充一点,因为在亚洲,人们更看重房地产。因此,我想说的是,酒店和住宅的结合也是亚洲酒店公司的非常强大的组成部分。

15:20—15:23
Thank you. Mr. Moy.
谢谢您,Moy 先生。

15:24—17:55
Yes. Sure. What I would add is that, you know, we look at competency, because Asia is very diverse, and you have different, you know, different preferences, different nationalities and different ethnic groups. So the competencies in China would be different from the competencies in Southeast Asia as well as in India, and also compared to some of the hotels that we manage in Western Europe and Americas. But for us, it's that you know our company was founded by Mr. Horst Schulze. He was the man who established Ritz-Carlton you know in the early days until the time when it was sold to Marriott. So we manage our hotels whether it is in Europe and Americas or Asia with two things. Number one is service excellence. So we are a customer-centric company, because we only play in the luxury and ultra-luxury space. So wherever we are, we would try to understand the customers, what is their preference. I think our fellow guests mentioned about spa and F&B. Families and kids is another thing I would highlight here as well. Asian families and Asian guests tend to have a bigger emphasis on kids. So, I think

China, and this one, it's China, I think China is, you know, a large percentage of the hotels, maybe with the exception of Shanghai, and Beijing and Guangzhou, you will tend to see you know a high majority of Chinese guests. So you know, we will look towards you know, leveraging you know, our operating processes to ensure that you know, we understand how the you know, what the Chinese guests like and dislike, and ensure that you know, we can drive the highest level of customer satisfaction. And that process would be different you know for a Southeast Asia hotel, which we have you know, in Singapore and Bali, and whether it is a city or resort hotels, you know, the competencies are also very different. But, I think two things for us. Number one is service excellence, which goes to the heart of customer-centricity [centric]. Now that you're making sure that customer is satisfied and wants to come back and would recommend other guests to come as well. And then secondly, it's obviously when we do development, the design and the program of hotel would be very important to ensure that the competency is captured into every single hotel that we manage.

　　是的，的确。我想补充的是，我们关注的是能力，因为亚洲是非常多样化的，有不同的偏好，不同的国籍和不同的民族。因此，中国的竞争力将不同于东南亚和印度的竞争力，与我们在西欧和美洲管理的酒店相比也不尽相同。但对我们来说，您知道我们的公司是由Horst Schulze先生创立的。就是他在早期建立了丽嘉酒店，后来丽嘉酒店卖给了万豪酒店集团。因此，我们管理我们的酒店，无论是在欧洲、美洲还是亚洲，通过两个方面来管理。第一是通过卓越的服务。我们是一家以客户为中心的公司，因为我们只经营豪华和超豪华酒店。所以，无论我们在哪里，我们都会试图了解客户，了解他们的偏好。其他嘉宾提到了水疗、餐饮。家庭和孩子是我在这里强调的另一点。亚洲的家庭和亚洲客人往往更注重孩子。所以，我认为在中国，大部分的酒店，也许除了上海、北京和广州，您会发现绝大多数的顾客都是中国人。所以我们会利用操作流程，以确保了解中国客人喜欢什么，不喜欢什么，并确保我们可以达到最高的客户满意度。这个过程不同于东南亚的酒店，我们集团在新加坡和巴厘岛都有酒店，不论是城市还是度假酒店，其竞争力都非常不同。但我认为有两点很重要。第一是卓越的服务，是以客户为中心。确保客户满意，成为回头客，并会推荐其他客人前来。其次，显而易见，我们开发酒店项目时，酒店的设计和服务项目都非常重要，确保我们管理的每一家酒店都具备这样的竞争力。

III. 实战练习二

1. 演讲背景

　　下文同样摘自"亚洲酒店论坛集团高管会议"的小组讨论内容，讨论的主题为

"亚洲酒店核心竞争力"。嘉宾们普遍认为,亚洲酒店的核心竞争力就在于亚洲人的热情好客、良好的口碑、训练有素和具有服务精神的员工。因此他们反复强调需要吸引合适的人才,提供培训,建立忠诚度,留住员工。鉴于中国出境游客大幅增加,嘉宾们认为需要满足中国游客的基本需求,包括提供开水、酒店里配备说中文的员工、改进服务设施、提供中国食物、建设购物场所和水疗设施。

2. 预习词汇

exemplary 示范性的;典范性的
butler 管家
innate 天生的;特有的
instinct 本性
mobilize 动员;调动
Balinese 巴厘人
Caribbean 加勒比海
Filipino 菲律宾人;菲律宾语;菲律宾的;菲律宾人的
moonlighting 兼职
consulate 领事馆
in a nutshell 简而言之
swarm 蜂拥而至
Phuket 普吉岛
Pattaya 芭堤雅
Jakarta 雅加达
Everest 珠穆朗玛峰
patronize 惠顾
F&B outlet 餐饮店

3. 演讲文本

00:00—00:50

Thank you! I just heard that some of you mentioned is the service; some of you mentioned actually is the design. People feels with the western style of hospitality. So I get the idea that, you know, most of you agree that the people, the people, elements affect the people is the key ingredient to make Asian hotels very different. But how do you keep up your, you know, this kind of promise? Or how do you actually deliver this exemplary services that make Asian hotels, a lot of Asian hotels top the list of the world's finest. I will start with Suparat.

谢谢您!我刚才听你们当中的有些人提到服务,有些人提到设计。人们会被西方式的款待所触动。所以我认为,你们大多数人都同意,员工或员工特质是亚洲酒店与众不同的关键。但是,您如何兑现您的这种承诺?或者您如何传递这种典范性的服务?这种服务让亚洲酒店,许多亚洲酒店成为了世界上一流的优质酒店。我们从 Suparat 开始发言。

00:50—02:24

You know, we have been really lucky. You know, I come from Thailand. I think people is knowing about the Thai hospitality. You know, in the old days, when you walked into the house, the people will put the water in front of the door. You know, if you get tired, you basically you go get the water. And sometime [sometimes] people invite you to the house. You know, we have that culture. Also for us, you know, Centara, you know, we sell Thai hospitality. So we try to export that to everywhere that we go, you know, in every hotel, even in the eight countries, you know, we have Thai people that we have in all the hotels. You know, HR, you know, tries to teach our local staff, you know, like the one in Maldives that we have. It becomes very very successful. They teach the Maldivian people to have a culture to some extent, you know. You cannot turn the people from another part of the world to be Thai, you know. We have something like that, you know. So that is what we try. Because we hope that you know, when customer come and experience that, you know they can [be] touched by wider service. And after they get touched by the service there, they talk, so make them understand our products more. That is how we try to differentiate our products. I think everyone tries to differentiate the products. That is just how we do it.

我们真的很幸运。我来自泰国。我想人们都知道泰式款客。以前,当你们走进房子的时候,人们会把水放在门前。如果您累了,您会去拿水,有时人们邀请您到房子里来。我们有这样的文化。对我们来说,森塔拉酒店集团的卖点就是泰式款客。所以我们尝试把它出口到我们去的任何地方,包括我们集团在八个国家的酒店,那里都有泰国人。人力资源部尝试去教导我们的当地员工,就像在马尔代夫那家酒店一样。它是非常成功的。他们教导马尔代夫人在某种程度上也拥有这样的文化。您不能把世界上其他地方的人变成泰国人。我们有类似的东西。这就是我们进行的尝试。因为我们希望顾客来体验的时候,他们可以被更贴心的服务所打动。他们被打动后会与他人分享,因此,让他们更多地了解我们的产品。这就是我们如何尝试着去使得我们的产品与众不同。我认为每个人都试图使得产品差异化。这就是我们的策略。

第四单元　酒店管理 Hotel Management

02:24—02:26
Word of mouth, you mean?
口碑吗，您的意思是？

02:26—03:04
Yes. You know, in our company, you know, they have, you know, the strategy called viral marketing. Actually I don't really like the word "viral marketing". But basically it is the word of mouth. You know we get the people to talk, you know. Now, you know, it is a little bit easier that we have the cyberspace. We have Facebook. We have those kind of things that you know, when people come to talk about our hotels, you know, they have the peers to talk. And actually, our good work relies heavily on to make sure that when people say something about our hotels, people in the cyber world know about it.

对。我们的公司有一个策略，叫"病毒营销"，实际上我不太喜欢"病毒营销"这个词。但基本上就是做口碑。您知道我们让人们分享。现在这更简单了，因为我们有网络空间，我们有脸书，我们有这样的东西，所以当人们在谈论我们的酒店的时候，他们有同伴一起讨论。事实上，我们的工作能做好，很大程度上取决于当人们评价我们的酒店时，这些评价能在网络上得以传播。

03:04—03:09
Thank you. What about you, Mr. Kent Sun?
谢谢您。您呢？Kent Sun 先生？

03:09—06:03
We don't have that kind of fortune, you know, like you guys in Thailand. So I think all of the hotel operators, we are facing big challenge—talent. We don't have well-trained people. Sounds strange. We have 1.3-billion population in China, but don't have enough well-trained, skilled force staff. And now they have the passion; they have willingness to do the hotel business any more. So this is the biggest challenge. I witness many many of our hotels, or some of the competitors, in particular, in tier-one cities, all of a sudden, most of the service staff, they are not from local. We need to build a dormitory, big dormitory for all the staff as well. So if we rely on people to provide very good service, the best service, try to build our core competency, I don't think it is sustainable any more, in particular, in China, in these days. One is we lack of people. Two, the labor cost increasing dramatically. So this is we need to do something very differently. I know, very few luxury hotels, they have 170 rooms, but meanwhile, they

55

have 700 staff. I don't think any other brand, any other hotel can afford to have this kind of luxury. So, for instance, our company, Holiday Inn, our target is very simple. The staff ratio will be 1∶1. One room, one staff. Maximum. Compared to other part of the world, it is still a very, very high staff ratio. So we need to do something very differently. On the other hand, I think, different consumer, different level of customer, they have very different need. If we use airlines as a benchmark, a lot of people, they don't care, they don't want to do check-in as the traditional way anymore. Automatic, you know, by themselves, self-service. Not every customer, including myself, always expect a so-called butler service. Why do I need it? I am very young; I am very self-driven. So not every customer like Mercedes-Benz; some of the people like BMW. BMW already… I don't want to, you know, promote their brand. Different customers, they have different habit, different philosophy. So this also give us, to have very different thinking. So why we have very different brand? I think our fellow colleagues are sitting here. So different company, we have very different vision and also very different brand. We have very different way [ways] to do business.

我们没有这么幸运，没有你们泰国人这么幸运。所以我认为所有的酒店运营商，都面临着巨大的挑战——人才。我们没有训练有素的人才，这听起来很奇怪。中国有13亿人口，却没有足够的训练有素、技能娴熟的员工。现在他们有热情，他们愿意做酒店行业。所以这是最大的挑战。我目睹了许多我们的酒店，或一些酒店竞争对手，特别是在一线城市，突然间，大部分的服务人员不是来自当地。我们需要建一个宿舍，一个大宿舍给所有的员工。因此，如果我们依靠员工来提供优质的服务，最好的服务，努力建立我们的核心竞争力，我认为这不再是可持续的，特别是在中国，在当今社会。一是我们缺乏人才。二是劳动力成本大幅上升。所以我们需要采取不同的措施。我知道，极少数的豪华酒店，他们有170间客房，但与此同时，他们有700个员工。我不认为任何其他品牌，任何其他酒店能如此的奢侈。所以，比如我们公司假日酒店，我们的目标很简单。客房和员工的比例为1∶1。一个房间配一个工作人员，最大值。与世界其他地区相比，这仍然是一个非常非常高的人员比率。所以我们需要采取不同的措施。另一方面，我认为不同的消费者、不同层次的客户，他们有着非常不同的需求。如果我们以航空公司为基准，很多人不在乎，不想再以传统的方式办理登机手续了，而是喜欢自助服务。不是每个顾客，包括我自己，总是期望有所谓的管家服务。为什么我需要管家服务呢？我很年轻，我很有上进心。所以不是每个顾客都喜欢梅赛德斯-奔驰；有的人喜欢宝马。宝马已经……我不想推广他们的品牌。不同的客户有不同的习惯，不同的理念。所以这也给我们带来了不同的思考。所以为什么我们有不同的品牌？我想我们的同事们都坐在这里。不同的公司有非常不同的愿景和不同的品牌。我们做生意的方式完全不同。

06:03—06:09
I will come back to you, but I will pass it to Mr. Steven Pan first.
我会再与您讨论,现在我先把麦克风交给 Steven Pan 先生.

06:09—07:02
Well, we hire people for their innate instinct to you know share, and then to… So we hire for attitudes. And then we would like to hire people who have actually no experience. So we train. And we are able to mobilize. We're sending the Balinese to the Caribbean in the summer and then we are sending Filipinos to Europe. So there is something that one can do to really mobilize this Asian workforce globally. Not very easy though. Some visa restrictions. But we have been doing a lot of that, controlling off-seasons and peak seasons. So we yeah…
我们招人是基于他们愿意分享的天性,还有……是基于他们的态度。我们想招那些没有经验的人。所以我们做培训,我们做动员。我们夏天的时候把巴厘岛人派到加勒比海地区,然后将菲律宾人送往欧洲。所以我们可以采取行动,真正地动员亚洲劳动力,在全球范围内发挥他们的价值。虽然不是很容易,会有一些签证限制。但我们已经做了很多这种工作,控制好淡季和旺季。所以我们……

07:02—07:11
So you have been moonlighting for the Filipino consulate? For their…?
所以您一直在菲律宾领事馆兼职?为了他们的……?

07:11—07:14
Something like that. We have a very strong relationship with them.
类似这样,我们之间关系很稳固。

07:14—07:19
So he declares. So let's have Mr. Moy's view.
所以这就是他的观点。现在我们来听听 Moy 先生的看法。

07:19—09:47
Yes. Sure. I think the process for our staff… No.1, attracting the talent. And I fully agree with Kent. The talent pool in China, although it is vast, but it is very tight because of… a lot of new hotels are being built. So there is the competition for talent. So the ability to attract people…I think if you are, you know, if you are a multi-brand, like InterContinental, you have a bigger pool. For us, we only play in the five-star

luxury. So the benefit is that you know we focus on that segment of the market to attract our people. I see it as the biggest challenge, attracting people. And once we attract them, then we have a very thorough and vigorous selection process, not just in terms of your skill set but also looking at their attitude of willing to serve from the heart. Because we believe in the philosophy that you know a good service staff, you know if they have that DNA or it is in their blood, then the training is the easy part. So once the selection process is done, then the third thing we do is obviously the continuous training, and depending on the depth of the skills set of the market, different level of training [will be, like,] would be required. I think in China, because again, talent pool is tight, we tend to, have to hire people which are less experienced. And therefore, the level of training is a lot more intense. Then after training, you know it is actually the monitoring process, the employee satisfaction. Survey. And that goes through the quality measurement that we do every measure. You know how employees are doing as well as you know whether they and themselves are happy. Because we believe that if the employees are satisfied and happy, then the true service would then be able to be extended to, you know, to our guests. So that five-step process of, you know, quality management, as we call it, you know, we practice it across all of our hotels to try to drive you know this operation processes.

是的。当然。我认为这个过程对于我们的员工来说第一是吸引人才。我完全同意 Kent 的看法。中国的人才库，虽然很庞大，但也非常紧张，因为……有很多新的酒店正在兴建。因此，存在着人才竞争，吸引人才的能力很重要。我认为如果您是一个多品牌的酒店，比如洲际，您就有一个更大的人才库。对我们来说，我们只经营五星级豪华酒店。因此，好处是我们专注于这一部分市场来吸引人才。我认为这是最大的挑战，吸引人才。一旦我们吸引了人才，我们就有一个非常彻底和严格的筛选过程，不仅仅要看他们的技能组合，也会看他们的态度，是否愿意真心实意地服务。因为我们认为一个好的服务人员，如果他对真心实意的服务非常认同的话，那么培训是很容易的事。因此，一旦完成筛选，我们做的第三件事显然是不断的培训，基于市场对技能组合的要求，我们需要开展不同层次的培训。我认为中国人才库很紧张，我们倾向于招那些经验不足的人。因此，培训力度会更大。培训后是一个监控的过程，监控员工的满意度，做调查。我们采取的每一项措施都要进行质量测量，您知道员工表现如何，也知道他们是否开心。因为我们认为如果员工满意、开心，那么真正的服务会延伸到客人身上。因此，您知道质量管理的五个步骤，这是我们的说法，我们在我们所有的酒店践行这五个步骤，以落实整个操作过程。

09：47—09：54
Thank you. Mr. Masi. You want to add to this topic on service quality assurance?
谢谢您，Masi 先生。关于服务质量保证这个话题，您还想说些什么吗？

09：54—11：40
Yeah. You know. Truly, it is a tough market. It is probably tougher to get associates in a hotel than it is we're actually to find hotels to manage. What you do, you know, is really starts from their group and process. You know. I think everyone has mentioned here. You want to find the right DNA, obviously the right attitude and someone that has the service, you know, mentality. And that's a lot easier said than done. And there are fewer and fewer of those associates out there that are genuinely hospitality-minded. You know, once obviously we find the right people and teach them our core values, and really what are all about and get into them, we can get in our service delivery. And our training, and really start to build the loyalty. I think that is really an important part of this whole processes. It's building the loyalty among the staff, to try and have them stay working for your retention. Because you know if you continue to recruit, and hire and train, and they don't stay, it is really costly. And it is not good for, you know, obviously for the business. So we focus a lot on loyalty through different programs and such. And then obviously, you know, building a bench strength for us is important so that we could deploy existing staff to new projects or, you know, as we need them in different locations throughout Asia. So you know kind of in a nutshell, that is really kind of we have. We approach our issues.

是的。事实上，这是一个艰难的市场。为酒店聘请员工比我们找酒店来管理要困难得多。您要做的事是从他们的群体和流程开始的。我想每个人在这里都提到过。您想找到对的人，显然指的是态度端正、有服务精神的人，这说起来容易做起来难。那些真正有服务精神的人越来越少。显然，当我们找到了合适的人，教给他们我们的核心价值观，真正融入他们，我们就可以把我们的服务传递出去。培训有助于建立忠诚度，我认为这是整个流程的重要部分，建立员工忠诚度，留住员工。因为如果您不断地招人，不断地培训，他们都呆不长久，代价真的很大，这显然不利于公司的业务发展。我们通过不同的项目来提高忠诚度。显然，储备力量也很重要，这样我们就能把现有的员工派去开展新的项目，或者把他们派到亚洲的不同地方去。简而言之，这就是我们的措施，我们就是这样来处理问题的。

11：40—11：47
So your strategy is mainly to retain and really to equip them with the tools to serve.
所以您的策略主要是留住他们，让他们具备服务所需的技能。

11: 47—12: 00

Exactly. Yes. That is a big part. It's building the royalty and retention. You know, obviously, we will continue to train them over time, but if we keep them and build the loyalty, that is key.

确实是这样,很大一部分是这样,就是建立忠诚度、留用员工。显然,我们会不断地进行员工培训,但如果我们要留住他们、建立忠诚度的话,这就是关键。

12: 00—13: 09

I promise to come back with a question to you. Mr. Kent Sun. You just mentioned about this. It depends on the brands. Maybe some Chinese, probably they don't really need a lot of attentions. So I just give you one question that while the foreign arrival you know to Asia is not increasing too quickly, it is falling. I wouldn't use the word "falling". But the Chinese, you know the mainland Chinese are swarming every single destination in Asia. You know, everywhere you go, Phuket, Pattaya, or you know Indonesia, Jakarta, and even the Mountain Everest, you know you see Chinese. So how actually you know your brand gear up to cater to the needs of these Chinese, you know, new-income, out-bounded travelers/tourists?

我说过会再问您一个问题,Kent Sun先生。您刚刚提到取决于品牌。也许有些中国人,也许他们并不需要太多的关注。所以,我只想问您一个问题,来亚洲的外国游客数量增长并非很快,实际上是在下降。我不会用"下降"这个词。但中国人,您知道中国大陆的人涌向亚洲的各个旅游目的地。无论您去哪里,普吉岛、芭堤雅,或者印度尼西亚、雅加达,甚至是珠穆朗玛峰,都能看到中国人。那么,您怎么知道您的品牌已经可以满足这些中国人的需求,这些富裕的出境游客呢?

13: 10—14: 51

OK, I think it is a very good question. Like you mentioned, a lot of Chinese goes overseas. During this year's Spring Festival, I start to use, to learn Weixin [WeChat]. Tracy is a Weixin Daren. So one of the first thing I learned from Weixin, a lot of my good friends, they took their family overseas. They went overseas to visit different part of the world, either, you know in Japan, in Thailand. Because of 《泰囧》, one film is so funny (A very famous movie I suppose). I know, also in Europe, in the US, everywhere, a lot of places. Amazing, you know. So I would dream to go with my family as well. So you are absolutely right. According to the latest data, basically last year, in 2012, the Chinese outbound business, first time, reached 18 million. 18 million travelers go to overseas. The top ten destinations name Hong Kong, Macau, Taiwan, Thailand, South Korea, Vietnam, Japan. Basically, I think, top ten, except the US market, all are in Asia. All are in Asia. So basically, talking about the Chinese consumers, it is no big difference compared to the Western visitors. To me, we call it fits the basics.

好的,问的非常好。就像您提到的,很多中国人出国了。今年春节期间,我开始学习使用微信。Tracy是微信达人。所以,我从微信朋友圈里得知的第一件事就是,很多好朋友把家人带到了国外,去世界各地旅游,有的去了日本、泰国,因为《泰囧》,一部非常有趣的电影(我认为这部电影很出名)。有些去了欧洲、美国,世界各地,很多地方,非常棒!所以我也想着和家人一起旅游,所以您是完全正确的。根据最新数据,去年,2012年,中国出境游客第一次达到1,800万。1,800万名旅客出境。十大旅游目的地是香港、澳门、台湾、泰国、韩国、越南、日本等。前十位,除了美国以外,都在亚洲。所以,中国消费者与西方游客相比差别不大。对我来说,就是要满足游客的基本需求。

14:51—14:55
Except, you know, they buy a lot of milk powder.
除了他们会买一堆奶粉。

14:55—16:04
So what means fits the basics is for certain degree, for some of the Western company, their feel is so different. Why? Because Chinese consumer, we like hot water; western like ice water. We like congee, you guys like you know western food. We like Chinese language, speak in Chinese language; even now, myself, watch the Chinese TV channels. So of course, for westerner, they want to watch the English channel and to speak in English. So all these kind of things is so basic need. If you ask our company, we just try to fit the basics is we try to provide Chinese food, hot water, the Chinese language speaking staff and also Chinese TV channels. Again, I think this is so-called fit the basics. Fundamentally, looks very different, but the need is so the same compared to the western travelers.

因此,满足基本需求意味着,某种程度上,一些西方公司认为基本需求也存在差异。为什么呢?因为中国的消费者喜欢喝开水;西方人喜欢冰水。我们喜欢喝粥,你们喜欢吃西餐。我们喜欢说中文,甚至现在,我自己也看中文电视频道。当然,对于西方人来说,他们想看英文频道,用英语交谈。这些都是基本需求。如果您问我们这个问题,我们满足他们的基本需求就是提供中餐、开水、会说中文的员工和中文电视频道。我认为这就是所谓的满足基本需求。从根本上说,具体需求看上去差别很大,但中西方游客的总体需求差不多。

16: 04—16: 07

So what about you, Mr. Pan?

那么您呢，Pan 先生？

16: 07—17: 15

I totally agree with Kent. And I think language is one area though. We try to have Chinese language speaking personnel in the right place in a hotel or resort. And we also have VIP programs, VIP service managers. And some of them actually follow key Chinese clients around the world. Yeah. So it's because I think it is very important to have a, so like relationship-based service. And you also have to gear your facility to be ready for multi-generational travelling, because, you know, not only parents, or kids, from their grandparents, big groups, so you need to have your facility flexible enough. For instance, multi-bedroom villas and so to accommodate the needs for multi-generational travelling. Thank you!

我完全同意 Kent 的看法。我认为语言是一部分。我们尽量让讲中文的人呆在适当位置上，在酒店或度假村里。我们也有 VIP 项目，VIP 服务经理。他们中的一些人实际上会关注世界各地主要的中国客户。因为我认为建立基于良好关系的服务非常重要。您还需改进设施，为多代游做好准备，因为您知道，不仅仅有父母，孩子，还有他们的祖父母，大的旅游群体，所以您的设施要足够有弹性。如多居室别墅，可以满足多代游的需求。谢谢大家！

17: 15—18: 13

Before Mr. Moy addresses this question, I modify the question a little bit, because recently I saw a Weibo message online. Weibo is the Twitter equivalent in China. And there is a little note about a Maldives resort. The GM actually, they told the staff stop providing hot water, you just mentioned hot water, to the Chinese guests. The reason is if they have the hot water, they could make their noodles, instant noodle in the room. And then they won't you know patronize the F&B outlets. So how are you gonna address this you know? Chinese, hot water. Mr. Kent Sun just said hot water. But what about you? You running this Maldives resort, do you give hot water? Mr. Moy.

在 Moy 先生回答这个问题之前，我稍微改一下这个问题，因为最近我在网上看到一条微博。微博类似于推特。有一则关于马尔代夫度假村的消息，总经理让工作人员不要提供开水，您刚才提到开水，不提供开水给中国客人。原因是如果有开水，他们会在房间里吃方便面。然后他们就不去餐饮店了。那您怎么解决这个问题呢？中国人要喝开水。Kent Sun 先生刚刚提到了开水的问题。那您呢？您经营这个马尔代夫度假村，您提供开水吗？Moy 先生。

18:13—19:42

Actually, we do. You know, in Maldives property, you know the past couple years, actually it has changed a lot you know. Before we had the lead market is German and UK, but now become Chinese. You know Chinese is No. 1 traveller to Maldives now. It is a very expensive destination. You know I tell you what's Chinese like. Actually you know, it is very similar to all Asian countries you know. No. 1 is food. Food have to be good. Second one is shopping. Even in the island, small island, you have to have place for them to shop. (Host: Nowhere, nothing to shop in Maldives.) We try. We try to put some store and so that they can shop. And third you know, this is new. You know it's they like to go to spa. OK. We get asked about hot water. Yes. We get a lot of requests that we have to put the hot water in. And surprisingly, we get a lot of requests to put the instant noodle in the room. Actually, so we do that. And also we provide the free Internet for the younger generation, for Chinese, too. That is what we have to do. So you know, you know, when, you know, you have to cater, you know, the different kind of the traveler, you know, you have to adapt your products to fit the market. That is normal. I think that is what everyone would try to do, too.

事实上,我们提供开水。马尔代夫的酒店在过去几年里发生了很多变化。之前在我们这儿主要的游客来自德国和英国,但现是中国。您知道马尔代夫游客中中国人最多,这儿消费非常高。我告诉您中国人是什么样的,他们和其他亚洲人都非常相似。排第一的是吃,一定要吃好。第二是购物。即使在小岛上,也要有地方让他们去购物。(主持人:没什么地方,没什么可在马尔代夫买的。)我们试着建一些商店,这样他们就能买东西了。第三点是一个新现象。他们喜欢去水疗。您问我有关开水的问题,对,很多人要求我们提供开水。令人惊讶的是,很多人还要求客房里也提供方便面。事实上,我们照做了。此外,我们提供免费网络给年轻一代,给中国人。这是我们应该做的。所以要迎合不同游客的需求,要自我调整,适应市场,这很正常。我认为大家都会这样做。

19:42—19:48

So you wouldn't tell your staff to stop providing hot water to the Chinese?
所以您不会让员工不给中国人提供开水?

19:48—19:50

I don't think that you can eat instant noodle every meal, you know.
我觉得您不会每顿都吃方便面的。

19:50—19:53
Some could.
有的人会。

19:53—20:05
When you go to the beautiful location like that, you know so I think, I don't know, but we provide hot water in the room and also instant noodles, too.
当您去到像马尔代夫那么美丽的地方,我想,我不知道,但是我们也在客房里提供开水,还有方便面。

20:05—20:11
OK. Let's return the mic to Mr. Moy. Mr. Moy, you want to address this?
好的。让我们把麦克风还给 Moy 先生。Moy 先生,您想谈论这个问题吗?

20:11—21:40
Yes. I think, you know, we are seeing the same phenomenon of Chinese outbound travelers to the key major cities. Our property, example of properties in Singapore and Bali, Chinese represent the biggest percentage of foreign guests. At each of these two hotels, it's the same strategy. We, you know, we try to cater to their needs, you know, language is one. You know, I think that is very important because not many Chinese guests speak English. So being able to communicate in Chinese, having somebody there is important. The menus have to be in Chinese. Chinese newspapers have to be, you know, provided for. You have to have, you know, some of the Chinese food as well, congee, and dim sum etc. So it is no different to how you know we look at other guests as well. I think we welcome the Chinese. I think they represent the new affluent travelers. I see that you know in the next decade or two, and the growth is phenomenal. So we have to you know we have to change our way of running the hotels to ensure that their needs you know are met.
是的。我们看到同样的状况,出现在中国出境游客身上,他们前往各大城市旅游。我们的酒店,例如在新加坡和巴厘岛的酒店,中国人在外国客人中占的比重最大。两家酒店采用同样的策略。我们努力迎合他们的需要,语言就是其一。我认为语言很重要,因为很多中国客人不会说英语。所以能够用中文交流,有会说中文的员工很重要。菜单要用中文。中文报纸要提供。要有中餐、粥、点心等。所以这跟我们对待其他客人的方式没什么不同。我们欢迎中国客人,他们代表了新一批富裕的游客。我知道在接下来的十年或二十年里,中国游客增长会相当惊人,所以我们必须改变我们酒店的经营方式,满足中国游客的需求。

第五单元　金融服务
Financial Service

I. 有稿同传

1. 什么是有稿同传？

有稿同传也被称为视译，指"同传译员拿着讲话人的发言稿，边听发言、边进行同声传译"（仲伟合，2008：71）。

有稿同传一般有以下几种情况：（1）会议的组织者既提供发言的原稿，也提供发言的译文。这种情况下，译员只需要边听发言，边做"同声传读"。（2）会议的组织者只提供发言的原稿，译员则需要在同传前自己做好视译准备。（3）会议的组织者提供发言人讲稿的提纲或幻灯片。这是大部分会议最常见的情形。

2. 如何准备有稿同传？

无论是有稿同传的哪一种情况，译员在拿到材料后都应当认真做好译前准备。一般来说，译员需要在会议前两周就开始准备，应和会议主办方或者发言人充分沟通，争取尽量多地拿到材料。在实际情况中，有些主办方和发言人可能出于各种原因，不太愿意提供发言材料。译员应直接或者通过翻译公司向主办方或发言人说明同传工作情况，让其了解材料对于同传工作的重要性。

如果译员拿到的是源语版的发言稿，在有充分时间准备的情况下，可以把讲稿中较难的词语、语句笔译出来，在讲稿上做一定的语篇分析和断句标识。译员如果对讲稿的内容很有把握，可以在发言稿上做一些标识，可以用箭头、下划线、五角星等符号标注出发言人讲话的思路及语篇标识；对于一些关键性的词语，如术语、机构名称、职务头衔，译员可以先笔译出来，在有稿同传的过程中就可以直接照读，这样既可以节省精力，又可以避免因临时翻译而出现差错。

如果译员在会议开始前才拿到发言稿，这时译员只能跳读或扫读，了解讲稿大意，应着重看引言和结尾，并掌握正文部分的逻辑关联。如果时间允许，可以把引言和结尾的重要词语翻译一下。准备好引言有助于译员进入良好的口译状态，准备结尾部分有助于译员掌握讲话的主要内容。此外，译好引言和结尾往往会给听众留下良好的印象，从而增加译员的工作信心。

3. 如何练习有稿同传?

同声传译的训练一般都是从有稿同传开始,同传学习者可以按照以下步骤进行练习。

首先,可以做"同声传读",即使用一些有译文的讲稿,边听发言录音,边读译文,通过这种方法,同传学习者可以初步感受同传的语速和状态。

其次,只看源语讲稿进行口译。要求同传学习者在较短的时间内通读原文,把握原文的主要内容,针对词语、语句等少数难点做译前准备。

有稿同传训练可以先从段落开始,再逐步过渡到篇章的练习。由于中英两种语言在句子结构上存在较大差异,因此同传学习者在视译中经常出现的问题是译文翻译腔较重,表达不顺畅。口译学习者平时应加大有稿同传练习。

II. 实战练习一

1. 演讲背景

英国驻广州总领事馆的代理总领事应邀参加"2016 英国—广东金融人才培训高峰论坛"并发表开幕致辞。他在致辞中提到了开展"优质教育在英国"活动的初衷,英国在金融服务业方面享有的优势以及与广东的合作项目。

2. 预习词汇

British Consulate-General in Guangzhou 英国驻广州总领事馆
UK-Guangdong Financial Talent Training Forum 英国—广东金融人才培训高峰论坛
UK Trade & Investment/UKTI 英国贸易投资总署
Guangdong Financial Affairs Office 广东省金融工作办公室
Guangzhou Financial Bureau 广州市财政局
UK-China Joint Statement 《中英联合声明》
Guangdong Finance Society 广东金融学会
International Capital Market Association 国际资本市场协会
University of Reading 雷丁大学
Guangdong Nottingham Advanced Finance Institute 广东诺丁汉高等金融学院

3. 演讲文本

00:00—00:18

My name is David Pool. I am Acting Consulate General at the British Consulate-

General here in Guangzhou today. My normal role is actually as UK Trade & Investment Senior Point of Contact for Southern China.

我叫 David Pool，我是英国驻广州总领事馆的代理总领事。我平时的身份其实是英国贸易投资总署在华南地区的高级联络人。

00：18—00：53

Dear official leaders, distinguished guests, ladies and gentlemen, I would like to warmly welcome you to the Education Is Great, UK-Guangdong Financial Talent Training Forum organized by UK Trade & Investment, the British Consulate-General Guangzhou with Guangdong Financial Affairs Office, Guangzhou Financial Bureau, as well as municipal and provincial associations as our supporting organizations.

尊敬的各位领导、各位来宾，女士们，先生们：热烈欢迎你们来到"优质教育在英国——英国—广东金融人才培训高峰论坛"。本次论坛由英国贸易投资总署、英国驻广州总领事馆主办，广东省金融工作办公室、广州市财政局，以及很多市级省级协会是本次活动的支持单位。

00：53—01：42

You may wonder why a campaign focusing on financial services industry is entitled "Education Is Great". We chose this title because we wanted to emphasize the importance of life-long learning as specialist vocational training in this incredibly important industry. *The UK-China Joint Statement* released during President Xi's historic state visit to the UK last year highlighted our shared commitment to boost cultural and educational links. I am delighted to see that UK Trade & Investment have correctly responded to this commitment in launching the "Education Is Great" Campaign across China this year.

各位可能想知道，为什么这场侧重金融服务业的活动主题却是"优质教育在英国"？我们选择这个主题，是因为我们想强调终身学习的重要性，它是这个重要行业的专业职业培训。《中英联合声明》是习主席去年对英国进行历史性访问时发布的，强调了中英共同承诺促进文化和教育领域交流。我很高兴看到英国贸易投资总署已经切实履行这个承诺，今年在中国举办这场"优质教育在英国"的活动。

01：42—02：20

The UK is a leading global financial services center. London and the UK more widely, boast some of the world most well recognized business schools and finance, finance qualifications, with an international reputation for quality, second to none. Professional bodies, particularly in the accounting sector, command worldwide respect, for their roles in setting standards of entry to the professions and for professional development covering ethical as well as technical standards.

英国是领先的全球金融服务中心。在伦敦和英国其他地方都有很多世界著名的商学院和提供金融专业文凭的教育机构,教育质量享誉国际,首屈一指。专业机构,尤其是会计学领域的,在全球都很权威,因为他们不仅负责制定行业准入标准,还制定行业发展的道德和技术标准。

02:22—02:46

Here in China, the continued strong economic growth has created an increased demand for highly skilled professionals. In Guangdong in particular, the 13th Five-year Plan focus on developing financial industry and building Guangzhou as an international financial city. There is a huge demand for financial talents with internationally recognized qualifications.

中国持续强劲的经济增长需要越来越多的尖端专业人才。尤其在广东,"十三五"规划强调发展金融业,将广州打造成国际金融城市。这就非常需要具有国际认可资质的金融人才。

02:46—03:26

I am very pleased to see that there has already been much cooperation between Guangdong and the UK in financial and professional services training sector. For example, Guangdong Finance Society who will deliver a case study later in the forum has a very successfully joint financial talent training program with International Capital Market Association and the University of Reading. Guangdong Nottingham Advanced Finance Institute in addition, is also a recognized program delivered under the joint effort of UK and Guangdong Governments.

我很高兴看到广东和英国在金融专业服务培训领域已经有很多合作。例如广东金融学会稍后会在论坛上展示一个案例分析,它与国际资本市场协会以及雷丁大学组织了非常成功的人才培训项目。另外,广东诺丁汉高等金融学院也是英国和广东地方政府组织的有名项目。

03:26—04:12

But, I believe there is much more that we can do together in this area, which why I am delighted that the "Education Is Great" Campaign this year brings 17 companies from the UK financial and professional services training sector to foster relationships between the UK Educational organizations and the Chinese FPS institutions. I hope UK delegates will take this opportunity to make new contacts and further explore this exciting market.

Likewise, I am confident that our Chinese guests will find the forum informative and a great chance to collaboration with the UK partners in education training qualification areas.

但我相信我们在这领域的合作远不止这些。因此我很开心今年"优质教育在英国"汇聚了英国金融专业服务培训领域的17家公司，搭建起英国教育机构和中国金融人才培训机构的桥梁。我希望英方代表可以趁此机会结交新的友谊，深入开拓这个令人兴奋的市场。同样，我相信我们的中国来宾会发现论坛资讯丰富，提供极好的机会，与英国在教育培训资质方面进行合作。

04：12—04：37

UKTI and the British Consulate-General Guangzhou have been striving to build more platforms like this to facilitate collaboration between both parties to share experience and exchange expertise. And on the personal level I hope it will go much further beyond the just financial services into other sectors. I believe that the "Education is Great" Campaign will do just that.

英国贸易投资总署和英国驻广州领事馆一直致力于打造更多类似的平台，促进双方的合作，共享经验、交流知识。从个人层面，我希望这种合作不仅仅是金融服务领域，还延伸到其他领域。我相信"优质教育在英国"活动可以实现这一点。

04：37—05：10

Once again, I would like to express my gratitude to Guangdong Financial Affairs Office and the Guangzhou Financial Bureau for the invaluable support for this event. Finally, I would like to wish you all a successfully and fruitful afternoon and I am looking forward to hearing more about the successful collaborations which will hopefully restart here today. Thank you very much for your time.

再次感谢广东省金融工作办公室和广州市财政局对这次活动的宝贵支持。最后，预祝你们下午的活动圆满成功，硕果累累。我非常期待听到更多成功的合作在今天开启。谢谢大家！

III. 实战练习二

1. 演讲背景

英国贸易投资总署伦敦总部教育产业（中国）及金融专业培训副总监应邀参加"2016英国—广东金融人才培训高峰论坛"并发表主旨演讲。她在演讲中提到了中国现在是英国国际学生最大的来源国，中国人到英国去是出于各种不同的原因；英国金融服务业在全球占据领先地位，历史悠久，许多古老的金融机构都是起源于英国。英国金融服务业成功的关键在于能理解、倾听、回应合作伙伴面临的挑战和需求，快速给出经过检验并行之有效的解决方法。

2. 预习词汇

City of London 伦敦金融城

Tianhe CBD 天河中央商务区

highlight 强调

high level dialogue 高层对话

people-to-people dialogue 民间对话

foreign direct investment 外国直接投资

bond 债券

financial and professional service 金融专业服务

Lord Mayor of London Show 伦敦市长展

Chartered Banker Institute Scotland 苏格兰特许银行家协会

Chartered Institute of Bankers 特许银行家协会

Chartered Accountants of Scotland 苏格兰特许会计师协会

Institute of Chartered Accountants in England and Wales/ICAEW 英格兰及威尔士特许会计师协会

provision 规定

3. 演讲文本

00：00—01：30

This is my last stop, so my voice is going. But good afternoon, ladies and gentlemen, distinguished guests. Please first of all, let me add my thank you to Guangdong Finance Office, and Guangzhou Finance Office. I just want to pick up before I go to my speech. I just want to pick up three points Mr. Zhang made. I thought the whole speech was very very useful and informative. Three particular points, first of all, the recognition of market and industry driven qualifications is what China needs. It's not what the government tells you to have but is what the industry needs. To me, I think that is a very realistic comment. And also challenges that you're facing, lack of, for example, international knowledge and information, and also, perhaps some challenges that we as your international partner would face in terms of localizing our services and products to find the most suitable products as well as we can find the synergy to work together. And that's why we are here. Absolutely based on those three points, we are here as a strong UK delegation.

这是最后一站了,我声音都哑了。下午好!女士们,先生们,尊敬的各位来宾。首先,请允许我感谢广东省金融办公室和广州市金融办公室。我想先提一下,在我演讲前,我想讲一下张先生提到的三点。我认为他讲的非常有用,信息量很大。三大点,第一点是市场认可和行业资质,这正是中国需要的。这并不是政府要求你们做的,而是这个产业的要求。对我而言,这是一个非常现实的看法。第二点就是贵国面临的挑战,比如说缺乏对国际知识和信息的了解。第三点是作为贵国国际合作伙伴,我们也会面临一些挑战,包括如何让我们的服务和产品本地化,以便找到最合适的产品,实现协同效应。这就是为什么我们今天来到这里,完全是基于这三点,我们率领了一个强大的英国代表团来到这里。

01:31—03:46

Guangzhou hosts a very special place in me, and because this is the place where I lived for 4 years since 2011 until two months ago. I have many friends. I have met many friends, familiar faces this afternoon. And also this is where, when I first time, seriously consider my next career move, and this is where I decided I want to get into education and training, and I want to continue to contribute to UK and China in that particular area and field. I also remember my first official meeting was with Tianhe CBD, where we discussed to bring City of London and Tianhe closer. We made progress. We made slow progress, but we are there now. So many congratulations to all colleagues involved. Sorry. As I said, this is our last stop, we have been to, since Monday, me and our delegation have been to Beijing, Shanghai, and we keep hearing, you know, opportunities, wonderful opportunities. We also keep hearing challenges, some similar challenges, some different challenges. So Mr. Zhang's speech again just highlighted some of those areas. And this is what we think. UK is absolutely the partner of choice. UK is your number one partner in this area. So in 2013, when our chancellor Jorsben visited China in Beijing, he said UK wanted to be China's best friend in the west. I think we are. We are China's best friend in the west today, some recent evidence of that. In financial services in particular, we want to work closer.

广州对我来说是一个非常特别的地方,我在这里住了四年,从 2011 年开始直到两个月前。我交了很多朋友。我遇见了很多朋友,很多熟悉的面孔,今天下午就碰到了他们。就在广州,我第一次认真考虑了下一个职业目标,也是在这里,我决定从事教育和培训行业,我想继续为英国和中国的这个领域做贡献。我还记得我第一次参加的正式会议是和天河中央商务区一起洽谈,我们讨论了有关伦敦金融城和天河区加强合作的事宜。我们取得了进展,尽管进步很慢,但我们有了进展,祝贺所有参与的同事们。我刚刚说过这是我们的最后一站,从周一开始,我和我的代表团去了北京、上海,我们一直听到你们讲了很多好的机遇,我们也听到了一些类似的挑战，和一些不同的挑战。张先生的演讲再一次强调了这些领域，我们也是这样认为的。英国绝对是中国首选的合作伙伴，这个领域的首选。2013年英国财政大臣Jorsben访问北京时曾说过，英国想成为中国在西方最好的朋友。我认为我们是中国在西方最好的朋友了。最近有很多这方面的迹象，尤其在金融服务方面，我们希望加强合作。

03：47—04：39

Before I get into financial services training and education, I just want to bring us back to some basics. I want to talk a little bit about culture and little bit, touch a little bit on history. So I think, the one very important reason, why UK and China would work really well together is that we both have very rich culture and history. We actually, the two nations respect each other's culture and history. That's why we also had, in addition to all sorts of high-level dialogues, we also have people-to-people dialogue trying to encourage more interactions, communications, activities, just at very ordinary people level.

在我讲金融服务培训和教育之前，我想回到一些基本问题上，我想稍微谈一谈文化和历史。我认为英国和中国之所以能有良好的合作，很重要的一个原因就是我们两国都有着非常深厚的文化和悠久的历史，我们尊重彼此的文化和历史，因此，除了各种高层对话外，我们还有民间对话，是为了激发更多的互动、交流和活动在普通百姓层面开展。

04：40—05：42

So I went to UK some 25 years ago, I went to study. And there are more, and many more people nowadays, many more Chinese nowadays in the UK. And people go to UK for different reasons. Young children going to UK for education because their parents want them to. And also they go to UK because they want to learn some magic tricks from Harry Potter. Older children, or young adults, they go to UK for Shakespeare, for UK universities, for some great career prospects, and of course to enjoy British beers. Most of people, who just go to UK just want to chill and enjoy the environment, enjoy the history, enjoy all the museums that UK presents. Young and professional people, come to benefit from the education system we offer and we have.

我去英国是在约25年前，我是去学习的。有越来越多的中国人在英国，人们去英国出于不同的原因，一些小孩子去英国上学，是因为他们的父母希望他们去，他们也是为了从哈利·波特那里学一点魔法。大一点的孩子或是年轻人去英国是因为喜爱莎士比亚，喜欢英国的大学，获得好的职业前景，当然他们也是想去试试英国的啤酒。大多数人去英国是为了感受寒冷，享受环境，了解英国历史，参观英的博物馆。年轻的专业人士去英国是想从我们的教育体系中获益。

05：43—07：37

China is now the largest source of international students in the UK. We have about 100,000 Chinese students studying in the UK. Why? Because UK education is not about straightforward teaching and learning experience. It's actually about giving students, giving you inspiration to develop your knowledge and skills, to give you the freedom to be creative, and to support you to achieve your best, and to achieve the most desired performance, and to follow your passion and to follow your passion to actually to learn and to gain qualifications. And those qualifications are well respected by your future employers as well as academics worldwide. For Chinese students, when you first come to UK, you may have different difficulties even to start. Because the learning experience as I said can be quite different. In the UK, the learning is not about how you learn, and what you know, it's actually about working with other people to share what you know and to learn together, to then achieve a result as a team that you deserve. This mentality continues to influence people's behavior when they are in the business world. We are keen to share our knowledge, and we constantly shape the way we think, the way we do business, especially the way we do business with our international partners.

中国现在是英国国际学生人数最多的来源国，我们有10万中国学生在英国学习。为什么？因为英国的教育不是简单的教与学，它还能给学生灵感，帮助学生学习知识和技能，给你们发挥创造力的空间，让你们能做到最好，取得最理想的成绩。你们还能根据自己的爱好去学习，并获得相关的资历证书，这些证书很受重视，不管是未来的雇主，还是各大高校都会非常看重。对于中国学生而言，当你们第一次去英国，你们开始会碰到各种各样的困难。因为学习体验，就像我刚刚说的，是非常不同的。在英国，学习并不是说你们怎么学、你们知道什么，而是与别人合作、分享知识、共同学习，然后组成学习小组共同进步，这是你们应该做的。这种思维方式会继续影响你们的行为，即便是进入生意场上也是如此。我们热衷于分享我们的知识，我们一直在塑造我们的思维方式、开展业务的方式，尤其是我们和国际伙伴开发业务的方式。

07：38—08：29

In the world of financial and services sector, this is particularly true. As this industry touches our lives in many ways, we rely on them to safeguard our money, to help us save for the future, and to protect us from many risks that we face. Therefore, a well trained professional financial workforce is the key to achieve those intentions and ambitions. We have already heard from Mr. Zhang that what type of talent is actually needed here in particular in Guangzhou. And that is very very important to fulfill those gaps. I hope we can be very much a part of that journey to support you to do that.

金融服务业尤其如此。这个行业涉及到我们生活的方方面面，我们依赖金融服务业，来确保我们的资金安全，帮我们存钱，保护我们免受许多风险。因此，训练有素的专业金融人士是实现目标和雄心的关键。张先生刚刚已经讲过什么样的人才在广州是急需的，这些专业人士对于填补这些空缺非常重要。我希望我们能够参与其中，帮助你们达成目标。

08：28—09：29

As many of you already know that financial professional services in the UK is the cornerstone of UK economy, it counts about 12% of total UK GDP output. And UK is the number one financial center, and UK is also the most internationally focused marketplace in financial services world. That's because the global leadership of London, the long tradition of innovation to remain a center of leading and forward-thinking practices. It is the number one destination for foreign direct investment projects in Europe and recognized as the most business-friendly environment to do business in the world. Half of the world's top 8 international firms are based in the UK.

你们很多人都知道，英国的金融专业服务是英国经济的基石，占英国GDP总值的12%。英国是首屈一指的金融中心，也是金融服务界最注重国际化的市场，这是因为伦敦具有国际领先地位，长期以来保持创新传统，努力保持最具前瞻性的领先创新中心地位。它是欧洲外国直接投资项目的首要目的地，也被认为有世界上最优良的营商环境。世界前八强公司中，有一半总部在英国。

09：29—10：45

The UK also have the Europe's largest asset management and insurance industries. This sector employs 2.1 million people right across the country, not just in London. In fact, two thirds of those people based outside of London. On trade, UK is the world's leading exporter of financial and professional services with a surplus of over 60 billion pounds. London also remains a premier international center for trading of international bonds. In 2013, UK became the first western country of RMB trading center and issued the first RMB bond in western country and again in 2014. UK now is the third largest center for foreign exchange trading of RMB after the mainland China and Hong Kong, way ahead of Singapore.

英国还有欧洲最大的资产管理和保险业，这个行业为全国210万人提供了就业机会，不仅限于伦敦。事实上，三分之二的从业人员都不在伦敦。贸易方面，英国是世界领先的金融专业服务出口国，贸易顺差超过600亿英镑。伦敦也是主要的国际债券交易中心。2013年,英国成为拥有人民币交易中心的第一个西方国家,也是首个发行人民币债券的西方国家,2014年也是如此。英国目前是第三大人民币外汇交易中心,仅次于中国大陆和香港,遥遥领先于新加坡。

10:46—12:55

So I touch down a little bit culture there, and I want to let you know the history also happened in financial and professional services. Do you know the first Lord Mayor of London Show is one of the oldest surviving traditional ceremonies started in 1237? The world's oldest banking institute is the Chartered Banker Institute Scotland, now based in Edinburgh. The world's second oldest banking institute is Chartered Institute of Bankers; their Vice Principal Martin Dave is here with us today. The world's oldest law firm in operation is in UK, is in Tunbridge Wells, called Thomas Snail Pasmont. They have a very clear line of developments. Partners working within the firm passing on traditions, cultures, the expertise, the way of doing business from one generation to another since late 16th century. The world's oldest professional body of accountants is Institute of Chartered Accountants of Scotland, received its Royal Chartered in 1854. And guess what, the world's second oldest professional accountants body is still a UK organization, founded in 1880, Institute of Chartered Accountants in England and Wales, ICAEW. One of the directors is also with us today. So let's fast forward to today's picture. The UK's now home to 150 professional bodies and world-class education services, that's well pressed internationally. Some of them are here today.

这里我想稍微谈一谈文化,我想让你们知道金融专业服务领域的历史。你们知道吗?第一届伦敦市长展是保留下来的最古老的传统典礼,始于1237年;世界上最古老的银行组织是苏格兰特许银行家协会,总部现在在爱丁堡;世界上第二古老的银行组织是特许银行家协会,他们的副会长马丁·戴夫今天也来到了会议现场;世界上运营时间最久的律师事务所在英国的坦布里奇韦尔斯,被称为Thomas Snail Pasmont,它们的发展历程非常清晰,公司的合伙人将传统、文化、专业知识和商业模式一代又一代传承下来,从16世纪末期开始就是如此。世界上最古老的会计师专业组织是苏格兰特许会计师协会,于1854年获得皇家特许资格;世界上第二古老的专业会计师组织依然是一个英国机构,也就是成立于1880年的英格兰及威尔士特许会计师协会,简称ICAEW,其中的一位总监今天也在我们的会议现场。我们快进到目前的情况。如今英国有150个专业组织和世界一流的教育服务机构,这在全世界都非常突出,其中一些今天也来到了现场。

12:57—15:02

Why we can be successful for so long, for so many years? That's because we understand, we listen, we respond to our partners' challenges and demands quickly with our well tested and measured solutions. You will be hearing more from later case study and panel discussions. In China's case, we understand China's ambition. We understand, we want to understand a bit more about Guangdong ambition to develop yourself as international financial services center, one of the centers. This, of course, is driven by your speedy economic wonderful contribution and achievements, but also driven by the desire to access global capital market. As a result, as we heard before already from Mr. Zhang, the demand for tailor-made appropriate financial professional services, education and training is significantly high here in China and in Guangzhou, in Guangdong. We believe, those qualifications, those UK qualifications are increasingly important for individual mobility, the growth of business, and government economic development plans, whether central government, or provincial and multi-municipal development plans. So all've been said, you can't really have a better partner than the UK to achieve the best result you deserve. The benefit is absolutely clear. And I hope you would agree.

  为什么我们的成功能持续这么久、这么多年？是因为我们能理解、倾听、回应合作伙伴面临的挑战和需求，快速给出经过检验并行之有效的解决方法。接下来你们会从案例研究和小组讨论中了解更多信息。就中国而言，我们了解中国的抱负，我们想多了解广东的抱负，那就是广东要发展成为国际金融服务中心之一。这当然得益于广东快速的经济发展及取得的经济成就，这也因为广东渴望加入国际资本市场。因此，正如张先生所讲的那样，对定制金融专业服务的需求，对教育和培训的需求在中国非常大，广州及广东尤为如此。我们认为这些英国学历会越来越重要，比如对个人流动性、商业发展以及政府经济发展计划都日益重要，对中央政府、省市级政府发展计划也都如此。因此，你们最好的合作伙伴就是英国，英国能帮你们实现最好的发展，益处显而易见，我希望你们能同意我的说法。

15∶02—16∶00

  And in summary, the UK offers historical reputation and status, breadth and flexibility of provision that would actually lead us to localize our services and products to tailor and suit for your demand, your particular demand. We also have strong governance and supporting structure. So please enjoy today's discussion. And we have travelled long way to be here in Guangzhou, and we hope today's dialogue will be a beginning of a closer, deeper, better relationship. I look forward to meeting as many people as I can later today. Thank you very much.

  最后，英国拥有历史悠久的良好声誉、崇高地位，广泛、灵活的规定能让我们的产品和服务实现本地化，适应你们的需求，具体需求，我们也有强大的管理方式和支撑体系。请尽情参与今天的讨论。我们不远万里来到广州，希望今天的对话能够开启一段更紧密、更深厚、更美好的合作关系。我希望接下来能结识更多的人，谢谢大家！

第六单元　行业介绍
Introduction to Industries

I. 数字处理

数字口译一直是难点，在同传中更是如此。原因在于两个方面，一是英汉两种语言数字的表达方式不同，即分段方式不同；二是译员需要在很短的时间内迅速进行两种语言之间数字的转换，同时还要跟上发言人语速，译出其他信息。

在同传中，译员通常也会准备好纸笔，听到数字立刻记下来。同传中的数字口译常常需要团队合作，轮休的译员通常会帮正在口译的译员记下数字。

1. 数字转换的基本方法

（1）点线法。

"点线法"是针对英汉两种语言数字分段方式不同而专门设计的。英文数字是三位一段，记录方式为从右向左每三位一个逗点；中文数字是四位一段，记录方式是从右向左每四位一条斜线。这样数字在两种语言中的记录和转换就比较清晰，如下例所示：

1,000,000,000,000
1/0000/0000/0000

上面的例子中中英文数字同样都为1兆，数字在英文表达方式下三位一段，共隔了四段，从右向左每个分段处的单位分别是thousand，million，billion和trillion，每一段起始位为"百"位。而中文表达方式下四位一段，共隔了三段，从右向左每个分段处的单位分别是万，亿和兆，每一段起始位为"千"位。

（2）小数点移位法。

对于一些以thousand，million，billion，trillion以及万、亿和兆为单位的大位整数，采用小数点移位法，转换起来更快，如下例所示：

637 million

末位数字7后面单位为百万，可转换成中文的单位亿，则小数点向左移动两位，中文数字为6.37亿。

78万

末位数字8后面单位为万，可转换成英文的单位thousand，则小数点向右移动一位，英文数字为780 thousand；或者转换成英文的单位million，则小数点向左移动两位，英文数字为 0.78 million。

2. 倍数

英语中常用 times 来表达倍数，但中英文的倍数用法却有所不同。英语在表述或比较倍数时，无论使用什么句型，都包括基数倍数在内，因此都不是净增净减。

Asia is 4 times larger than Europe.

译：亚洲的面积是欧洲的 4 倍。/亚洲比欧洲大 3 倍。

The cotton output in the county has increased 4 times.

该县棉花产量增加到 4 倍。/增加了 3 倍。

3. 数字的趋势和数值

在进行数字口译的时候，出现在上下文当中的数字通常不能忽略。如果数字有加上单位，如美元、千克等，一定要连同单位一起译出。另外一些与数字有关的常用表达法，如趋势、数值等，也应为口译学习者所熟知。

（1）表示向上的趋势：

增加 increase, rise, grow, go up

爬升 climb

飙升 skyrocket, soar, surge, shoot up

（2）表示向下的趋势：

下降 decrease, fall, drop, go down

稍降 slip

暴跌 plunge, plummet

（3）数值：

总数达 reach, be up to, stand at, amount to, total, add up to

占百分比 account for, occupy

大约 about, around, approximately, roughly

多于 more than, over, above

少于 less than, under, below

4. 模糊处理

在遇到语速快、数字位数较多、连续的数字较多、信息密集的讲话时，译员想要准确译出数字和相关信息难度比较大。译员"在遇到一连串复杂的数字时，采取模糊处理的策略还是必要的"（仲伟合、詹成，2009：286）。一些比较重要的数字可精确译出，而相对不是那么重要的数字则可以使用约数。

237.2 吨　　over 237 tons

501.3 万元　　approximately 500 million RMB

II. 实战练习一

1. 演讲背景

全球前四大市场研究公司之一的 GfK 捷孚凯公司的家电部全球大客户副总裁应邀出席"2017年广交会系列论坛——中国电子家电品牌与创新高峰论坛"并发表题为"智能家居演变"的演讲。他开门见山地指出，中国引领着智能家居领域的发展。麻省理工学院每年发布的全球 50 家最智能企业名单中，五家中国企业名列前茅。接下来他详细分析了每种智能联网设备的发展趋势，包括可穿戴设备、虚拟现实应用、无人机。最后他还分享了智能大家电和智能小家电的市场表现。

2. 预习词汇

Canton Fair 广交会
CCCME/China Chamber of Commerce for Import and Export of Machinery and Electronic Products 中国机电产品进出口商会
consumer technology 消费者技术
MIT/Massachusetts Institute of Technology 麻省理工学院
Facebook 脸书
value proposition 价值主张
wearable 可穿戴设备
health and fitness tracker 健康与健身追踪器
virtual reality/VR 虚拟现实
virtual showroom 虚拟展厅
augmented reality/AR 增强现实
head-mounted display 头盔显示器
critical mass 临界物质；临界质量；临界点
drone 无人机
cooktop 嵌入式灶具
personal scales 体重秤
espresso machine 浓缩咖啡机
toothbrush rechargeable/electric toothbrush 电动牙刷
robotic vacuum/robotic vacuum cleaner 机器人吸尘器
multi-cooker 多功能电饭煲

3. 演讲文本

00:00—01:20

Hello，你好。So my name is Peter Goldman, and what I'm going to try and do is first bridge our last two speakers, so thank you Jack and thank you Bill. I think what I do is I take off my jacket. So I'm not too dressed. I'm not too underdressed. I also want to thank the leadership of the Canton Fair and the leadership of CCCME. They are great partners of GfK. We are always pleased to attend these events to be asked to participate and to work with Canton Fair organizers and to work with CCCME. It's really a great pleasure. So thank you very much. I also want to thank my colleague, David Ding, Jiang Ling, sitting over here. So David is my business partner and assists me because unfortunately my Mandarin is not so good. OK, so I'm going to move to my presentation and as I go through my presentation, I will try to highlight many of the key points, but keep the presentation moving. I realized that we're a bit behind schedule, and we have this great panel and these are really, really smart people who have great insights to share, they are actually much smarter than I am, and so we want to get them up here quickly. So to do this, I'll try to move through my presentation a little bit more quickly than I planned.

大家好。我叫 Peter Goldman。我想先试着拉近和刚刚两位发言人间的距离。谢谢 Jack 和 Bill。我想先脱掉我的夹克衫，显得不那么隆重，也不那么寒酸。我还要感谢广交会的领导和中国机电产品进出口商会的领导，他们是 GfK 的好伙伴。我们一直以来都很高兴能参与这些活动。很高兴受邀参与其中，和广交会主办单位及中国机电产品进出口商会合作。我们真的很高兴，非常感谢你们。我还要感谢我的同事 David Ding 和 Jiang Ling，他们就坐在这里。David 是我的商业伙伴，他会帮我，因为我的普通话不太好。好了，言归正传。在演讲的过程中，我会尽量突出重点，但保持连贯性。我发现我们的进度有点落后。我们有一个很棒的小组，小组成员真的非常聪明。他们有很棒的见解要分享。实际上他们比我聪明得多，所以希望他们快点上台来。所以我会尽量讲快一点，比我原先计划的快一点。

01:24—02:37

OK, just make sure I can get my technology working. OK, so, the consumer technology industry, consumer technology goods industry is poised for a digital leap forward. This is for sure. And I believe very strongly that China is poised to lead the way. So why do I believe this? I believe this for a few reasons. First of all, there's certain technology market dynamics which is every 10 or 20 years we do see some major shifts in technology and developments that rearrange the marketplace, so we could go back 20 or 30 years when the Japanese were able to take advantage of the home appliances marketplace, and that consumer technical goods marketplace and make a name for themselves. I think we saw it about 15 years ago with some Korean brands, and we are really in a place today right now where things are shifting quickly and China is absolutely in a leadership role here. So as you're going to see in some slides that I'll present in a few minutes, China is already leading the way with smart home technologies. Here in China, and this gives you tremendous knowledge, tremendous learnings and tremendous advantages to bring to the rest of the world.

我想先确保我的幻灯片能放出来。好的，消费者技术产业、消费者技术产品行业正蓄势待发，迎接数字飞跃，这是毋庸置疑的。我坚信中国将引领这个产业。为什么呢？有几个原因。第一，技术市场动态是存在的，每十年或二十年，我们确实看到一些重大的技术变革和发展，对市场重新洗牌。我们可以回顾二三十年前，那时日本利用家电市场和消费者技术产品市场闯出名堂。我们看到十五年前，一些韩国品牌也是如此。我们现在身处的时代，发展日新月异，而中国是当之无愧的领导者。我将在接下来几分钟向大家展示，中国已经引领智能家居技术的发展。在中国，大家可以获得更丰富的知识、学问和巨大的优势，并惠及全世界。

02：37—04：08

So this is what I believe. And perhaps I'm not the only one who's talking about these things or thinking this way. So many of you may be familiar with MIT, it's a very prestigious technical school in the United States. And MIT lists each year the 50 smartest, smartest companies, and in June of 2016, they came out with their list and if you look here, we see NO.1 Amazon, NO.8 Alphabet which is the parent of Google, and a few other companies which I think we're all here as global technology and global thought leaders day to day. But what we also see on this list：Amazon may be NO.1, but Baidu NO.2, Alphabet NO.8, Huawei NO.10, Facebook 15, Tencent 20 and on and on. And actually if you look at this list published by an American university by the way, 5 companies, 5 Chinese companies make the top of this list. So I think what we are seeing is the rest of the world beginning to acknowledge that China is no longer about being a fast follower, Chinese companies are about innovation and leadership. We also see this in the action of some of the big Chinese particular home appliance and technology companies. So just to save time, I won't go through all of this, but you know there's been tremendous amount of global acquisitions and investments that are very, very strategic and led by Chinese companies.

这是我的看法。也许不只我一个人这么说或这么想。你们中很多人可能熟悉麻省理工学院，它是很有名的理工院校，就在美国。MIT每年都会列出五十家最智能的企业。2016年6月,他们公布了名单。如果你们看这里,会看到第一是亚马逊,第八是Alphabet,它是谷歌的母公司,还有一些其它企业。我想这里的都是全球的技术和思想领袖。但我们还在名单上看到:亚马逊也许是第一,但百度第二,Alphabet第八,华为第十,脸书十五,腾讯二十等等。事实上,如果你们看看这名单,它是由美国一所大学发布的,但有五家中国企业名列前茅。所以,我想我们看到的是,世界开始承认中国不再是快速的追随者,中国企业就是创新和领袖的代名词。我们也能从中国一些大企业,尤其是家电技术企业采取的行动看出这一点。由于时间关系,我不会一一详述,但是我想告诉大家,现在大量的全球收购和投资都极具战略意义,而它们是由中国企业主导的。

04:08—04:59

We also hear from consumers. So GfK is a market research company and this will be the first of my data slides that I'll present to you today. So what we hear from consumers when we ask them, percent of consumers who feel that smart home technology will have an impact on their lives over the next few years, a whopping 75%, 75% of Chinese consumers tell us that smart technologies are going to have an impact on their life far beyond what we see in the rest of the world, and you know this is a major shift that used to be particularly home appliance trends. They came from Europe. They came perhaps from Korea. Now we see again consumers telling us that a lot of the thought leadership is right here in China.

我们也聆听消费者意见。GfK是一家市场调研公司。这也将是我第一张带数据的幻灯片。我们从消费者那里得到什么反馈呢,当我们询问他们看法时,部分消费者认为智能家居技术将会影响他们的生活,未来几年就会如此。有非常多,有75%的中国消费者告诉我们,智能技术将影响他们的生活,影响的程度远大于我们在世界其他国家所看到的。这是一个重大的转变,而这个转变在过去尤其出现在家电领域的趋势。这些趋势始于欧洲,也许是韩国。现在,我们再次听到消费者告诉我们,很多思想领袖就在中国。

04:59—06:28

So what's the status today? There is a challenge and the folks who spoke before me, Jack and Bill who spoke before me touched upon some of these things. There are barriers. So one barrier or set of barriers is caused. Smart goods are more expensive than non-smart goods. Consumers don't necessarily understand the value proposition yet, and there is this issue of privacy which I hope to talk about some more with the panel. But beyond this, there's something that Bill touched on quite a bit, which is, there's no standardization today in the smart home industry. If you look on the left side of the chart, you see what some of the Chinese clients and manufacturers and large international retailers are doing. On the right-hand side of the chart you see the rest of the world, but the problem is, unlike the smart phone industry where there is a lot of standardization, we don't see that yet in the smart home space. And given that and probably also given to some natural and organic technology developments, what we're seeing for now is that there is not necessarily a next big thing, but many, many small things. Individual connected items each with its own value proposition but not yet in an interconnected or entirely an ecosystem, let's say of smart.

那么今天的情况如何呢？我们面临着一大挑战，之前的演讲嘉宾Jack和Bill谈到了一些。现在有各种阻碍。个别或某些阻碍是某些原因造成的。智能产品比非智能产品贵。消费者不一定会理解这一价值主张，但就隐私问题，我希望多跟小组成员进行探讨。但除此之外，有一些东西Bill提到了很多，那就是标准化还没有在智能家居产业实现。如果你们看左边的图表，会看到一些中国客户、制造商和大型国际零售商在这行业的作为。在图表的右边，你们能看到其它地方的数据。但问题是，不像智能手机产业实现大量标准化，智能家居产业则缺乏标准化。再加上自然和环保技术的发展，我们看到的是，目前未必会出现下一个大热门，但小玩意儿不断。所有独立联网的物件都有各自的价值主张，但还没在彼此互联或全面互联的生态系统中达到智能的程度。

06：28—07：45

So from our studies what we learn is that the average consumer has somewhere between three and four smart connected devices, and yet they're all individual devices and so I want to spend a little bit of time talking about the trends for each of these technology devices and then I'll talk about some of the trends for home appliance devices. So first of all, you can see that smartphone is huge, and of course smartphones are the centerpiece and at least for now there, well, let's say the remote control of the smart world and our smart lives. Wearables is just 10% of the smart home, smart phone market place, really quite small but developing of course. Virtual reality glasses and virtual reality solutions are just 14 million units, so just 1% of the overall smart phone world and just 10% of the wearables marketplace, and then of course drones. So I'm going to focus on these three for a minute because they each have an impact I think, each have an impact on what comes next.

从研究中我们发现，消费者人均拥有3~4台智能联网设备，但它们都是独立的。所以我想花点时间谈谈每一种设备的趋势，然后谈一谈家电的趋势。首先，你们可以看到，智能手机比重很大，当然，它是最重要的，至少目前如此，我们可以称之为遥控器，控制着智能世界和我们的智能生活。可穿戴设备市场规模只是智能家居、智能手机市场规模的10%，真的很小，但在持续增长，这点是肯定的。虚拟现实眼镜和虚拟现实解决方案只有1,400万台，其规模仅相当于智能手机市场规模的1%、可穿戴设备市场规模的10%，当然还有无人机。我将重点关注这三种产品，花点时间讲讲，因为每一种产品都有一定影响，我认为它们影响着后来出现的产品。

07：45—10：02

So with regard to wearables, in Europe what we see is that there are about 13 million wearable units sold. And when we talk about wearable units, we're talking about smart watches, we're talking about health and fitness and then we're talking about sort of other parts or components in the market that are bit smaller. So if you look at this, health and fitness trackers, health and fitness trackers make up 50% of the wearables market in Europe. One in every three wearables purchased the 32% number here is smart watches, so it seems a respectable number and it feels like at least in Europe smart watches gain some attraction. But when we look at Asia, we see really a very, very different picture with only 17% of consumers purchasing smart watches. So this becomes interesting right? Because… is smart watches the next platform? Is smart watches, the device that will take a leadership role over smart phones and so we're not carrying something so bulky? We're wearing something on our wrists. That's effective and can help us manage the world around us, and the environment around us and I think we see different things happening in different markets, but it calls into question the platform or it calls into question the device just as media tablets I think in many ways were expected to be the next big thing, and it didn't turn out that way. My guess is that smart watches may not turn out to be the next big thing, yet nevertheless when we look at the overall wearables market, what we see is a 50% growth rate led by China at something like 60 million units and North America at 62 million units, so pretty comfortable in size. It goes to show you still the importance of China to the smart connected world and it goes to show you that this is still a large market, but smart watches may not be the next big thing. So if not smart watches, then what?

谈到可穿戴设备，在欧洲我们看到的是，1,300万台可穿戴设备已售出。当我们谈到可穿戴设备，我们指的是智能手表，是健康与健身追踪器，我们指的是市场的其它部分，份额更小的部分。如果大家把目光放到这里，健康与健身追踪器占可穿戴设备市场一半的份额，这是欧洲市场的情况。三分之一已出售的可穿戴设备，也就是这里的32%都是智能手表。看起来这是个不错的数字，似乎至少在欧洲，智能手表有一定的吸引力。但当我们把目光投向亚洲，看到的是极其不同的情况，只有17%的消费者购买智能手表。很有趣对吧？因为……智能手表会成为下一个平台吗？智能手表会取代智能手机的领导地位，使我们摆脱笨重的手机吗？我们手腕上戴着的东西，它能有效地帮助我们管理周围的一切和周围的环境。我们看到不同的情况发生在不同的市场，但这让人们质疑这个平台，或者质疑这个设备，就像以往多媒体平板电脑在很多方面都被认为是下一个大热门，但它并没有像我们预期的那样。我猜智能手表可能不是下一个大热门，然而当我们把目光投向整个可穿戴设备市场，我们看到的是50%的增长率，其中中国和北美领先，中国大约是6,000万台设备，北美是6,200万台，这是相当大的数字。这告诉大家的仍然是中国在智能联网领域占据重要地位，仍然是一个巨大的市场，但智能手表可能不是下一个大热门，那会是什么？

10：03—13：14

So virtual reality, everybody is probably quite familiar with virtual reality applications for games, and there are of course many creative applications for virtual reality and of course many other consumer and consuming let's say applications for virtual reality, but the one that I really want to focus on, especially given time constraints, the one I'll spend time talking about is virtual showrooms. So GfK did a study recently, the study was completed at the end of 2016, and what consumers told us is that future shoppers expect innovative shopping experiences, and they would be more likely to visit a retail store that offers some augmented reality or virtual reality showroom. In fact, something like 41% of consumers told us this and if we look at the leading edge consumers, the consumers that are of a more technical background. 70% of consumers, 69% of consumers told us that they are more likely to visit a retail store with virtual reality experiences. So think about this for a minute, it could really change the nature of retail, right? Today a retailer is limited by what they can merchandise, tomorrow they could be merchandising many, many more products. So consumer walks in, talks to them about their dimensions of their kitchen let's say, or laundry room but let's say kitchen. So I walk in, I talk about the dimensions of my kitchen, I talk about the things that I am interested in, I put on a pair of goggles, I stepped into an empty room and behold in front of me the empty room becomes alive, functional, essentially virtual or augmented kitchen where I can see what my cabinets would look like, I can see what my counters would look like, I can see what every one of the appliances looks like. This has the power to change the experience for retail, and it even has the power to change the experience for internet retailers, if this capability or same capability is ever delivered at home, I don't even have to leave my home. In three to five years, commercially, I'm not talking about as consumers, but commercially, this really has a potentially very big impact on our world. If we look at the consumption piece and what

第六单元　行业介绍 Introduction to Industries

consumers are doing, you know I just share these European numbers with you. In Europe what we saw in 2016 is that the virtual reality was a 250-million-dollar market, and it was led by head-mounted displays, these are just displays with the actual or head-mounts with the actual display inside, not a phone that you attach, and in the last quarter what we saw was a 180 million of that 250 million market developed, so OK we're seeing a lot of critical mass towards virtual reality but still compared to smartphones a very, very small, small market.

关于虚拟现实，大家可能都很熟悉虚拟现实游戏应用，当然，有很多有创造性的虚拟现实应用，很多虚拟现实的消费应用。但我想重点关注一个方面，由于时间关系，我想重点谈谈虚拟展厅。GfK 最近进行了一项研究，于 2016 年底结束。消费者告诉我们，在未来，他们期望有创新性的购物体验，他们更可能去的零售店是那些有增强现实或虚拟现实展厅的店。事实上，41% 的消费者都这么认为。如果我们看看前沿的消费者，就是那些有更多技术背景的消费者，70% 的消费者，准确地说 69% 的消费者都表示他们更倾向于能提供虚拟现实体验的店。请大家用一分钟想想，消费者的期待真的会改变零售业的本质，对吧？今天，零售商受限于自身售卖的货物。明天，他们可能售卖的产品会多得多。消费者走进店里，说出自家厨房的大小、洗衣间的大小。以厨房为例吧。我走进店里，说出自家厨房的大小，说出自己想买的东西。我戴上一副虚拟现实眼镜，走进一间空房间，看着眼前的一切变得生动、实用起来。这实际上是虚拟或增强现实的厨房，在这里，我可以看到橱柜的样子，柜台的样子，还可以看到每一件电器的样子。虚拟现实的力量足以改变人们的购物体验，甚至改变网上购物的体验。如果这种体验能送货上门，我甚至不需要走出家门。在未来的三至五年里，在商业上，我现在谈的不是消费者，而是商业，这真的有可能深刻地影响我们的世界。如果我们把目光投向消费品和消费者行为，我刚刚也跟大家分享了欧洲的数据。在欧洲，我们看到的是，2016 年虚拟现实的市场价值为 2.5 亿美元，由头盔显示器引领市场，它们都内置了虚拟现实的显示器，并没有用手机联接。在上一季度，我们看到 1.8 亿的增长出现在价值 2.5 亿美元的市场上。我们看到了虚拟现实市场已达到临界点，但比起智能手机，这仍然是一个极小的市场。

13：15—14：20

So as long as we have drones listed here and we can see the developments of drones on this slide. I'll just talk about drones very quickly as well and their potential impact for your consideration, you know I'm always trying to look out, so now what's necessarily happening in the market today but where we may be a few years from now. And when we think about drones, OK, we all know JD.COM and Amazon and others are talking about how to deliver packages using drones, but, and this will change how products are delivered to consumers and this will change our lives as consumers in terms of how quickly we can get our hands on things. But it could also change our lives. As manufacturers you know, for those who were manufacturers in the room, why does your product need to leave your factory by anything other than a drone, and why couldn't it go from your factory directly to a consumer using a drone, yeah, the product still may sell on JD. COM, the product still may sell on Amazon. com, but this is another potential game changer too soon to say, but potential game changer for our industry.

因为这张列表上有无人机的数据，我们就可以看到无人机的发展情况，就在这张幻灯片上。我会快速地谈一谈无人机，谈谈它们的潜在影响，供大家思考。我总是试着去留意外部情况，比如留心当下市场的状况以及从现在起的几年内市场的变化。当我们想到无人机，我们都想到京东、亚马逊和其它公司都在谈论如何使用无人机投递包裹，这将改变包裹投递给消费者的形式，也将改变消费者的生活方式，改变我们拿到货物的速度。而这也可能改变制造商的工作模式。对于在座的制造商来说，为什么把你们的产品送出工厂要用其它方式，而不用无人机呢？为什么产品不能直接从工厂送到消费者手上，用无人机送达呢？产品可能还是在京东上出售，可能还在亚马逊出售，要是说这很可能改变现有的游戏规则，或许还言之过早，但这很可能改变我们所处行业的游戏规则。

14：20—16：28

So let's look at smart home appliances. So, as many of you know, GfK tracks retail point of sale information in 80 countries around the globe. This is fact-based point of sale information that comes to us from retailers, and every one of these markets in Europe as well as many, many other countries around the world, and so what we see when it comes to smart home appliances is double-digit growth and in many cases, triple-digit growth. If we look at France, if we look at Germany, we see 128% year over year growth in the sale of smart home appliances, smart major appliances. If we look at the impact on pricing smart technologies bring, you know, the top item there is a refrigerator, then a washing machine and then cooking appliances, below that a cooktop and an oven, so you can see that there's a huge, huge value impact on the price index of smart connected appliances, so the question now is, OK, we're in the early stages and can we hold on to this same value proposition? Think this is going to be a trick, right? Because when 50% or 75% of appliances are actually smart, it becomes perhaps more difficult and competition may also threaten this, but for those of you who aren't in here or in the beginning stages, there's a tremendous, tremendous opportunity to, for a small investment in a chip or a board that will make your product more intelligent, there's a huge, huge payback. I mean we hear numbers between 10 dollars and 25 dollars depending on who we talk to, to make a product smart. But look at the return here.

我们来看看智能家电。你们中很多人都知道，GfK 追踪零售点的销售信息，覆盖全球 80 个国家。这是以事实为依据的销售点信息，它们来源于零售商、欧洲每一个市场及很多其它国家的市场。我们看到智能家电有两位数的增长，在很多情况下有三位数的增长。在法国市场，在德国市场，我们看到 128% 的同比增长出现在智能家电，智能大家电领域。如果我们看看智能技术对定价的影响，首先受到影响的是冰箱，其次是洗衣机，然后是烹调用具，后面跟着的是嵌入式灶具和烤箱。所以大家可以看到，巨大的价值影响存在于智能联网电器的价格指数上。现在的问题是，我们现在处于早期阶段，我们能否守住同样的价值主张？大家觉得这会是一个骗人的花招，对吗？因为当 50% 或 75% 的家电都变得智能，坚持价值主张可能变得更难，竞争也可能对此构成威胁，但如果您目前还未达到这个阶段，或刚处于起步阶段，您就有一个绝好的机会，可以小额投资一个芯片或电路板，这将使您的产品更智能，这会给您带来巨大的投资回报。我说的数目是 10 至 25 美元，数目的多少取决于我们找谁合作，由谁来打造智能产品。现在来看看投资回报。

16：31—19：37

OK, and then to quantify a little bit further, smart technologies and smart major appliances in particular, in 2014 GfK measured about 200 models, globally 200 models of smart major appliances. By 2015 selling globally there were 800 models of major appliances and today in 2016, while year ended 2016, there's something like 2,200 different smart appliance models, major appliance models available in the marketplace today. If we look at the markets where these products are being purchased, first of all, well let's look at the left hand side of the screen first, you can see that these 2,200 models represented something like 7.5 million units in sales, 7.5 million units sold globally excluding North America, so the market from 2015 to 2016 doubled excluding North America and what we see the truly interesting and when we talk about, when I talk about China and China's leadership role, as it relates to smart technologies is, we see that China essentially makes up 44%, 44% share of the smart global market. It's staggering. So there's two ways to look at this: one way to look at this is, well the market is here and the market is home and we can continue to develop this market and learn from this market and build knowledge and move this out globally over time; of course the other way to look at this is already 55% of the market, one in every two appliances is bought outside of China, right? And so if you're not already thinking about your overseas strategy, if you're not already in the marketplace with smart products in the overseas marketplace, with smart products, then you're missing an opportunity, yeah, in fact, one in every two. So again just to illustrate the importance of China if we look at washing machines, and when we look around the world at that ten biggest smart washing machine markets, you can see that China by far is the biggest smart washing machine market. Yeah, the next couple of countries combined don't even equal the size of China, yet again one in every two appliances sold is a smart appliance, every… one in every two smart appliances sold is sold outside of China. And so if you're looking for your overseas strategy, it's South Korea; it's Iran; it's Great Britain; it's Russia, etc.

好。然后再进一步量化智能技术和智能大家电，2014 年。GfK 测量了约 200 个型号，在全球测量了 200 个智能大家电型号。截止 2015 年，全球约售出 800 个不同型号的智能大家电，现在，虽然这一数据只截止到 2016 年底，现在约有 2,200 种不同型号的智能家电和大家电出现在市场上。如果我们把目光投向市场，看看出售这些家电的市场。首先，让我们看看左边屏幕，你们可以看到 2,200 个型号，即约 750 万台设备在售，这是全球的数据，但不包括北美。所以市场规模从 2015 年至 2016 年翻了一番，这不包括北美市场在内。我们看到一个十分有趣的现象，就是当我谈到中国和中国的领先地位，就是中国在智能技术上的表现时，我们看到中国基本上占了 44% 的份额，占了全球智能市场的 44%。这是很惊人的。我们可以用两种方式看待这个问题：第一种方式是市场就在中国，就在家居领域，我们可以继续拓展这个市场并向中国学习，建立知识并逐渐拓展至全球。当然，另一种方式是从剩余的 55% 的市场份额看，这意味着每两台家电中就有一台不是在中国售出，对吧？如果您还没有考虑海外市场的策略，如果您还没有进军海外市场，没有将智能产品打入海外市场，那么，您正错过一次机会，没错，就是每两台家电中就有一台是在海外市场出售。我又要再一次强调中国的重要性，大家可以看看洗衣机的情况，纵观全球，在全球十大智能洗衣机市场中，中国就是老大。排在后面的国家加起来甚至都比不上中国。同样，每两台售出的洗衣机中就有一台是智能的，每两台智能洗衣机就有一台在海外售出。所以，如果您在寻找海外市场，那就是韩国、伊朗、英国、俄罗斯等国家。

19:41—22:47

OK, and to turn our attention away from major appliances into small appliances just for a moment, I'm not going to spend too much time on this slide. Another thing to say that we see a lot of developments in the small appliance marketplace, these include personal scales with mobile connection, espresso machines, fully automatic espresso machines with mobile connection, toothbrush rechargeable, toothbrush with mobile connections and of course, of course robotic vacuums with mobile connections. So this is something like, two… almost 170 million, or a little over 170-million-dollar market globally today again excluding North America. So here are some of the products that I just mentioned in some additional, some additional products as well would give you an idea of what consumers are purchasing and where there is global interest around the world for smart small appliances. And if we are there to try again to quantify this and convey the importance of this, if we look at Germany for instance, and we look at rechargeable toothbrushes, in 2015, 10% of the market, 10% of all electric toothbrushes were smart. Today it's 17%. If we look at multi-cookers, it was 13% moves to 18%, so you might imagine in 2017 these numbers will easily achieve 20% for more of the marketplace, which means if you're selling toothbrushes, one in every five toothbrushes that sell, one in every five multi-cookers that sell are going to be smart toothbrushes and smart multi-cookers. Similarly, if we look at China and we look at robotic vacuums in 2014, GfK tracked zero, zero robotic vacuums that were smart and connected sold in China. A year later it was 11% of the market, and this past year it's 28% of the market, so now one in every four robotic vacuum cleaners sold is smart connected. And a similar story for personal scales, yeah, in the Netherlands, so OK, these things differ market by market and opportunities exist, depending on the category whether it's refrigerators, whether it's washing machines, whether it's scales, robotic vacuum cleaners or otherwise. The markets are different from place to place. The opportunity is slightly different from place to place, but clear one Chinese manufacturers are leading the way and clear two there's still tremendous upside, if you know where to go and you find the right marketplaces to export these products.

好，现在我们把关注点从大家电转移到小家电，就一会儿，我不会花太多时间讲这张幻灯片。要谈的另一点是，我们看到了很多的新发展出现在小家电市场，包括与手机联网的体重秤、浓缩咖啡机，这是与手机联网的全自动咖啡机，还有电动牙刷，能够与手机联网的电动牙刷。当然，还有联网的扫地机器人。所以这是约1.7亿，1.7亿多美元的全球市场，不包括北美在内。这些产品是我刚刚提到的。另外的一些产品也会让你们了解到消费者在买些什么，全球在关注小电家的哪些方面。如果我们再次尝试量化这一点并传达它的重要性，例如德国，看看德国的电动牙刷，在2015年，10%的电动牙刷都是智能的，今天这一数字是17%。如果我们看看多功能电饭煲，它的比例已经从13%增长到18%。你们可以想象，在2017年，这些数字会轻而易举地达到20%，占据更多的市场份额。这意味着如果您在销售牙刷，每五支牙刷里就有一支，每五个多功能电饭煲里就有一个是智能的。同样，我们看看中国，看看扫地机器人在2014年的情况。GfK追踪到，当时并没有扫地机器人，那种智能联网的扫地机器人一台也没能在中国售出。一年后，这种扫地机器人就占了11%的市场份额，而过去一年是28%。所以现在每卖出四台扫地机器人，就有一台是智能联网的。同样的情况出现在体重秤上。在荷兰，不同产品市场情况不同，机遇取决于产品的种类，看该产品是不是冰箱、洗衣机、体重秤、扫地机器人或其它。市场因地域而异。机遇也因地域而略有不同。但目前清楚的是：第一，中国制造商引领着市场；第二点，这行业仍存在着巨大的优势，只要在座各位明确自己日后的发展方向，并找到合适的市场出口这些产品。

22：48—24：27

So in summary, from my point of view, technologies ascent is astounding, and we're very much in early days. You know companies like Google and Baidu and Tencent and Amazon, these are companies only fifteen or twenty years old. The Internet itself is just like twenty some years old, so there is a tremendous opportunity here and tremendous upside for growth, and this technology as I said earlier is going to change our industry, it's going to change the home appliances/consumer technical goods industry dramatically, and I believe that China is really well poised for this, given what we saw 40%, yeah 40% of major appliances sold in China are smart appliances. There's a tremendous amount of knowledge here. There's a tremendous amount of expertise here. There's a tremendous amount of innovation here in China. And we see this, we visit a lot of different clients, we attend a lot of different trade shows, and we see it we see they are on the trade show floor over the past couple of days, we see it when we meet with our clients, innovation from China is leading edge, and exporting that innovation is the next big challenge. You know, I'll just leave it at that. So I thank you very much for your time, and what I'd like to do now is bring up our panelists and we'll have some discussion about smart technologies in the future—the SmartGo. So please warmly welcome our…oh, I'm sorry, actually, David yeah.

总之，在我看来，技术的进步是令人震惊的。我们还处于早期阶段。像谷歌、百度、腾讯和亚马逊这些公司只有 15 到 20 年的发展历史。互联网本身就只发展了二十来年，所以这里蕴含着巨大的机遇和增长潜力。而这一技术正如我早些时候所说，会改变我们的行业，它会改变家电或消费者技术产品行业。我相信，中国已经做好准备，毕竟我们看到 40%，对，40% 中国销售的大家电都是智能的。这里蕴含着丰富的知识、大量的专业知识。万众创新在中国如火如荼，我们都见证了这一点。我们拜访了很多不同的客户，出席了各种不同类型的展会，我们都亲眼见证了这一点，看到技术就蕴藏在展馆中，就在过去几天一直举办的展会里。在我们会见客户时能清楚看到，中国的创新占据领先优势，而出口创新将是下一个巨大的挑战。我的演讲到此结束。非常感谢在座各位的聆听！现在我想做的是有请我们的小组成员，我们将探讨未来的智能技术——SmartGo。所以请以热烈的掌声有请我们的……抱歉，是有请 David。

III. 实战练习二

1. 演讲背景

印度京德勒集团代表应邀参加"不锈钢产业发展大会"并发表主旨演讲,他在演讲中简要地介绍了公司的发展历程、产品系列,具体谈到了 200 系不锈钢的发展史,他所代表的公司由于当时镍价暴涨,决定自主研发低镍不锈钢产品系列。随后他还分享了 2016 年全球各国不锈钢的产量,中国是名副其实的第一生产大国,印度第二,最后还谈到了不锈钢的终端用途。

2. 预习词汇

stainless steel 不锈钢
manganese 锰
raw material 原材料
Jindal Group 京德勒集团
Jindal Stainless 京德勒不锈钢有限公司
Jindal Steel and Power 京德勒钢铁和电力有限公司
JSW JSW 钢铁有限公司
Jindal Saw Limited 京德勒索有限公司
plain chromium stainless steel 纯铬不锈钢
ferritic grade 铁素体等级
utility grade 多用途等级
molybdenum 钼
duplex grade 双相系
lean duplex 精钢
austenitic grade 奥氏体系
chromium 铬
nickel 镍
Band-Aid 创可贴
nitrogen 氮
copper 铜
end use 终端使用
dairy industry 乳制品行业
beer industry 啤酒行业
household appliance 家用电器

kitchen and white good 厨房用具和白色家电
AISI/American Iron and Steel Institute 美国钢铁学会

3. 演讲文本

00：00—00：27

A very good afternoon, friends. It's indeed, a great pleasure and honor for me to stand before you today, in your special events dedicated to the manganese industry. I come from the stainless steel background, and manganese in recent years has become one of our important raw materials.

下午好，朋友们。今天，我很开心、很荣幸能站在你们面前，参加你们专门为锰业举办的活动。我来自不锈钢行业，但锰在近年来已成为我们重要的原材料之一。

00：35—01：23

Can I change it? OK. This is a small slide to give an introduction of our group companies. We have four large corporates in the Jindal Group, Jindal Stainless, Jindal Steel and Power, JSW, Jindal Saw Limited. Together, we produce around 25 million tons of steel in India, which includes one million ton of stainless steel. So definitely our relation with manganese is very long. Well, I don't want to take your time about how our journey of stainless steel starting in 1970 going to a million ton today.

我能不能换一页PPT？好的。这张幻灯片上展示了我们集团的子公司。我们京德勒集团旗下有四家大公司，包括京德勒不锈钢有限公司、京德勒钢铁和电力有限公司、JSW钢铁有限公司、京德勒索有限公司。我们共生产大约2,500万吨钢铁，都在印度生产，其中包括100万吨不锈钢。所以，毫无疑问，我们和锰业的联系非常紧密。我不想浪费你们的时间来讲我们的不锈钢发展史，从1970开始做到现在的100万吨产量的历程就不进了。

01：23—03：02

Now this is an important slide. As you can see the stainless steel family tree, stainless steel family tree we call it. This part of the plain chromium stainless steel. Ferritic grades, utility grades, molybdenum comes here. So those become duplex grade. Lean duplex. These are all austenitic grades which are with nickel, chromium, molybdenum and this is a new development of the 200 series which is chrome and Ni (nickel) and a very little of nickel in this. What are the key elements to produce 200 series stainless steel? You can see chromium, without chrome no stainless steel. Chromium is the element which gives the properties of stainless in a steel. It is like really a shield or like a bodyguard. It is on the top of the stainless steel surface. So even if you damage, you scratch stainless steel sheet or any stainless steel material, all it needs is air in the atmosphere to reform and it's like a human body. You know you get a scratch, you put a Band-Aid and you heal yourself. Similarly, without chromium, there is no stainless steel. When we talk of 200 series specifically, then chromium is in moderate range. Manganese is very high. Nickel is low. We add a nitrogen and copper to improve the quality of stainless steel.

这张幻灯片上的内容很重要。你们可以看到这张不锈钢产品系列图,我们把这个图叫做不锈钢产品树。左边是纯铬不锈钢,铁素体等级、多用途等级和钼都属于纯铬不锈钢,这些属于双相系。精钢等,这些都是奥氏体系,这些产品含有镍、铬、钼,是200系的一个新产品,含有铬和镍,非常少量的镍。200系不锈钢的关键生产元素是什么?你们可以看到是铬,没有铬,就没有不锈钢。铬是一种元素,它赋予了不锈钢的特性。它像一个盾牌、一个保镖,位于不锈钢的表面。所以即使损坏了、刮花了不锈钢或者任何不锈钢材料,只需空气便可以重新塑形,像人的身体一样。你们知道,当人被刮伤后,贴一个创可贴就可以治愈。同样的,没有铬,就没有不锈钢。我们特别谈到的200系,铬含量适中,锰含量非常高,镍含量低。我们还通过加入氮和铜来提高不锈钢的质量。

03:03—04:37

Now what is the history of 200 series of stainless steel? Initially in fact they were developed in 1930, but the use limit remained very very limited. It had in those days, chemistry of 15% chromium, 12 manganese, 1.5 nickel. And these were used in Germany 1940s. Major applications was the dairy industry, beer industry and household appliances. Now in early 50s, during the Korean War, the US government put a restriction because of nickel shortage to use nickel and bring out some grades which are below 1% restriction there. So therefore companies like Allegheny developed proprietary grades IA 201 which are just little less than 1% nickel. It had high chromium and high manganese. As you can see manganese is as much as, manganese is 15%, chromium 14.5, nickel is below 1. And post Korean War we needed softer alloy and therefore these 200, 201, 202 grades came into AISI standards in 1955. But after that, what happened is there was no nickel shortage. There were no issues of that kind. So it remained like a sleeping giant without further growth in this scenario.

200系不锈钢有何发展史?最初,人们在1930年开发了200系,但它的使用范围非常有限。那时,200系不锈钢含有15%铬,12%锰,1.5%镍。20世纪40年代的德国使用这个品类的不锈钢,主要应用于乳制品行业、啤酒行业和家用电器。在50年代早期,朝鲜战争期间,美国政府限制了镍的使用,因为镍非常短缺,有一些产品,镍的使用甚至要控制在1%以下。因此,像阿勒格尼这样的公司开发了专利产品 201 系，镍的含量略低于 1%，铬和锰的含量很高。你们可以看到，锰的含量是 15%，铬 14.5%，镍在 1% 以下。朝鲜战争之后，我们需要更软的合金，因此这些 200 系，201 系，202 系在 1955 年就形成了美国钢铁学会标准。但在那之后，镍并未出现短缺的问题，没有这样的问题。所以它就像一个沉睡的巨人，在这种背景下没有进一步的增长。

04：37—06：03

Now this is the most important slide of my presentation, friends, because it was India which took the lead in development of 200 series in 1990s. Our production was only 250,000 tons for the whole year in 1990 and 95% of what we produced was 18 chromium, 8 nickel, and 85% of stainless steel used only for the housewives, for the kitchen and kitchen related. And as you know in 1989, the nickel prices went to $18,568. We had to import 100% nickel from outside. You are also paying a 55% import tax and therefore and we had certain problem with our foreign exchange balance sheet. End use was kitchen. So we looked at that scenario and started looking at what Allegheny had done, what happened in World War II and we were able to develop our own stainless steel grades going forward. And as you know also in 2007 nickel touched an all-time high $52,179 in the May of 2007 and the average of May, 2007 was $37,000. So how much volatility in nickel prices was a big worry for our industry.

这是我的演讲中最重要的一张幻灯片，朋友们，因为印度在 200 系的发展中处于领先地位，当时是 20 世纪 90 年代。我们的产量在 1990 年全年只有 25 万吨，而我们生产的 95% 的产品含有 18% 的铬和 8% 的镍，85% 的不锈钢主要为家庭主妇使用，是厨房和厨房相关用品。正如你们所知，在 1989 年，镍价涨到了 18,568 美元。我们所需的镍百分之百从外面进口，此外，我们还要缴纳 55% 的进口税。因此，我们的外汇资产负债表出现了一定的问题。终端用途是厨房用品。所以我们在这个背景下，开始研究阿勒格尼所做的事情，在第二次世界大战中发生了什么，我们能够开发出我们自己的不锈钢产品系列。正如你们所知道的，2007 年 5 月，镍的价格达到了历史最高的 52,179 美元，而 2007 年 5 月的平均价格是 37,000 美元。因此，镍价的波动是一个很大的担忧，对我们的行业来说是如此。

06：09—06：37

Now this is our own company's growth story of what all we have developed in all these areas. We have done 15 years of research and development for end use bases. We have been able to develop all these grades of stainless steel and you can see later on in your presentation copy that what is the 201, 202, 204 with copper deep drawing qualities. And you will be able to see the applications.

这是我们公司的发展历程，关于我们在所有这些领域所开发的产品。我们的研发持续了15年，为终端用户服务。我们已经能够开发出所有这些系列的不锈钢，你们可以在后面的演示中看到什么是201系，202系，204系，有铜的深拉特性。你们还能够看到这些产品的应用范围。

06：37—09：07

Just a quick look at the stainless steel industry, you can see the 2016 production, India became the second largest producing country after China. But the gap is huge. China produced almost 25 million tons. We produce 3.2 million tons, so we are the second largest producer but the China has gone so big in a short time. In fact, China in 2010 was only 11 million, gone up to 24～25 million tons. So today half of the stainless steel produced is coming from China and all the grades. So everybody in the world is looking at the story of India and China as far as stainless steel is concerned. This is again if you see from 2006 to 2016, you will find that the growth invested in Europe is almost negative or flat. Central/Eastern Europe is very small anyway. Americas also is not great. The green one is all that is you can see in China alone. And this is Asia without China, which means four countries Japan, Korea, Taiwan, and India. So this is how the scenario is there at the moment. For this audience here, this one you can see that 20% of stainless steel produced in 2016 was of 200 series which means nine million tons from almost zero. When India we started the world production of 200 series was just 14,000 tons for the whole year. Today we are talking about nine million tons. So this is definitely a success story on its own, right? And again to demonstrate the role of China, as you can see in 2005 China had a 39% of the world market share and they are at 54% already. So this the big story about China, but I don't know how long that growth can be sustained, because they have grown sometimes even on 20% year-on-year, sometimes 25%, but having reached 40, 26, 27 million tons production, I think the growth will be moderated, I'm sure in China, and India will be and this is again, this is a quarterly production. Third quarter is not relevant in this meeting here.

稍微看看不锈钢行业数据，就能看到2016年的不锈钢产量，印度成为第二大生产国，仅次于中国。但差距巨大。中国生产了近2,500万吨。我们生产了320万吨，所以，我们是第二大的生产国，但中国在很短的时间内发展如此迅猛。事实上，中国在2010年只有1,100万，后来产量达到了2,400万～2,500万吨。所以目前生产的各个系列的不锈钢有一半来自中国。因此，世界上每个人都在关注印度和中国的发展，特别是不锈钢行业。看2006—2016年的数据，你们会发现欧洲的投资增长率几乎为负或与之前持平，中欧、东欧的增长率也都非常小，美洲的增长率也不太好。绿色表示的是中国。另外，这个是不包含中国的亚洲产量，是亚洲四个国家和地区——日本、韩国、台湾和印度的产量。这是目前不锈钢行业的基本情况。在座的各位，你们可以看到，2016年生产的不锈钢中有20%是200系，这意味着200系几乎从0吨增长到900万吨。印度在全球范围内开始生产200系时，当时的年产量只有14,000吨。今天这个数字达到了900万吨。所以这绝对是一个成功的故事，对吧？这再一次证明了中国的作用，你们可以看到，2005年中国占世界市场份额的39%，而现在已经达到了54%。这是中国不锈钢行业的辉煌成就，但是我不知道这种增长能持续多久，因为中国产量有时甚至同比增长20%，有时25%。但在达到4,000万，2,600万和2,700万吨产量后，我认为增长将放缓。我相信在中国和印度的增速都将放缓。这是一个季度的产量，第三季度产量与本次会议无关。

09：07—09：52

Now again coming back to India, what has happened is today although the world average is 20% of the 200 series which requires chrome manganese, a little bit of nickel and copper and nitrogen. In India, 58% of what we produce is of 200 series. So India is an important market for the manganese industry. It is for the manganese industry to give us the right material whether it is the ferro-manganese, whether it is manganese metal or any other product form so that our cost can be contained and we have about 30% of stainless steel in India which will be nickel chrome molybdenum grade, four ferritic grades, 400 series, pure chromium steel, around 12%.

回到印度，现在的情况是，尽管世界平均水平是20%的200系不锈钢需要铬锰，少量的镍，铜和氮。在印度，我们生产的不锈钢产品有58%是200系。因此，印度是锰业的重要市场，锰业为我们提供合适的材料，不论是锰铁，还是锰金属或任何其他锰产品。这样可以控制成本。印度有大约30%的不锈钢属于镍铬钼系，四个铁素体系、400系、纯铬钢，占大约12%。

09：54—11：08

Where does stainless steel go in the world? If you look at the world averages, 39% is the metal products, mainly related to kitchen and white goods, whereas in India our housewife is our number-one customer without doing much marketing, without doing much. They know for their cooking, for serving, for washing, anything in the kitchen. It is stainless steel all the way. So we are very happy that still 52% again. 39% what we have grown in recent years is what we call the automotive railways. In transport sector we have reached around 7% still almost half the world average. 13% in architecture, building and construction. We are very low compared to the rest of the world. And so an important part is that our per capita use in India is only two kilograms per person. World average is six kilograms, the three times the Indian story and all the developed economies in Europe and Americas is 10 kilos, 15 kilos. In Taiwan, nickel is even somewhere 35 kilos in the past.

世界范围内不锈钢行业的情况如何？如果你们看看世界平均水平数据，就会知道39%是金属制品，主要与厨房用具和白色家电有关。在印度，家庭主妇是我们的头号顾客，不需要太多市场营销，也没有做什么别的宣传，她们知道烹饪、盘子、洗刷等等厨房里的任何东西都是不锈钢的。所以我们很高兴，这个数据达到了52%。近年来，我们的增长主要在所谓的汽车铁路领域。在交通领域，我们占了7%左右，几乎是世界平均水平的一半。建筑、楼房和建设约13%。与世界其他地区相比，我们的水平很低。所以很重要的一点是，印度的人均使用量只有2公斤。世界平均水平是6公斤，是印度的三倍，欧洲和美洲的所有发达经济体的人均使用量分别是10公斤和15公斤。在台湾，镍的人均使用量以前甚至接近35公斤。

11:09—13:01

So what we did that after all the R&D we did? We asked the Bureau of Indian Standard to give some specific grades for our end use. And after doing all the study in food contact, in the year 2012, they came out with these standards for a low nickel high manganese 200 series and then and 2017 these grades were also approved for general applications and general purpose applications. I don't want to take you to detail, but these are the three Indian grades at the moment, besides a lot of proprietary grades which we produce, which will have manganese from as low as 6% to 8% to as high as 10%. And of course the nickel will be reduced substantially on these grades from 1% to maybe 4 to 5%. And these are just to give you an idea of what, if you use this grade which is a 9% manganese and 1% nickel, the shallow or deep drawn items for normal house application, you can use this grade which is not deep drawing, which is not critical. If you need to produce a little more of these products again for miscellaneous use, the nickel can be 2%, manganese 5%. So this is just to demonstrate and if you want to go for all other fancy products like a kitchen sink and deep drawn item in your breweries for beer, or for any of those applications, we go to 7% manganese, 4% nickel grades. So these is just an example of what can happen here. Finally, these are again items which are using the 200 series chrome manganese stainless steel.

那么我们在研发之后做了什么呢？我们要求印度标准局为我们的终端使用制定一些具体的标准。我们做了所有关于食物接触级不锈钢产品系的研究，是在2012年，在这之后，他们制定了低镍高锰200系的标准，然后在2017年，这些标准也被批准用于一般用途。我不想细说这一部分。这是目前印度的三个不锈钢系列，除了我们生产的许多专有的系列等级，锰含量可低至6%到8%，最高可达10%。当然，这些系列中的镍含量从4%到5%大大减少到1%。这些数据只是为了给你们一个笼统的概念。如果你们用的不锈钢产品含有9%的锰和1%的镍,那么对于普通家庭使用的具有浅度或深拉特性的产品,可以用这个系列的产品,不具有伸拉强度,这不是关键。如果你们需要生产更多的此类产品以供杂用,镍的含量可以是2%,锰5%。所以这只是为了证明如果你们想要购买其他的高档不锈钢产品,比如厨房水槽和啤酒厂酒槽,或者任何类似的不锈钢产品,我们可以买锰含量为7%,镍含量为4%的不锈钢系列。这只是一个例子,说明一些可能的情况。最后,这些是使用了200系铬锰不锈钢的产品。

13:01—14:43

So in summary, I would say that high manganese austenitic 200 series stainless steel have been noticed when nickel prices rise and India is credited for its initial growth in volume terms in 1990 onwards, because as I said when that trigger point came, the world production was only 40,000 tons mainly the United States as a utility grade. It was not used for any other application but today it is the talk of the town that and then the Chinese market after 2005 were picked up. The development of these 200 series and today of course they produce a very large volume if we say 9 million, we may produce about 2~2.5 million out of that. The major portion, balance portion are coming from China. Also I am glad that 200 series are accepted worldwide and has started showing its presence in standard and various specific end use application because the cost is more stable. The price of manganese or our scrap and the nickel is very limited quantity, so the volatility in prices is minimized. So therefore, it has a secure future. To say once again that 200 series chrome manganese stainless steel have a secure future and end use applications in two largest producing countries China and India will continue to grow. Thank you very much for your kind attention! I'm ready to take any questions from you. Thank you once again for inviting me!

所以总的来说,我认为高锰奥氏体200系不锈钢备受关注,因为镍价格上涨,印度产量自1990年以来一路上涨。因为就像我刚刚说的,触发点来的时候,世界只有40,000吨,主要生产美国多用途等级系列,当时不锈钢产品没有用于任何其他场合。如今,不锈钢产品被广泛地运用于各个领域。2005年后,中国市场崛起。200系不锈钢产品在整个不锈钢行业占有重要地位。如果说不锈钢产量为900万,那么200系占200~250万吨。主要部分,剩余部分来自中国。我也很高兴200系在世界范围内被接受,并且已经开始存在于标准和各种特定的终端应用,得益于它稳定的成本。锰、废铁和镍的价格非常有限,所以价格的波动对其影响可以最小化。因此,200系不锈钢有一个稳定的未来。最后再说一次,200系铬锰不锈钢拥有安全的未来,终端用途在两个最大的生产国——中国和印度,还将继续扩大。非常感谢你们的聆听!我已经准备好回答你们的提问了。再次感谢你们邀请我参加本次活动!

第三部分 同传实战

第七单元　研发合作
R&D Cooperation

I. 实战练习一

1. 演讲背景

斯科尔科沃是俄罗斯最大的政府创立的科技园,该园区驻华代表应邀参加"建设世界一流高科技园区国际会议"并发表主旨演讲。他在演讲中指出,斯科尔科沃基金创立的初衷就是为初创企业和创新公司提供联邦贷款,并建设生态系统和基础设施。斯科尔科沃拥有斯科尔科沃科技学院(Skoltech),入驻的企业中除了初创企业,还有全球知名公司,另外还有5个产业集群:生物医疗集群、IT集群、能源集群、核集群和航空业集群。最后还谈到了企业入驻享有的税收等优惠政策。

2. 预习词汇

Skolkovo 斯科尔科沃
Skolkovo Foundation 斯科尔科沃基金
incubator 孵化器
ecosystem 生态体系
Bloomberg report 彭博社报告
federal loan 联邦贷款
start-up 初创企业
Silicon Valley 硅谷
angel investment 天使投资
Start-up Village 创业村
resident 入驻企业;入驻公司
biological and medical cluster 生物医疗集群
profit tax 利润税
VAT/value added tax 增值税
tax benefit 税收优惠
3D printing 3D打印
mentorship program 导师项目

venture capitalist 风险投资人

3. 演讲文本

00: 00—00: 43

Good morning, everybody. First, I have to apologize that I have to speak English because my Chinese is not that good enough to give presentation, but I'll try to speak slowly so that probably translation will have, to give you a good picture of what I'm trying to say. My goal is to show you what we do in Russia in terms of financing and technology development through technological parks and I'm representing Skolkovo Foundation. Skolkovo is the biggest government technological park in Russia.

各位早上好！首先，抱歉，我只能用英语做展示，因为我的中文还不够好，但是我会尽量讲慢点，这样译员可以把我想讲的内容清楚地传达给你们。我今天是想向你们介绍我们在俄罗斯的融资和技术开发，途径是通过建立科技园。我是斯科尔科沃基金的代表。斯科尔科沃是俄罗斯最大的政府创立的科技园。

00: 43—01: 28

However, even though we are biggest in Russia, we are small compared to China, to Chinese counterparts. I was really impressed by previous speaker, Mr. Zhu. When he said that first Chinese incubator was established 30 years ago in Wuhan, for us it's very impressive 30 years ago, because Skolkovo is only six years old, so we are kind of baby compared to the China market. But anyway, we are trying to do our best and trying to solve the issues and challenges which are in front of our country and the start-up ecosystem.

然而，就算我们在俄罗斯规模最大，与中国同行相比我们还很小。上一位演讲嘉宾朱先生让我印象很深刻，他说中国第一个孵化器30年前就在武汉建立了，这让我印象很深刻，因为斯科尔科沃只有6年的发展历史，与中国市场相比我们还只是个"宝宝"。但是无论如何，我们一直在努力做到最好，努力应对我们国家和创业生态体系所面临的问题和挑战。

01: 29—03: 06

First of all, probably as you know, Russia is famous for its science, for its scientific researches and overall education system. According to Bloomberg report, couple of years ago, Russia was ranked number 14 globally in terms of innovations. Basically what it says is that Russia has brains, Russia has science, Russia has really smart people, but we are very weak in commercializing them. We can invent something, but we can not sell what we invent. This is the problem we share, most of our companies are facing. That's

103

why government decided to support start-ups and innovation companies in Russia and by federal loan, and the Government of Russia was established Skolkovo Foundation, which basically has three stages in its development. First, we create a critical mass of start-ups, adventure capital partners, programs and so on, so that we create the ecosystem, basically the example was taken from Silicon Valley or from Chinese science parks, from all over the world, where you need people come together and work together when they develop innovative products.

  首先，大家可能知道，俄罗斯因其科研和整个教育体系而闻名。彭博社报告称，几年前，俄罗斯的创新能力全球排名第14。这表明俄罗斯有人才，有科学，有非常聪明的人，但是我们的弱项是将创新商业化。我们能够发明创造，但是却不会出售发明。这是我们存在的问题，很多俄罗斯公司都面临这样的问题。这也是为什么政府决定支持俄罗斯初创企业和创新公司的发展，为它们提供联邦贷款。俄罗斯政府建立了斯科尔科沃基金，它的发展大体经历了三个阶段。首先，我们支持大量的初创企业、风险投资伙伴、项目等，创造生态系统。这种方式是从硅谷、中国科技园以及世界其他地方借鉴来的，生态系统需要人才聚集、共同开发创新产品。

03: 07—03: 36

  Then the next stage is to develop the overall system, and infrastructure ecosystem around this innovation sphere. From this and last year, we are trying to turn it to self-sustained system in terms of finance, because until now it was mostly financed by government, but now we also move in to direction when we implement various combined forms of financing.

  第二个阶段是发展整体生态系统，以及创新领域里的基础设施生态系统。从去年开始，我们就努力使其在融资上自给自足，因为直到现主要还是靠政府的资金支持。但是我们也正朝着融资多元化的方向发展。

03: 36—04: 26

  What Skolkovo is actually? Skolkovo is a special district near Moscow, southeast of Moscow which was developed from scratch, it was empty space, government-dedicated land. And on this land it was built technopark and offices, everything from scratch basically. Right now we have kind of nice campus for Skolkovo residents where they can have office, where they have labs, where we have space to host conferences, also we host some overall events like Start-up Village where not only Skolkovo start-ups, but other companies come together and share their experience.

  斯科尔科沃到底是什么？它是莫斯科附近的一个特区，在莫斯科的东南方向，是从无到有发展来的，最初是一块空地，归政府所有。我们在这片土地上建了科技园和办公楼，一切从零开始。现在，我们有非常棒的园区，入驻公司可以在这里办公、做实验、举办会议，同时我们也举办一些综合性活动，比如说"创业村"，斯科尔科沃的初创企业和其他公司可以相聚在此，分享经验。

04：26—04：59

The vision is that we want Russia to be, to sustain its technological age, and but we want this technological knowledge like science to be converted to commercial products, so that they can self-sustain themselves, they just don't just invent, but actually make money, which they can reinvest into themselves and to the society and bring the benefits to the rest of us.

我们的愿景是希望俄罗斯维持它的技术大国优势，我们更希望这些技术知识能够变成商品，这样公司才可以自给自足。它们不只是发明创造，还可以盈利，将利润再投资，回馈社会，造福所有人。

05：01—06：12

What's Skolkovo in parts? First, we have Skoltech. Skoltech is a joint venture between Skolkovo and MIT, Massachusetts Institute of Technology. It's basically an MIT branch in Moscow. Then we have start-ups, companies, small-and-middle-sized companies can apply to become Skolkovo residents, until now we have about 1,500 start-ups, companies, which became Skolkovo residents. Besides that, we have industrial partners like big companies, like Cisco, Intel, IBM, all those big global names. From China, it's Huawei, I think and others who also cooperate with Skolkovo and cooperate with start-ups which are residents of Skolkovo. And important part is the investors, private investors we see, institutional banks, everybody is there from angel investment to latest stage investment.

斯科尔科沃是由什么构成的呢？首先，我们有Skoltech，它是一家合资企业，由斯科尔科沃和麻省理工学院合办，是麻省理工在莫斯科的一个分支。其次，我们有初创企业，公司，中小型企业都可以申请入驻斯科尔科沃，目前入驻的初创企业已达1,500家。此外，我们还有工业合作伙伴，包括一些大公司，如思科、英特尔、IBM等全球知名的大公司，中国的华为及其他公司，他们也与斯科尔科沃入驻的初创企业有合作。另一个重要的组成部分是投资者，有私人投资者，也有银行机构，有初期的天使投资，也有后期投资。

06：12—08：35

We have five clusters. One is B&M, biological and medical cluster. Another one is IT, energy, nuclear and space. What does it mean? It basically means that any company which is working in this area, one of those areas can apply to become a Skolkovo resident and get some tax benefits, some financial support, office space, all typical services which served by such kind of organizations. For example, if a company becomes a Skolkovo residents, they can have profit tax zero, exemption from VAT and other tax benefits. Also companies can have financial support from venture funds and angel community which is also the part of Skolkovo ecosystem. Skolkovo itself has a grant program, so companies, usually small companies apply for the grant and they can have financial support without giving their shares to, as usually happens when they have, like, received financing. And they have research centers. They can use research centers and labs which are part of Skolkovo infrastructure. Grant financing, so far about 500 companies have got grant financing, almost one third of a billion was already pooled, and most of them already given to the companies. As you can see all those grants are kind of equally distributed between the sectors, so we try to support different sectors focusing on various fields.

我们有5个集群，生物医疗集群、IT集群、能源集群、核集群和航空业集群。什么意思呢？这意味着任何一家从事这5大领域的公司都可以申请入驻斯科尔科沃，享受税收优惠和财政支持、拥有办公区及其他科技园区提供的代表性服务。例如，入驻斯科尔科沃的公司可以享受零利润税，免除增值税，及其他税收优惠。还可以获得企业基金和天使资金支持，天使资金也是斯科尔科沃生态系统的组成部分。斯科尔科沃本身也有补助项目，因此公司，通常是小公司，都可以申请补助金，它们不需要出让股份就可获得资金支持，而通常公司想获得资金就需出让股份。入驻公司可以使用研究中心和实验室，这些都是斯科尔科沃基础设施的一部分。关于补助金资助，目前有500多家企业获得了资助，已经筹集了近3亿资金，大多数都已经拨给了公司。您可以看到，所有这些补助金在这五大行业中是公平分配的，所以我们支持不同行业不同领域的发展。

08：35—09：32

Also they can use other sectors' laboratories, about 35 labs are present in Skolkovo campus, so any of them could be used by the residents of Skolkovo. And they can make research, tests, proof of concept, 3D printing, everything. Besides that, we Skolkovo provides mentorship program usually also for small-and-medium enterprises, for small residents of Skolkovo. Basically it's the people from big companies, from universities, professors, from the government who come and give lectures, trainings, all monitor companies on the whole stage of the development of company from zero to a billion.

入驻企业还可以使用其他行业的实验室。斯科尔科沃园区中有35个实验室，入驻企业都可以使用。可以做研究、做测试、证实理念、3D打印等。此外，斯科尔科沃还提供导师项目给入驻的中小企业。导师通常来自大公司、高校和政府机构，他们过来做讲座、开展培训，监督公司从无到有的整个发展过程。

09：39—10：38

We cannot do it alone, so we have partners all over the world. In basically every country we have some kind of partnership with similar organizations, like for example in China, we partner with Zhongguancun Science Park, we partner with Tus-Holding, and we also open to any other new opportunities and new collaboration. International expansion for Skolkovo is kind of a new thing, because as I said, we are only six years old and so far I am the only one foreign representative for Skolkovo, we don't have any other representatives in Europe or America, so we started from China, because China is the priority at this moment, and we will develop this collaboration and this ties to China and other countries in the region and global as well.

我们无法独自完成，因此我们在世界各地都有合作伙伴，在几乎所有国家，我们都与类似机构展开合作。比如在中国，我们和中关村科技园合作，和启迪控股合作，我们还会寻找新的机会，开展新的合作。斯科尔科沃的全球扩张是一项新举措，就像我说的，我们只有6年的发展历史，目前我是斯科尔科沃唯一的驻外代表，我们在欧美没有其他代表，我们从中国着手，因为目前中国是发展重点，我们会将合作与联系拓展到中国、本区域各国及世界各国。

10：42—12：39

As the theme of this conference is technology and finance, I focus a little bit on the finance at this moment, as I said that we create the ecosystem which helps people with money to find people with ideas. And all angel investors and venture capitalist of Russia work with Skolkovo, because it's the best platform to find good and growing start-ups. We have business angel club. We have venture capitalist and we have kind of a few quite successful deals. If we look at Russia as a whole, all venture capital market, every third company would be Skolkovo related. So basically Skolkovo is kind of responsible for one third of Russian venture capital business ecosystem. Most of the investments are going to IT for some reason because other industries, other clusters like energy, biotech, space, and nuclear maybe sound a little bit more hard core, so IT is more popular this moment. But now we are trying to shift this to more equally distributed picture, so we are trying to find us partners, like we see it's who can invest and also nuclear or space and biotech. Biotech is very hot right now, so probably one or two years it will overcome IT. And energy, energy efficiency is also priority for the country, for Skolkovo in general.

本次会议的主题是科技和金融，现在我着重讲一下金融。我刚说到我们建立了生态系统，帮助有资金的人寻找有创意的人，俄罗斯所有天使投资人和风险投资人都在与斯科尔科沃合作，因为我们是发掘发展中的优质初创企业最好的平台。我们有商业天使俱乐部，有风险投资人，有许多非常成功的交易。如果我们将俄罗斯看作一个整体，所有的风投市场、第三方公司都与斯科尔科沃相关联。斯科尔科沃负责俄罗斯三分之一的风投商业生态体系。出于某些原因，大多数投资会集中在IT行业，因为其他行业，其他集群如能源、生物科技、航空和核能听起来是非常传统的行业，因此，IT现在是热门。但我们正努力改变现状，更公平地分配资金。我们正寻找合作伙伴，比如看看哪些投资商可以投资核、航空或者生物科技。生物科技现在也非常热门，可能一两年之后它会超过IT。总体来说，能源利用效率也是俄罗斯、斯科尔科沃的重点。

12：44—13：50

As I said that not only these, but also industrial partners, all the big names collaborate with Skolkovo and our start-ups. Skoltech is university. As you know that success of Silicon Valley is because of Stanford and Berkeley there and success of Haidian district in China is because of Beida, Qinghua there, right? So that's why in Skolkovo, we have Skoltech which is MIT in Russia. And also not only that university, but all universities, so Moscow like Physical and Technical University, Moscow State University, all the educational institutions also collaborate with Skolkovo. We have special programs with start-ups and supply workforce and ideas and creativity to Skolkovo residents. At the same time, we also collaborate with foreign universities as well.

除了科技和资金之外，我还说到了行业合作伙伴，各大公司与斯科尔科沃及初创企业有合作。Skoltech是一所大学，大家都知道硅谷的成功得益于斯坦福大学和伯克利大学，中国海淀区的成功得益于北大和清华。因此，我们在斯科尔科沃有Skoltech，它是俄罗斯的麻省理工学院，而且我们不仅有Skoltech这一所大学，还有其他大学，像莫斯科的物理技术大学、莫斯科国立大学等，都和斯科尔科沃有合作。我们为初创企业提供特殊的项目，提供劳动力、创意和创造力给斯科尔科沃入驻企业。同时，我们也与国外的高校合作。

13：51—14：46

Moscow is a big city in Russia, but not the only one. It has started from Moscow and so far we have campus only in Moscow. Last year we have open office in Vladivostok which is Far East, Haishenwai in Russia. And next two years we'll open another five offices across the country. So basically we are expanding cross the country

第七单元 研发合作 R&D Cooperation

and bringing this expertise and this experience to other parts of Russia as a country. And this is how we developed inside Russia and we are open to collaboration with Chinese and other countries, similar partners like technoparks and incubators. Welcome!

莫斯科是俄罗斯的大城市，俄罗斯也有其他这样的大城市。我们从莫斯科起步，目前只在莫斯科建立了园区。去年，我们在Vladivostok设立了办事处，它位于远东地区，也就是俄罗斯的海参崴。未来两年，我们会在全国开设五个办事处，因此我们正在全国范围内发展，将专业知识和经验带到俄罗斯其他地方。这就是我们在国内的发展模式，同时，欢迎中国和其他国家的类似机构与我们合作，比如科技园和孵化器等。欢迎!

II. 实战练习二

1. 演讲背景

美国律师Jeffery应邀参加"建设世界一流高科技园区国际会议"并发表演讲。他从律师从业经验的角度，谈了中国公司该如何吸引孵化器，并让新客户入驻他们的孵化器。开场伊始他分享了一个故事说明孵化器的关键所在就是创新，为初创企业创造附加值，包括建立新的人脉关系、合理分配资金、法律帮助、财务管理、产品分销、会计、管理、保护知识产权。

2. 预习词汇

incubator 孵化器
attorney 律师
added value 附加值
sapphire 蓝宝石
deploy 部署
bankruptcy 破产
seasoned 经验丰富的
ambiguity 模棱两可
lawsuit 诉讼
fiscal management 财政管理
CES/Consumer Electronics Show 消费电子产品展览会
Sony 索尼公司
Beta Beta 系统（是由索尼公司研制出的一种标清广播级录像机制式）
VHS/Video Home System 家用录像系统（是由日本JVC公司在1976年开发的一种家用录像机录制和播放标准）

109

Bill Gates 比尔·盖茨
Microsoft 微软公司
Steve Jobs 史蒂夫·乔布斯
Apple 苹果公司
Kickstarter 一个专为具有创意方案的企业筹资的众筹网站平台
Indiegogo 一个众筹平台
shark 坑蒙拐骗的人；诈骗者

3. 演讲文本

00：00—00：36

First, let me say that I'm an American attorney, and I'm going to be speaking differently than most of the people here before, frankly I've done a lot of bankruptcies. And instead of talking about different incubators, I'm gonna tell how can a Chinese company attract incubators and new clients to join their incubators with little bit different, more of an educational speech. Now I'd like to tell you a little, an anecdote first. As a lawyer, it's sometimes good to tell a story before you actually go into your presentation.

首先，我要跟大家说，我是一名美国律师，我下面的演讲会和前面大部分人的演讲不同。其实我处理过很多破产案件，我不打算讲不同的孵化器，而是会告诉大家中国公司该如何吸引孵化器，并让新客户入驻他们的孵化器。所以我分享的内容有点不同，更像是一个教育性的演讲。现在我想先和你们分享一个小故事。作为一名律师，有时候不妨先讲个故事再进入主题。

00：36—01：49

So once upon a time, there was a nobleman who had a beautiful sapphire, beautiful giant precious stone, and he showed it to all of his friends and he was very proud of it. And all of a sudden it got a crack, crack right down the middle. So he's a nobleman. He hanged the person who did it. But now what do you do with a sapphire that has a big crack? It's ugly now. So he went to all of the different jewelers in the land and one jeweler finally told him, "I can fix it, but you don't hang me if there is a problem." And so what he did was he took the beautiful sapphire and he took the crack and he edged a rose along the crack, making it a sapphire with a beautiful rose on it. So he made it more beautiful than it was before. And so the moral of the story is when you have a problem, then what's the opportunity and how do you make innovation? And the whole point for incubators is you have to make innovation. Now I'm gonna speak a little bit about how do you go with innovation with incubators.

从前有一个贵族，他有一块漂亮的蓝宝石，非常漂亮，又大又珍贵。他把它拿

第七单元　研发合作 R&D Cooperation

给所有朋友欣赏，非常自豪。但突然，这块宝石裂开了一条缝，从正中间裂开。于是这个贵族把弄裂宝石的人绞死。但又能怎么办呢？宝石已经裂了一条大缝，看起来很丑。所以他去找了全国所有的珠宝匠。最后，一个珠宝匠告诉他："我可以修好，但如果出了问题的话，您可不能绞死我。"珠宝匠拿来这块宝石，沿着裂缝镶了一朵玫瑰花作为花边，把它变成一块镶有玫瑰花的宝石。宝石比之前更漂亮了。这个故事的寓意就是：当您遇到问题时，要发现机遇在哪里，思考如何创新。而孵化器的关键所在就是必须要创新。现在我准备讲一下如何在孵化器方面进行创新。

01：50—03：00

First of all, most incubators here, everybody here has money and space for the clients who they are trying to attract, but you should know that nine out of ten of the companies that you are going to attract even though you fund them, you do everything for them, they are gonna run out of money, and they are gonna go bankrupt. Nine out of ten. Everybody knows this. The trick, however, is to add value. And if you offer an incubator or a start-up that you bring it to you, and you give them extra value, added value, then you can make the difference of them, succeeding or not. They can have the best technology there is, they can have the smartest people there is, but they very often need your value. Now China is growing, they say this is the 21st century. This is the century of China. But China is becoming very expensive. There is a consequence. China now has to bring in, and every region has to bring in new technologies, new start-ups, new incubators, so they can move on to the next generation of success.

首先，这儿大部分孵化器，在这儿的每一个人，都有资金和场地提供给你们想要吸引的客户，但你们应该知道百分之九十你们想要吸引的公司，就算你们提供资金、包办一切，他们还是会把钱耗光，还是会破产。百分之九十的公司都会这样。这一点大家都清楚。然而，窍门就是，提供附加值。如果您赋予孵化器或初创企业额外价值、附加值，意义会很重大，会影响他们的成败。他们可能拥有最好的技术，拥有最聪明的人才，但他们也非常需要您提供附加值。现在中国不断发展，有人说21世纪是属于中国的时代。但中国的成本变得越来越高，这就导致了中国每个地区都需要引进新技术、新的初创企业和新的孵化器，这样才能更上一层楼，获得成功。

03：01—03：38

So how do you keep an incubator from failing? One of the things, problems with incubators and with start-ups is the people who are in there are usually brilliant people with brilliant ideas and they know nothing about business and they think unfortunately that they are very smart because they are very smart, but how do they bring their technologies to the world? How do they deploy? How do they make their businesses work? That's something that they need help for, that's we need the added value.

所以您该如何避免孵化器失败？有一个问题，这些孵化器和初创企业面临的一个问题是，里面的人通常都是杰出的人才，有着绝妙的想法，但是他们对商业却一无所知，而且遗憾的是，他们认为自己非常聪明，因为他们的确非常聪明，但是他们如何向世界推广自己的技术？如何部署？如何经营公司？这一切他们都需要别人的帮助，也就是说，我们需要有附加值。

03：39—04：16

So one of the problems I've seen, I've done many many bankruptcies, is many of the new entrepreneurs believe their own lies and make up stories, and they tell you how is everything gonna be great, what's gonna happen next, but you got to help them. So the government offers different added value for them to join a new incubator, and let's talk about that. One of the things that they have to have in many of the young incubators is they need the advice of more seasoned business people, and you can help them do that and let the new technologies know that you're giving them extra value.

我发现有一个问题，我处理过很多很多破产案件，我发现的一个问题就是很多创业新手会对自己的谎言深信不疑，自己编故事。他们告诉您一切都会好的，告诉您接下来会怎样，但您要帮助他们。因此政府要提供不同的附加值吸引他们加入一个新的孵化器。我们来谈谈这一点。有一样东西是很多年轻的孵化器需要的，就是经验丰富的商界前辈的建议。这方面您可以帮助他们，让他们知道您在为他们的新技术提供附加值。

04：17—04：47

One of the first things is relationships. Many of these incubators with young engineers, young designers and they don't know anybody in the world. They know how to make a new machine and new device, new medical technology, but they don't know how to get to the international funds, how to get to the domestic funds, how to cooperate with other incubators. One of your tasks is, as a leader in incubators, is to give them the new relationships, so they are able to go to the next step.

你们能提供的帮助，其中一个就是人脉。很多孵化器都是由年轻工程师、年轻设计师组成，他们缺乏人脉关系。他们知道如何制造新机器、新设备、新医药技术，但他们不知道如何获得国际基金，如何获得国内资金，如何与其他孵化器合作。作为孵化器的负责人，你们的任务之一就是帮助他们发展人脉关系，以便他们可以进一步发展。

第七单元　研发合作 R&D Cooperation

04：48—05：17

Another thing is that China is a huge market with huge manufacturing capabilities. There are international distributors looking to come to China. I get them come to me every day, saying, "What can you bring me to New York? I want to sell something great made in China. I want to sell it in New York. What do you have?" Well, if you are an adviser to an incubator or a start-up, this is what you should be doing—you should be helping them make the different relationships.

另外，中国有一个巨大的市场和强大的制造能力。很多国际经销商想来中国，每天都有很多人来找我，问我："您有什么可以给我带回纽约的？我想卖一些中国制造的好货，拿到纽约去卖。您有什么推荐的？"如果您是孵化器或初创企业的顾问，这就是您应该做的，即帮助他们建立不同的人脉关系。

05：18—06：13

Another problem is that very often, the number one reason why incubators and start-ups would fail is they run out of money. OK? They don't know how to manage money. They've never had money before. And you as the people helping provide everything for them, you have to give them advice, so they don't foolishly spend their money. For example, I've seen the incubators, the start-ups, they spend their money on furniture. They overpay factories. They don't know how to negotiate with factories. I've seen incubators buy the website, pay fifty, seventy thousand dollars American for a website that they don't need now, maybe gonna need it two years. The smart advisers for incubators, give them this advice, they need help with distribution.

另外一个问题是，通常孵化器或初创企业失败的首要原因是资金链断裂。是的，他们不知道如何管理资金，他们之前没掌握过那么多资金。而你们是给他们提供一切的人，你们要给他们建议，防止他们乱花钱。例如我看到有些孵化器、初创企业，他们花钱置办家具，给工厂支付过高的费用。因为他们不知道如何与工厂谈判。我还看到有的孵化器购买网站，花了五万或七万美元买一个网站，而他们现在不需要这个网站，可能得过两年才用得上。聪明的孵化器顾问会给他们这方面的建议。他们需要你们的帮助，合理分配资金。

06：13—07：31

Next thing they need is legal help. Very, very often the start-ups have young inexperienced innovators, designers, engineers, and they don't know how to relate to other people. I've seen many cases where there are employees of start-ups, where they think that they are partners in start-up and he's an employee of the start-up, and there's no contract. They don't know what's the trade secret, who does the trade secret belong

113

to? Who's the boss? Sometimes you have an employee who is a worker in a start-up, and he thinks he is a partner in the start-up. All of these has to be clarified and you as the managers behind incubators, you have to give them advice and let them know that they're gonna have an advice that there can't be any ambiguities. There needs to be contracts. Everything should be set forward. One of the famous ideas in new businesses is: you have two brothers, you have two partners, and one of those say "he will never cheat me; he is my brother". And they both have a misunderstanding of what the relationship is supposed to be, the next thing you know they have a lawsuit. Everything falls apart, because this guy thinks that that guy is his brother. He's never gonna cheat him and now he thinks his "brother" is cheating him, he can't have that.

此外，他们还需要法律援助。绝大多数情况下，初创企业都是些年轻的经验不足的创新人员、设计师和工程师，他们不知道如何处理人际关系。我看到很多案例，就是初创企业的员工认为自己也是公司的合伙人，其实他们只是公司的员工，但没有签合同。他们不知道商业秘密是什么、这个商业秘密归谁所有、谁是老板。有时您雇了一名员工，他只是公司的员工，但他认为自己是公司的合伙人。所有这些都必须讲清楚。作为孵化器背后的管理者，您要给他们建议，让他们明白不允许任何模棱两可的情况出现，必须要有合约，所有事情都要提前说清楚。在很多初创企业中，很常见的情况就是，有两兄弟，是合伙人，其中一个说："他永远不会欺骗我的，他是我的好兄弟。"他们都误解了彼此之间应该是什么样的关系，接着您就发现他们打起了官司，一拍两散。因为这个人认为另外一个是他的兄弟，永远不会欺骗他，而现在他的"兄弟"却欺骗了他，他接受不了。

07: 32—08: 15

Next thing is fiscal management. The innovators very often don't know how to take care of their money. They don't know where to spend it. They need advice. They're gonna go to CES and they are gonna get themselves a beautiful booth in Las Vegas, and they can't afford it. But if you have people who can help them with financial management, they'll share the CES booth with somebody else. Later on, when they become Google, like they have their own giant booth, but at the early stages, they need help how not to spend the money, how not to overpay the factories, not to spend money on things that can be shared at an earlier level.

另外一个是财务管理。初创企业经常不知道如何妥善管理资金，不知道钱该花在哪里。他们需要这方面的建议。他们要去参加消费电子产品展览会，想在拉斯维加斯给自己弄一个非常漂亮的展位，却负担不起。但如果你们有人帮他们做财务管理的话，他们就知道可以和别人共用一个展位。以后，当他们变得像谷歌那么成功了，就可以有自己宽敞的展位了。但在前期，他们需要帮助，才能知道如何避免乱花钱，避免去工厂花冤枉钱，避免把钱花在一些前期能与别人共享的东西上。

08：15—08：55

Next they don't know how to do distribution, very often an incubator or a start-up or have a new product that's fantastic, and he thinks that everybody loves it and he doesn't know how to sell it. A very famous story is with Sony and with VHS when they came up with tapes. VHS, everybody said was inferior to Sony's Beta. Beta knew how to sell it, and VHS didn't know. And over the next few years, VHS dominated the market and Beta died. So if you're gonna help your start-ups, you have to help them with the distribution.

还有，他们不知道如何做分销。通常一个孵化器或初创企业有一款非常棒的新产品，他觉得人人都会喜欢，但他不知道如何卖这款产品。有一个非常有名的故事，有关索尼和 VHS 录像机，他们都研发了录像带。大家都说 VHS 录像机不如索尼的 Beta 录像机。但是 VHS 懂销售，而 Beta 不懂（译者注：原文为发言人口误，说反了）。过了几年，VHS 占据了市场，而 Beta 则消亡了。所以如果您要帮助初创企业，您得帮他们做好分销。

09：00—09：25

Next they need accounting help. Very often the incubators don't know what to do with taxes, don't know what to do with funding, don't know how to allocate their funds, don't know how to pay customs. And they think they know because they went to the best schools, they're great engineers, they think they know all the sort automatically. And it's not the way it is. They need the help.

然后他们还需要会计援助。通常，孵化器都不知道如何处理税收问题，不知道如何使用资金，不知道如何分配资金，也不知道如何付关税。他们以为自己知道，因为他们上的是最好的学校，是优秀的工程师，他们认为自己无所不知。其实并非如此，他们需要帮助。

09：26—10：03

And when back into management assistance, many people don't know that even though Bill Gates was a founder of Microsoft and Steve Jobs was a founder of Apple, they were not the CEOs of their companies when they started. They had to hire CEOs. They were innovators, they were founders, they were engineers, they were designers, they were brilliant, but they weren't CEOs. So what you have to do is actually help these start-ups to have the proper management. So if they're gonna go to the market, if they're gonna deploy, if they're gonna raise money, that they get the help that they are going to need.

说到管理协助,很多人都不知道,虽然比尔·盖茨创立了微软公司,史蒂夫·乔布斯创立了苹果公司,但他们创业时都不是自己公司的 CEO。他们得聘用 CEO。他们是创新人员,是创始人,是工程师,是设计师,是天才,但他们不是 CEO。因此,您要做的其实就是帮助这些初创企业进行合理管理,以便当他们要进军市场、进行部署、筹集资金时,他们能得到必要的帮助。

10∶04—11∶23

And finally one of the problems, of course, especially in China, is when you have come up with a new idea, there are people who are gonna steal it. Competition is unbelievable. I have represented companies. I have developed new products in Kickstarter and Indiegogo, and two weeks later, somebody else is making the same product. Even I've seen them steal the video from the Indiegogo or Kickstarter promotion and use it for competing product to sell against the actual designer and developer. You have to help them, give them the advice, so that the young designers and young engineers don't get fooled, because there are sharks who are looking to compete and steal the innovation of the new designers once they start raising money, get out in the public. But if you have proper advice for your innovators and let them know you are going to give them this advice, you will be able to attract, you will be able to explain to them and help them make a success. At the end, a lot of conflict is gonna be avoided. Everybody will make money. And instead of one out of ten incubators and start-ups surviving, more will survive because you give the added value. Thank you very much!

当然,最后还有一个问题,尤其是在中国,当您有一个新想法,就会有人来窃取。这种竞争真是不可思议。我做过一些公司的代理人。我在 Kickstarter 和 Indiegogo 这两个众筹平台开发了新产品,两周之后,就有人在做同样的产品。甚至我看到他们从 Indiegogo 和 Kickstarter 上窃取了宣传视频,用在自己的产品上,跟真正的设计者和开发者进行竞争。您得帮助他们,给他们建议,让刚入行的设计师和工程师避免上当。因为有一些骗子正虎视眈眈要打垮或窃取这些年轻设计师的创意,趁他们筹集资金推广产品的时候出手。但如果您能给孵化器提供合适的建议,并且让他们知道您能帮他们,您就能吸引他们。您就可以向他们解释清楚,帮助他们取得成功。最终,很多冲突也就可以避免,每个人都能赚到钱。而且,也不再只有十分之一的孵化器和初创企业能存活,更多的企业也能生存下去,因为您提供了附加值。非常感谢大家!

第八单元　商事仲裁
Commercial Arbitration

I. 实战练习一

1. 演讲背景

德和信律师事务所的律师应邀出席"国际仲裁峰会"并就"如何选择仲裁机构与仲裁员"发表主旨演讲。他在演讲中提到，机构仲裁优于临时仲裁，因为机构仲裁可以确保仲裁效率，避免拖延；裁决得以执行的概率更大。选择仲裁机构时需要考虑该机构的地区和国际竞争力、仲裁语言、声誉、仲裁规则。仲裁条款需要遵循 KISS 原则。选择仲裁员时需要考虑其所说的语言、专业背景、中立性等因素。

2. 预习词汇

arbitral proceeding 仲裁程序
award 仲裁裁决
arbitral institution 仲裁机构
CIETAC/China International Economic and Trade Arbitration Commission 中国国际经济贸易仲裁委员会
arbitration commission 仲裁委员会
ad hoc arbitration 临时仲裁
institutional arbitration 机构仲裁
procedural certainty 程序确定性
statute of limitation 仲裁时效
delaying tactic 拖延战术
confidentiality clause 保密条款
arbitration law 仲裁法
HKIAC/Hong Kong International Arbitration Center 香港国际仲裁中心
ICC/International Chamber of Commerce 国际商会（仲裁院）
contractual relationship 合同关系
competence 竞争力
arbitration rule 仲裁规则

panel of arbitrators 仲裁员名册
default number 默认数量
default rule 默认规则
scrutiny 仔细检查
legal review 法律审核
formal requirement 形式要求
value-based fee calculation 依据争议金额收取费用
LCIA/London Court of International Arbitration 伦敦国际仲裁院
hourly-based fee 按每小时计费
arbitration agreement 仲裁协议
jurisdictional dispute 管辖权纠纷
model clause 示范条款
discretion 自由裁量权
exhibit 物证
applicable law 准据法
tribunal 仲裁庭
engineering degree 工程学位
MBA/Master of Business Administration 工商管理硕士
neutrality 中立
impartiality 公正
biased 偏颇的，偏袒的
CV/curriculum vitae 简历，履历

3. 演讲文本

00：00—00：47

Thank you very much Gavin. Thank you. Now this afternoon, we're going to take you, "we", that means the speakers that will follow me and myself. We are going to take you through some of the most important steps of an arbitral proceeding and well, we will end with the enforcement of an award that was hopefully rendered in your favor. I will start at the very beginning and that is choosing your arbitral institution. Now we've already heard a lot of benefits about CIETAC in Hong Kong. But as Gavin pointed out to be fair to the other institutions, I am also gonna mention them, of course, in this place.

非常感谢您，Gavin，谢谢！现在是下午，我们接下来会带您走进今天的主题。"我们"指的是我本人以及接下来的发言人。我们会带您了解一些重要的步骤，是有关仲裁程序的，我们最后会谈及执行仲裁裁决，希望这会对你们有用。我会从最开始讲起，也就是如何选择仲裁机构。现在我们已经听说了很多成效，是中国国际

经济贸易仲裁委员会香港分会取得的成效。但是,就像 Gavin 提出来的,要对其他机构也公平点,所以这里我也会提及。

00:48—02:42

Now, before I get to the individual institutions, the question is, of course, "Why do I actually need an arbitral institution?" That question is easily answered in China, because you need an arbitration commission in order to commence a valid arbitration. However, even if your arbitration does not take place in China, we strongly recommend that you use institutional arbitration simply for the reason that the alternative that is ad hoc arbitration cannot provide you with the benefits that institutional arbitration can. And the benefits, I have put them on here, are definitely the efficiency of the proceedings. You get administration from arbitration professionals. You get tailor-made rules that are made to your very needs in an international arbitration. And you get procedural certainty. Especially, the last point can be very important and that it goes together, of course, with the administration. For instance, and Dr. Wang mentioned that before, you know when a submission is being submitted, when the arbitration is commenced, that is of course very important for statute of limitation. You get all the other services of the institutions in that they acknowledge receipt. They advise on the next step, so you basically avoid delaying tactics which may occur in arbitration that is not administered. Of course, you also have confidentiality clauses in most of the international arbitration rules, which is something you do not have in many arbitration laws in the countries where you may go. So a confidentiality can be very important aspect also in favor of institutional arbitration.

在讲具体的仲裁机构前,存在一个问题,"为什么需要仲裁机构?"这个问题在中国很容易回答,因为你们需要仲裁委员会启动有效的仲裁。然而,即使仲裁地不在中国,我们还是强烈建议你们使用机构仲裁,只因为另一种方式,也就是临时仲裁,无法给您提供只有机构仲裁才能带来的效益。所谓效益,我已经列举出来了,毫无疑问指的是程序的效率。仲裁专家可以帮您管理案件,您可以得到量身定制的规则,能满足您在国际仲裁中的需求。同时您可以获得程序确定性。特别是最后一点,非常重要,当然也要和管理相配合才行。例如,王博士之前也提到过,你们知道,当提交申请书、仲裁启动时,这对于仲裁时效来说非常重要。您会获得其他所有服务,因为他们承认受理您的案件。他们会为下一步出主意,所以您基本上可以避免拖延战术,拖延会出现在管理不善的仲裁中。当然,保密条款也是大多数国际仲裁规则要求的,这在很多仲裁法中是没有的,在您开展仲裁的国家中也可能没有。因此,保密非常重要,这也是选择机构仲裁的原因。

02:43—03:16

At the very end, I mean, the rules you will get and Dr. Wang has elaborated on that already, they are all very very detailed. They provide you with the arbitration process from the commencement to the very end. And I mentioned before, at the very end, of course, there is the enforcement. There is nothing on the enforcement as such in the institution rules. But if you have an award in hand that has a CIETAC or HKIAC or ICC stamp on it, you may have a much better chance in getting your award enforced in the end.

最后，我想说您获得的规则，王博士已经讲得很详细了，内容已经非常非常详细了。它们可以让您了解仲裁程序，从仲裁开始到结束。我之前提到过，在最后，会有执行环节。说到执行，机构规则对此没有规定。但是，如果您拿到了仲裁裁决，并且上面盖有中国国际经济贸易仲裁委员会、香港国际仲裁中心或者国际商会仲裁院的印章，您有更大的概率让仲裁裁决最终得以执行。

03:17—04:01

Now, this has been said why you actually need an institution. I'm just gonna have a very brief comment on which institution to choose. I don't think there is a clear answer to that. We have very compelling arguments in which situation to choose CIETAC Hong Kong or CIETAC overall. But of course, there is also some general criteria for HKIAC and the ICC in Hong Kong. What are the criteria that you should consider when choosing your arbitral institution? That's a difficult question to answer, because when you choose your arbitral institution, you most likely will not think about the dispute because that is at the early stages of your contractual relationship.

现在，我已经说过为什么您确实需要仲裁机构。我会非常简要地介绍一下应该选择哪一个仲裁机构。我认为没有明确的答案。我们有非常充分的理由，告诉大家什么情况下选择中国国际经济贸易仲裁委员会香港分会或中国国际经济贸易仲裁委员会。当然，也有一些一般性标准来选择香港国际仲裁中心以及香港国际商会。您需要考虑哪些标准来选择仲裁机构呢？这是个非常难回答的问题，因为当您选择仲裁机构的时候，您很可能不会考虑太多争议的问题，因为这只是在早期阶段，这时您的合同关系才刚刚建立不久。

04:01—05:04

But still, general considerations you may want to do are regional and international competence of the institution you choose. Services in the relevant languages you will need. That is of course not only language of the arbitration but also maybe the language of the parties that are all involved. All the contracts. The language of the contract is very often not the same as that of the arbitration. Finally, reputation. That's a key factor. It also, again, comes back to the enforcement issue. You want your award enforced in the end. And for that purpose, you want an award from a recognized, well-reputed, well-known arbitral institution. And in that respect, of course, all the three that I listed here, CIETAC, HKIAC and ICC, provide this first-class service that will assist you in this matter.

但是,一般而言,您想到的或许是您所选机构的地区和国际竞争力。相关语言服务您会用到。这当然不仅是仲裁语言,也包括所有当事人的语言。还有所有的合同,合同的语言通常与仲裁语言不同。最后是声誉。这是非常关键的一个因素。我会再次回到执行问题上。您希望您的仲裁裁决最终能够执行。为了实现这一目的,您希望您的仲裁裁决是由一个认可度高、声誉好、知名的仲裁机构给出的。在这一点上,我这里列举了三个,也就是中国国际经济贸易仲裁委员会、香港国际仲裁中心和国际商会仲裁院,它们能够提供一流的服务,会帮助您解决纠纷。

05:05—06:28

Now I put together a couple of the key features of the arbitration rules of the three institutions. I don't think we have the time to go through all of them. I just wanted to highlight a few. You will of course get this presentation after the seminar if you are interested and can have a closer look. It just compares how the institutions handle the various steps of the arbitration. For instance, the panel of arbitrators. The ICC, for instance, does not have a panel of arbitrators. That is something a lot of people don't know. Then the default number of arbitrators varies between the institutions. Of course, I should say all of these rules you see here are the default rules. They are subject to parties' agreement. But that again shows you the benefit of having an institution, institutional arbitration. If you forget to agree on one of these issues in your arbitration clause and you do not have institutional arbitration, you have a problem. However, if you have an institutional arbitration, you have your default rules here, which tell you, for instance, that you get three arbitrators in a CIETAC arbitration or one in an ICC arbitration. Well, I should have probably put that up first. It's the same in Chinese.

现在我总结一些重要的特征,是有关这三个仲裁机构的仲裁规则。我觉得我们没有时间过一下所有的内容。我只想重点讲部分内容。你们可以在研讨会结束后拿到这个PPT,如果您很感兴趣的话,您可以仔细看看。PPT上对比了仲裁机构是如何处理仲裁中的不同步骤。例如仲裁员名册。就拿国际商会仲裁院来说,它没有仲裁员名册。这也是很多人不知道的。然后仲裁员的默认数量是因仲裁机构而异。当然,我想说明一下,所有您看到的这些规则都是默认规则,当事人可以自行约定。但是这也再次表明找一个仲裁机构和选择机构仲裁的好处。如果您忘记在仲裁条款中就其中某个问题达成协议,而且您没有选择机构仲裁,这就麻烦了。但是,您选择了机构仲裁,您就相当于有了默认规则,这会告诉您,比如中国国际经济贸易仲裁委员会规定选择三位仲裁员,而国际商会仲裁院只选择一位仲裁员。我本来一开始就该把这一页PPT放给大家看,中文版本的内容是一样的。

06:28—07:55

Now that is some further features of the rules which I don't want to go through. As I said, Dr. Wang already mentioned the fees. There is of course always an issue in arbitration. One thing I wanted to point out though is the scrutiny. That is a factor which some institutions provide for. And it's a factor which many clients very much appreciate. The scrutiny, of course, should not be confinal with a legal review of the award. It's not, the institutions do not check whether the award is correct. They only check whether the formal requirements are fulfilled and you get an award that, on the face of it, is an enforceable award. And that of course is a very valuable service which, as you can see on the right-hand column, the ICC also collects quite high fees for. Now, on fees, maybe one comment that there is [are] two ways of calculating the fees. All the three institutions I mentioned here do the value-based calculation. There are some institutions, like the London Court of International Arbitration that have hourly-based fees, so based on the time you actually spend on an arbitration instead of the value.

现在这些是规则的其他特征,我不想讲。就像我之前说的,王博士已经提到了费用。这一直是仲裁中的一个问题。我想提出的第一点就是仔细检查。这是一些仲裁机构提供的服务,也受到许多客户的赏识。仔细检查当然也不应该和仲裁裁决的法律审核有交叉。否则仲裁机构不会检查仲裁裁决的对错与否。它们只会检查形式要求是否得以履行,您获得的仲裁裁决从表面上看是否是一个可执行的裁决。这当然是一项非常有价值的服务,您可以看看右边一栏的内容,国际商会仲裁院也会就这项服务收取相当高的费用。就费用而言,我想说,有两种计费方法。这三个我提到的仲裁机构会依据争议金额收取费用。也有一些仲裁机构,比如伦敦国际仲裁院按时收费,也就是说按照您在仲裁上真正花的时间计费,而不是按照争议金额计费。

07:56—09:20

Now, I don't think it would be fair to draw a conclusion saying it's, one institution is always the right institution or another one is the right institution. As I said, it very much depends on the specific situation you are in, on the specific situation of the contract, of the parties, where the seat of the arbitration may be. So that I think it's, I hope you forgive me if I say that it's not always correct to say you have to choose one same institution all the time. But what I did want to say though is: please don't forget how you actually get to the institution. And that is of course through a valid arbitration agreement and I cannot overstate the importance of agreeing on a valid arbitration agreement. Any mistake you make at the stage of the agreement on arbitration will be very costly both in terms of money and time. Because you will end up in endless jurisdictional disputes over whether you're actually in the right forum now or not and you will literally lose years and a lot of money until we actually get to the substance of the case. So it cannot be overstated how much attention should be paid to ensuring that you have a valid arbitration clause in your agreement. And it's actually fairly simple to do that.

我认为下这样一个结论是不公平的：某个仲裁机构总是最合适的，或者另一个仲裁机构是最合适的。我说过，这很大程度上取决于您的具体情况、合同和当事人的具体情况以及仲裁地是哪里。所以，希望您不要介意我这样说：总是选择同一个仲裁机构不一定就是对的。但是我真正想说的是，请不要忘记您找仲裁机构的初衷。这当然是通过一项有效的仲裁协议，我不能夸大有效的仲裁协议达成一致的重要性。您犯的任何错误只要出现在仲裁协议阶段，都会造成巨大的损失，不管是金钱还是时间。因为您会陷入无休止的管辖权纠纷之中，无休止地讨论您是否选择了合适的仲裁院，您会耗费多年的时间以及一大笔钱，才会真正触及到案件的实体问题。因此，再怎么强调都不过分，您应该投入精力确保您在协议中确立了有效的仲裁条款。这其实非常简单。

09：21—10：25

I, actually, this next slide should be read from the bottom up. The most important thing is keep it simple. We call it the KISS principle, keep it short and simple. That is the easiest way of ensuring that you get a good arbitration clause. Don't be creative. Don't try to invent anything. It will most likely end up in uncertainties which will cause trouble. Now while you are coming back to the question "which arbitration institution to choose?" While you're at that, you might as well already be online and check which institution may be good for you. While you're doing that, stay on the website, copy the model clause and put it into your agreement. That is the easiest way to do it. Most arbitration institutions provide for that. They have a model clause on their website. You should simply copy it in and then you are sure to have correctly identified the institution and you are sure to have included the necessary requirements and also those that should be required in order to make your life in the arbitration a lot easier.

其实，这张幻灯片应该从下往上看。重点是保持简洁，我们把它称为 KISS 原则，也就是保持简短、简洁。这是最简单的方式来确保您得到好的仲裁条款。不要创作，不要尝试发明任何条款。因为很有可能会导致诸多的不确定性，这会很麻烦。现在，当您回到这个问题"应该选择哪个仲裁机构？"当您面临这个问题，您不妨上网，核实哪个仲裁机构对您有好处。当您网上搜索时，停留在所在的网站，复制示范条款，将它加入您的协议中。这是最简单的方式。大多数仲裁机构都提供了示范条款。它们会将示范条款放在网站上，您只需将它复制下来，接下来您务必要找到合适的仲裁机构，您务必要将必要的要求以及那些必须的条款写进协议，这样可以让您的仲裁过程更简单。

10：26—11：26

Now, let me get to the second topic and that is choosing arbitrators. You all know that the institution rules we have discussed provide for the opportunity of the parties to appoint their own arbitrator. That of course leads to the question: "Who do you really want to appoint?" "What are the criteria you want to look for?" and "How do you actually find the suitable arbitrator in the end?" And Dr. Wang has already pointed that out. It is of utmost importance how you choose your arbitrator. Of course, arbitration can only be as good as the arbitrators that do. So and you should never forget that the three or one, or the one person of the three people that sit up there, they have a very wide discretion and great powers in deciding on your dispute. So, it is a step to be very carefully considered when you choose your arbitrator.

现在，我要进入第二个话题了，也就是仲裁员的选择。你们都知道，我们讨论过的仲裁机构规则为当事人提供了机会，来选择他们自己的仲裁员。这当然也会引起这样的问题："您真正想选择谁为仲裁员？""您选择的标准是什么？""最终您怎么找到最合适的仲裁员？"王博士已经指出了这个问题。最为重要的就是怎么选择自己的仲裁员。当然，仲裁的胜负取决于仲裁员的能力。所以，不要忘了三个仲裁员，或一个，或者他们当中的一个，也就是坐在那里的人，他们具有很大的自由裁量权，有很大的权力对您的争议进行裁决。所以，这一步需要仔细考虑，然后再选择您的仲裁员。

11：27—11：54

Now what are the personal qualifications you want to look for? Of course, the first thing is: the arbitrator should speak the language that proceedings are conducted in. That is a bit of a formal point but of course key. You may also look at arbitrators that don't only speak the language of the arbitration but maybe also understand what the parties actually are saying and a bit, maybe and sometimes exhibits and contracts are in different languages, so that is something to consider.

那么您会选择具有哪些个人资历的仲裁员呢？当然，首先就是仲裁员所说的语言应该是仲裁程序使用的语言。这是非常正式、也是非常重要的一点。您也许也会选择这样的仲裁员，他们不会讲仲裁中使用的语言，但可以理解当事人在讲什么，也许有时他们可以理解使用不同语言的物证和合同，这也是需要考虑的。

11: 54—13: 18

The professional background of course is crucial. You will want a legally qualified arbitrator that has experience in arbitration. You don't necessarily need someone that is qualified in the legal system of the applicable law. Familiarization with that legal system should, well, that certainly doesn't harm. It doesn't have to be qualified there. But what you will want is a lawyer, a qualified lawyer. There are sometimes cases where this is discussed, very technical cases in particular. Shouldn't we have an engineer on the panel instead of a lawyer? And that, it may sound intriguing. So you can actually, so you know that this person will understand the details of the case. However, in the end, the dispute is, in most cases, decided on legal questions. And you do not want to be the party that appointed one arbitrator that can rarely discuss in the end when it comes down to making the decision. So, non-legal professionals on the tribunal as your arbitrator are not very advisable. What is of course very advisable is if you have someone who is a lawyer and has additional qualifications, such as an engineering degree or an MBA, and can put that knowledge into the tribunal.

专业背景当然很重要。您想找具有专业法律资格的仲裁员，他们有仲裁经验。您不一定需要找准据法司法体系中具有专业资格的仲裁员。熟悉这个法律体系当然更好。但不一定非得在特定司法体系中具有专业资格。但是，您想要的是一位律师，有专业资格的律师。有时有些案件，就像现在讨论到的，非常有技术性。难道我们不应该找个工程师来代替律师作为我们的仲裁员吗？这听起来可能非常有趣。所以，您知道这个人会了解案件的全部细节。但是，最后争议在于，大多数案子是根据法律问题来定夺的。您不会想成为这样的当事人：您选择的仲裁员最后却很少讨论，即使到了做出裁决的时候也不开口。所以，请非法律专业人士上仲裁庭作为您的仲裁员我们是不太推荐的。当然，非常推荐的人选是律师，他们有额外资历，比如工程学位或者工商管理硕士，他们可以将所学知识用到仲裁庭上。

13: 18—14: 18

Now, all of these qualifications, if you look for them, it's fine. But sometimes these qualifications are even put into the arbitration clause, saying that the arbitrator appointed in the dispute has to have qualification A, B and C. That may seem attractive, but it also reduces the pool of available arbitrators significantly. There is only so many arbitrators and if you reduce them by adding qualifications in the arbitration clause, which excludes so many arbitrators, you may end up with having real trouble finding an arbitrator that is available for your dispute. And that brings me to the other criteria. Of course, you need someone who is available. And you need to consider the workload. That is a big issue together with the issue of conflicts these days. And that again brings us back to the criteria. The more criteria you add in the arbitration clause, the smaller the amount of people and the more likely these people will have a conflict in this very area.

所有这些资历,如果都是您想要找的,那也是可以的。有时这些资历甚至会写进仲裁条款中,要求选定的仲裁员必须有资历A、B和C。这看上去非常有吸引力,但这会大幅度地减少仲裁员人选。只有这么多仲裁员,如果您设定门槛,将资历加进仲裁条款中,这会减少可选择的仲裁员,您可能最后会碰到麻烦,找不到仲裁员来为您解决争议。这让我想到了另一个标准。当然,您要找的人必须可以用。您需要考虑工作量,这是个大问题,和当今争议的问题一样是个大问题。这再次让我们回到了这个标准。您往仲裁条款里加的标准越多,可以考虑的仲裁员数量就越少,很可能这些人在这个领域会有利益冲突。

14:19—15:03

Now, neutrality, of course, an exclamation mark there, independence and impartiality. That is something that is absolutely inherent in arbitration. There is often a misunderstanding that the party-appointed arbitrator should somehow be a party advocate within the tribunal. That is of course not the case. Impartiality is key in that a biased arbitrator will actually harm your case. As soon as a tribunal realizes that a party-appointed arbitrator is somehow biased and only argues in favor of the party that appointed him or her, that arbitrator will automatically lose weight within the tribunal.

中立,当然,这里是个感叹号,意思是独立、公正。这绝对是仲裁固有的特征。通常会有误解,认为当事人选择的仲裁员应该在仲裁庭上为当事人辩护。当然不是这样。公正很关键,因为偏颇的仲裁员实际上会对您的案件不利。一旦仲裁庭发现当事人选定的仲裁员有失偏颇,只为选定他的当事人辩护,这个仲裁员会自动在仲裁庭上丧失影响力。

15:04—15:49

Now, I've also put some other considerations here on the slide, which we don't have time to discuss in detail. It's just one final remark. How do you eventually find your arbitrator when you've decided on the criteria? We have said it before there are panels of arbitrators at many institutions. The CVs are online. You can check them. You go and also check the publications and lectures and of course, the word of mouth that is key in international arbitration. It's a fairly small community and people know each other. So the best advice is to ask people who are familiar with the arbitration scene, and I'm pretty sure you will then find your good arbitrator. Thank you!

我也将其他一些考量因素放在了幻灯片上,这些我们都没有时间详细讨论。我想说最后一点,您最终是如何找到您的仲裁员的? 也就是在您确定标准之后。我们之前提到过,很多仲裁机构都会有仲裁员名册,他们的简历都挂到了网上,您可以查看。您也可以去查看出版物和讲座,当然,口碑在国际仲裁中是非常重要的。这是个非常小的圈子,人们彼此认识。所以最好的建议就是去问别人,问熟悉仲裁的人,我敢肯定您会找到好的仲裁员。谢谢!

II. 实战练习二

1. 演讲背景

德和信律师事务所的代表应邀参加由香港仲裁事务所主办的"国际仲裁峰会"并发表主旨演讲。她在演讲中比较了国内法院判决与国际仲裁裁决在其他国家得以承认与执行的要求,包括正当程序和互惠原则;而仲裁裁决需要区分国内仲裁裁决与国际仲裁裁决。国际仲裁裁决要得以承认与执行,必须满足以下要求:(1) 有效的仲裁协议;(2) 有可以通过仲裁解决的裁决事项;(3) 仲裁庭组成合理;(4) 正当程序;(5) 裁决不违背公共政策。

2. 预习词汇

arbitral reward 仲裁裁决
enforce/enforcement 执行
procedural law 程序法
due process 正当程序;法定诉讼程序
enforcement law 执行法
reciprocity 互惠
court ruling 法庭判决
New York Convention 《纽约公约》
arbitrable dispute 可以通过仲裁解决的裁决事项
insolvency dispute 破产纠纷
proceeding 审理程序

3. 演讲文本

00:00—01:03
Thank you very much for this praise, I will, I hope I can live up to that. Ladies and

gentlemen, now you have chosen the best institution you can find, you have put into your contract a very good arbitration clause. You have respected all the eight winning ways, and you've won your arbitration, but your opponent doesn't pay, so what do you do then? You have spent all this time, all this money on winning this arbitration, and now you are stuck with the award and you need to look can you enforce it and how can you enforce it? So as a matter of fact, when I am asked by a client to advise on arbitration, I always ask first the question which comes last, can we enforce the award? Because otherwise it doesn't really make sense to start the arbitration, and you should rather look for other ways to solve your dispute.

感谢您的赞誉,我将努力也希望自己能配得上这种称赞。女士们,先生们,你们已经尽力选择了最好的仲裁机构,并在合同里添加了严密的仲裁条款。各位都使用了八大制胜法宝,也赢得了仲裁,但对方当事人不肯支付费用,那您应该怎么办呢?您已花费了大量时间和金钱才赢得了这起仲裁,而现在又卡在了裁决上,您需要看看自己能不能执行这份裁决,如何执行?事实上,当客户请我给仲裁提建议时,我总是先考虑最后一个环节:我们能执行裁决吗?原因是,如若不能,就没有必要寻求仲裁,您更应该寻找其他解决纠纷的方式。

01:03—02:52

Now while this is the bad news, the good news is that what advantage and this is truly a big advantage of international arbitration is that, in very many countries, international arbitration awards are recognized and can be enforced. As a matter of fact, I would venture to say that, international arbitral awards are easier enforceable than are court decisions. Before I start to go into the details regarding the enforcement of arbitral rewards, let me just briefly remind you, and I am sure you know about that, how state court judgments are enforced in another country. The recognition and enforcement of state court decisions is always subject to the procedural law of the enforcement state. And I think we can say that in general, in all the states, the requirements are more or less similar, but they may vary to a certain extent and these differences may be very important. The general requirements are due process, usually the states also have a provision in their enforcement law that there should be no violation of fundamental principles of justice and morality.

虽然这是不好的一面,但好的一面是,国际仲裁有一个很大的优势,在很多国家,国际仲裁裁决普遍得到承认和执行。事实上,我敢说,国际仲裁裁决比法院判决更容易执行。在详细阐述执行仲裁裁决之前,我想先简要地提醒各位,我相信大家也都知道,国家法院的判决是如何在其他国家执行的。承认与执行国家法院的判决必须遵照执行国的程序法。我认为可以这样总结,大体上,所有国家的要求是相似的，但也存在一定的差异，这些差异值得注意。总体要求是正当程序，通常国家的执行法规定了不应违背正义和道德的基本原则。

02：52—04：33

And there should be reciprocity. What does reciprocity mean? Reciprocity means that if one state is willing to enforce the judgment from another state, this state will look at whether the state where the judgment comes from, would also enforce their own state court judgments. And this reciprocity requirement is often very problematic. I've been looking into that from the German point of view, in order to be able to answer maybe your questions which I anticipate on what is the situation between Germany and China. The good news is that there are two court rulings, which have expressly recognized Chinese court judgments. Although the situation in China seems to be a little bit unclear, the German courts have held that, if nobody starts reciprocity, so if we don't start accepting and enforcing Chinese judgments, then there will never be reciprocity, because we cannot expect the other country to start first. So basically, in Germany, Chinese state court decisions have a very good chance of being accepted and enforced. This was just the basic principle.

还有互惠原则。这是什么意思呢？互惠原则指如果一国愿意执行来自另一国家的判决，那么执行判决的国家要看做出判决的国家是否也承认并执行本国的判决。这种互惠要求通常很有问题。我一直都从德国学派的角度研究，也许能够回答各位的问题，我预测可能会提到中德之间的情况。好消息是有两个法院判决明确承认了中国的法庭判决。虽然中国的情况似乎还不明朗，但德国法院认为，如果没有一个法院开始实行互惠原则，如果我们不承认并执行中国的判决，那么就永远不会有互惠，因为我们不能等对方先实行互惠原则。所以，总体来说，在德国，中国法院的判决得到承认和执行的机率很高。这可以说是条基本原则。

04：33—07：05

Now turning to arbitral awards, we have to differentiate between domestic arbitral awards and foreign awards. Domestic arbitral awards are in the terminology and the definition, awards, which are rendered in the same state that the enforcement is going to take place. Foreign arbitral awards are awards which are rendered in a different state than the enforcement state. For example, if you want to enforce an arbitral award in China and the award has been rendered in Hong Kong or in Europe somewhere, this is going to be a foreign award in the international terminology. The recognition and the enforcement of domestic awards usually is dependent on national arbitration law of the country where you want to enforce it. In many states, the national enforcement requirements are similar to the international requirements written down in the *New York Convention*. But they may differ, so we might have to look into that in detail. What is the most interesting to all of you, I would assume, is the enforcement of foreign awards. For example, in China, the enforcement of foreign awards is subject to the requirements of the *New York Convention*, which was already adopted in 1958, and which in the meantime has been signed by 149 countries, all European states are signatory states to the *New York Convention*, China is, including Hong Kong, for example, Russia, the United States, Singapore. So all of the main countries, the important countries you can think of, have signed the *New York Convention*. And this means that in those states, even the awards which have been rendered in countries which have not signed the *New York Convention* will also be enforceable, if they fulfill the following requirements.

现在谈谈仲裁裁决，我们区分开国内仲裁裁决和外国仲裁裁决。国内仲裁裁决的定义是，该裁决作出和执行都在同一个国家进行。外国仲裁裁决指裁决作出和执行在不同国家进行。比如，如果您想在中国大陆执行一项仲裁裁决，而裁决是在香港或欧洲作出的，那么从术语的角度来分析这就是一个域外仲裁裁决。承认和执行国内仲裁裁决通常取决于本国仲裁法，以执行国家法律为准。很多国家的执行要求和国际要求相似，和《纽约公约》中的要求相似。但各国的要求也有不同，因此我们应该研究细节。大家最感兴趣的一点，我觉得会是外国仲裁裁决的执行。比如，在中国，执行外国仲裁裁决就要遵循《纽约公约》，公约是1958年签署的，现在共有149个签署国。所有欧洲国家、中国（包括香港）、俄罗斯、美国、新加坡等，所有您能想到的主要国家，都签署了《纽约公约》。这意味着在这些国家，即便作出裁决的国家是未签署条约的国家，同样需要执行，前提是它们符合以下要求。

07:05—08:34

I have put together the requirements without referring to the articles, because I don't think that matters here. I have just set out the main requirements for enforcement of international arbitral awards, and you will see here that, it's basically concerning formal requirements, such as there has to be a valid arbitration agreement, and I can tell you that state courts in all the countries are very strict on that. They really look into the details whether the arbitration agreement the parties rely on is valid. It should be an arbitrable dispute. What does that mean? In some countries, certain disputes are not arbitrable, like for example, family disputes, governed by family law, sometimes insolvency disputes are not arbitrable, sometimes even shareholder disputes may not be arbitrable in that particular country. So one has to really look into the question is the dispute which we are dealing with, a dispute which can be dealt with in arbitration or is that reserved for the state courts of the country we are talking about.

第八单元 商事仲裁 Commercial Arbitration

我已经将这些要求整理在一起，但不涉及具体的法条，因为我认为这不是主要部分。我列出了主要的要求，是关于国际仲裁裁决的执行，大家可以在这里看到，基本是关于格式要求，比如必须有有效的仲裁协议，可以说所有国家的法院对此都有严格要求。法院会详细研究双方签订的仲裁协议是否有效。应该有可以通过仲裁解决的裁决事项。这是什么意思呢？在某些国家，特定的纠纷是不能通过仲裁解决的，比如家庭纠纷受家事法管辖，有时破产纠纷也不可仲裁，甚至一些股东纠纷也不能仲裁，在有些国家就是如此。所以要认真研究我们正在处理的纠纷，看它能否通过仲裁解决，还是要提交到这些国家的法院来审判。

08：34—09：02

Very important is the proper constitution, composition of the arbitral tribunal. If there has been an arbitrator on the panel who was not impartial and this has been raised during the arbitration, then the arbitral tribunal has not been constituted properly, then the arbitral award risks of not being enforced.

非常重要的一点是合适的组成，即仲裁庭的人员组成。如果有仲裁员并非中立，并在仲裁期间有一方提出该问题，那么仲裁庭的组成就不合适，仲裁裁决也面临无法执行的风险。

09：02—09：45

Of course, very important is the obedience to due process. Due process, you probably all know means, first of all, the rights of both parties to be heard, so if there is one party, he did not participate in the proceedings, it is extremely likely that this award will not be enforceable. But even more so, if there has been evidence which is offered by the arbitral tribunal for some reason decide not to hear it, then it will be very difficult to enforce this award.

当然，程序正当也很重要。正当程序，大家应该都知道，首先意味双方具有申辩的权利，如果有一方没有参加审理，这份裁决极有可能无法执行。但如果有证据呈上仲裁庭，而出于某些原因没有被采信，也很难执行裁决。

09：45—11：10

The award should not be contrary to public policy. Public policy meaning again should not be against the fundamental principles of the law of the country where the award needs to be enforced. And of course the award needs to be binding. I am not talking here about the challenge of an award. The challenge of an award needs to be very closely differentiated from the enforcement of the award. Because the challenge of the award needs to be done under the laws and in the country where the award has been issued. Like for example, if you have an award which was rendered in Hong Kong, and which so be enforced in China, the example which Doctor Wang made prior to when she was giving her introductory speech, then the challenge of the award would be under the laws of Hong Kong, while the enforcement of the award would be under the rules of the arbitration law in China, governing in China. So be sure to make this differentiation, because there may be differences.

裁决不应违背公共政策。公共政策不应违背国家法律的根本原则，即执行裁决的国家的法律。裁决也应有约束力。我今天并不讲对裁决提出异议，对裁决提出异议应和执行裁决区分开来。因为异议需要根据法律提出，还需要在作出裁决的地区提出。例如，如果您的仲裁裁决是在香港作出，而在中国大陆执行，就是王博士之前在开场演讲中提到的例子，那么应当根据香港法律对裁决提出异议，而执行裁决应当根据中国大陆现行的仲裁法的规则。所以要分清这两种情况，二者也许有很大不同。

11：10—11：43

Now what we think might be most interesting for you is the question how can foreign awards be recognized and enforced in China. And of course not being a Chinese lawyer, I would not be able to tell you about that, but we have a Chinese lawyer in our law firm and I will now hand over to Iris Wang. Thank you very much!

现在大家最感兴趣的也许是外国裁决如何在中国得到承认和执行。当然我不是中国律师，所以我无法向大家讲述，但我们律所有一位中国律师。我现在就把麦克风交给 Iris Wang。谢谢大家！

第九单元 时尚潮流
Fashion Trend

I. 实战练习一

1. 演讲背景

2014年11月1日,在线时尚潮流预测公司Fashion Snoops的亚太区总监应邀参加"广交会设计潮流趋势研讨会",发布2015—2016秋冬女装时尚趋势。下文摘自其中一个主题的内容"叛逆少女",他在演讲中详细介绍了该主题产生的背景、色系、材料、印花图案、设计细节、重要单品。演讲的部分内容抽象难懂。

2. 预习词汇

delinquent 罪犯(尤指少年犯),有过失者,叛逆少女(少年)
American horror story 美国惊悚故事
Salem 塞伦(镇)
mood board 情绪板
oak panel library 橡木面板库
moody color 暗色系
electric purple 荧光紫
eggplant purple 深紫色;茄紫色
mauve 淡紫色
maroon 紫褐色;栗色
forest 森林绿
pine 松绿色
strong accent color 重点色;对比色;强调色
navy blue 海军蓝
moody 喜怒无常的
cobweb lace 蛛网蕾丝
metallic Swiss dot 金属质地的点子花薄纱
silk chiffon 真丝雪纺
sheer nylon netting 透明尼龙网

crushed velvet 拷花丝绒

lurex 金银纱

herringbone 人字形布料

cotton poplin 纯棉府绸

plaid 格子呢

blurred vision 模糊图案

clouds of smoke 烟云

pagan symbol 异教徒符号

crest（鸟的）羽饰；羽冠

contrast collar 对比色领

contrast cuff 对比色袖口

Peter Pan collar 彼得潘领；小圆领

cut-out/peekaboo 镂刻

high slit 高开叉

crest applique 羽毛缝饰

soft bow tie 软领结

peasant sleeve 扎袖

dark embroidery 深色刺绣

key item 重要单品

cardigan 羊毛衫

long layer/layering 长长的层次感

elongated layer 长款的层次感

cropped pants 半截裤

dropped shoulder 落肩

rounded shoulder 圆肩

rounded top 圆领上衣

prim and proper 整洁得体

bow front blouse 蝴蝶结在前的女衬衫

dirndl skirt 阿尔卑斯式紧身连衫裙

blazer 休闲西装

3. 演讲文本

00：00—02：24

The next theme that we have, the second theme that we have for young contemporary market, for young casual womenswear is something we've called Delinquent. This is probably my favorite theme for the season. The story or the idea behind this story is that we were very much, our design team were very much inspired by a TV show that we have in the US called American Horror Story, and we are about to get it in HK, which stars Kathy Bates who is a fantastic actress. Really what this theme is playing into is that we take a dark autumn night in Salem, if those of you who know American history, Salem is a town, a small town in the 18th century in America that went crazy because they accused each other of being witches and lots of people were put to death on nothing more than hearsay. So it's all forever since being known as a town for witchcraft. So it's looking into history, and it's really sort of taking that witchcraft element along with American Horror Story. But it's not only about witchcraft, we are mixing it in with schoolgirl. Now in the young women's market, there is always a schoolgirl theme. You know, in everybody's young casual collection there is always a schoolgirl theme. For the past 6 to 7 years, it's been preppy. You know, I think we've got that point where everyone pretty much has enough preppy pieces in their wardrobes to have a preppy look. So we've taken a different twist at shcoolgirls, and we mix that sort of little bit of a darker witchcraft element into the theme. You can really see that sort of in this particular mood board here where you can see the witchcraft element being brought in through the, particularly through the main picture here with the pendent necklace with sort of the odd-seeing eye. But it's mixed, it's still very much a schoolgirl theme, so you still have your oak panel library there as your inspiration as well.

我们的下一个主题，也是我们第二个围绕年轻时尚市场、年轻休闲女装的主题，这个主题我们称之为"叛逆少女"。这可能是本季我最喜欢的主题。这个故事还有背后的故事或想法。我们自身及我们的设计团队极大地受到一档电视节目的启发，它是美国一个叫做"美国惊悚故事"的节目，即将在香港拥有节目版权，由凯西·贝兹（Kathy Bates）主演，她是个很棒的女演员。主题内容是我们在塞伦度过一个黑暗的秋夜，那些了解美国历史的人就知道，塞伦是一个镇。18世纪，美国的这个小镇变得很疯狂，因为这里的人互相指控对方是女巫，许多人因谣言被处死。因此塞伦一直被称为"巫术之城"。所以主题考察的是历史，可以说真正将这种巫术元素与"美国惊悚故事"结合。但它不只是关于巫术，我们还正将巫术与少女主题混合。现在在年轻女性的市场上，总是有一个少女主题。在各自的年轻休闲服装系列中总是有一个少女主题。过去的六至七年，少女主题一直走的是学院风。我认为我们已经有这样的观点，每个人的衣柜里都有足够数量的学院风服装，可以走走学院风。所以少女主题有了新的突破，我们在主题中混合了一丝黑暗的巫术元素。您可以在这个情绪板上看出这种结合。从这里您可以看出巫术元素的引入，通过……尤其借助这幅主图，这幅图上有一串吊坠项链，项链上带有怪异的眼睛。虽然风格是混搭的，但仍是一个少女主题，所以仍然可以把橡木面板库作为灵感来源。

02:24—02:52

We are moving to the video. So it is important if you are working to this particular theme to keep those two elements present in your design and product development. Have that schoolgirl element as the base, and then pushing that sort of witchcraft element. I think that our video here really really brings out this feel, so please… here's our video.

接下来我们要播放视频。如果想要围绕这一特定主题,将这两个元素保留在设计和产品开发中就很重要。把少女元素作为基础,然后推出巫术元素。我认为我们的视频真的使得这种感觉呼之欲出,请观看视频。

02:52—03:09

So I hope you saw that there we use that sort of antebellum southern mansion to give you that school house feel, but also to add that sort of mystery and a little bit of creepiness that associated with witchcraft.

所以我希望你们看到,我们使用那种南方的战前宅邸,带给大家那种校园的感觉,也增加几分神秘感和与巫术相关的惊悚感。

03:09—04:12

So the colour palette here for Delinquent is really, as you would expect, one of the sort of darkest and moodiest colour palettes that we have for this season. One thing where we bring in that sort of mystery and the witchcraft element, we use a lot of different purple here, so you have your electric purple, your eggplant purple as well as mauve which is a purple but a lighter tone purple. Maroon comes into play here as well, really as an accent color. Then you have your navy and your green like forest and pine. Really the navy and the green are the ones that sort of speak more to the schoolgirl aspect whereas the purple speaks more to the witchcraft aspect. So again your color usage you can see that we brought in that sort of very dark moody color palettes combinations, a lot of your purple and your black and your use to get the combination to create that sort of very moody atmosphere.

"叛逆少女"的色系如您所愿,是我们这季最深、最暗的色系之一。在引入这种神秘和巫术元素的地方,我们会在这里使用很多不同的紫色。所以可以使用荧光紫、茄紫色以及淡紫色,淡紫色也是一种紫色,只是颜色较淡。紫褐色也起到了作用,在这里作为一种强调色。您还可以使用海军蓝和绿色,如森林绿和松绿色。实际上,海军蓝和绿色色调更多地用于少女主题,而紫色则更多地用于巫术元素。所以从颜色的使用上,您可以看到我们推出的是非常深色、暗色的色系组合,您使用的紫色、黑色和其他颜色组合在一起,营造出这种喜怒无常的氛围。

04:12—05:18

I am gonna have to go a little bit faster because I am running short of time as I always do. There's someone speaking at 3:30, so I am gonna have to pretty much push it. So let's go through some of the slides a little bit quicker. The materials here, very delicate, but really a little bit of mystery is the key, so we're looking at transparency which always gives you that sense of mystery. So you have No. 1 Cobweb Laces, No. 4 Metallic Swiss Dots, No. 7 your Silk Chiffons and No. 5 your Sheer Nylon Netting. So that sort of transparency gives you the sense of mystery, but also you have that notion of luxury with Crushed Velvet at No. 9 and your Lurex. Then going back to the school girl roots, right in the middle, you have your Herringbone and your Cotton Poplin which brings in that schoolgirl element into playing.

我得加快速度，我的时间总是不够用。三点半有人发言，我得尽快讲完。现在我们快速浏览其中一些幻灯片。这些面料非常精巧，实际上，有点神秘感才是关键，所以我们一直在寻找透明的材质，这种透明总会带给您神秘感。1号的蛛网蕾丝、4号金属质地的点子花薄纱、7号真丝雪纺和5号透明尼龙网，这种透明面料会带给您一种神秘感，同时也会有9号拷花丝绒和金银纱的奢华感。然后回到主要构成元素少女元素，就是中间部分，人字形布料和纯棉府绸引入少女元素。

05:18—05:57

Your prints and patterns really goes well beyond looking at your Darker Plaids. Obviously by using Darker Plaids, anytime you use plaids in a young girl's collection, casual women's collection, you are playing to schoolgirl. But of course then that sense of witchcraft and mystery comes in through your Blurred Vision, your Clouds of Smoke at No. 3, and Pagan Symbols at No. 8, your Cob Webs, No. 5, you have your Crest which again push you back into that schoolgirl realm.

实际上，印花图案比深色格子呢更能起作用。很显然，使用深色格子呢，无论什么时候，在年轻女孩系列、休闲女装系列中使用格子呢都是在走少女风。但巫术元素和神秘感来自于模糊图案、3号的烟云、8号的异教徒符号和5号的蛛网，使用羽饰就再次回到了少女时代。

05:57—06:52

Your next slide here is your design details. Things like Contrast Collars or Contrast Cuffs really work here. At No. 1 you have your Peter Pan Collar. Anyone who've seen the movie the *Ring* probably, as soon as I see the Peter Pan collar I think of the *Ring* and I am scared out of my wits because it's really a very scary movie. So that gives you that sort of really hint of horror into this particular theme. But you have other details such as

Cut-outs, your High Slits, your Crest Applique for schoolgirl, your Soft Bow Ties, your Peasant Sleeves, No. 7, your Dark Embroidery and so on and so on to really create that sort of cross between schoolgirl and witchcraft.

下一张幻灯片是设计细节。像对比色领或对比色袖口这些都是细节设计。1号是彼得潘领。可能任何看过电影"午夜凶铃"的人，只要一看到彼得潘领，就会想到"午夜凶铃"，会很害怕，因为这确实是一部非常恐怖的电影。所以这个设计给这个特定主题带来一丝恐怖感。但还有其他的细节，例如镂刻、高开叉、少女的羽毛缝饰、软领结、7号的扎袖以及深色刺绣等等，真正把少女元素和巫术元素结合。

06：52—07：25

So looking at your key items here, your key items again would be the long cardigan sweaters as I mentioned many times before. But again elongated for that layering and of course the cardigan always ties in with the schoolgirl aesthetic. You have your cropped pants that rounded, dropped shoulder top again that rounded look are very very important for autumn/winter 2015—2016 and your asymmetric skirt.

现在看的是重要单品，这些重要单品就是我之前多次提到长款开襟毛衣。但是，这种长款的层次感和开襟毛衣总是与少女的审美相关。半截裤，圆肩、落肩圆领上衣，对2015和2016年秋冬季服装和不对称裙子来说至关重要。

07：25—08：00

Looking at more of the key items, and really keeping things more prim, and proper, and more schoolgirl-like, so you have your Bow Front Blouse, your Drindl Skirt, both of which are very fit in that sort of schoolgirl aesthetic, your Men's Coat bringing in that sense of the blazer and your quilted skirt. So here is your Style Guide for Delinquent, really my favorite theme for the season. I love this particular theme.

再看看更多的重要单品。若真让服饰更整洁得体，更有少女感，蝴蝶结在前的女衬衫和阿尔卑斯式紧身连衫裙，这两款都非常符合少女的审美，男士大衣带有休闲西装和绗缝裙子的感觉。这是"叛逆少女"的款式指南，是本季我最喜欢的主题，我特别喜欢。

II. 实战练习二

1. 演讲背景

下文同样摘自"广交会设计潮流趋势研讨会"，演讲嘉宾介绍了新的时尚潮流趋势"嘲弄艺术"，他介绍了该主题产生的背景、色系、造型、材料、印花图案、

第九单元　时尚潮流 Fashion Trend

设计细节、重要单品。由于时间问题，简单提到了"北极冰雪"这个主题。演讲结束前还讲到了主题划分的原则，并鼓励观众免费试用公司网站。演讲的部分内容同样抽象难懂。

2. 预习词汇

Artisan Journey 工艺之旅
Ironica 嘲弄艺术
Andy Warhol 安迪·沃霍尔（美国波普艺术的领袖人物）
young casual market 年轻休闲服装市场
color palette 色系
scarlet red 猩红色
cobalt blue 钴蓝
golden yellow 金黄色
clementine orange 甜橘色
sky blue 天蓝色
lavender 薰衣草紫
leggings 打底裤
acid wash denim 酸洗牛仔布
ice blue denim 冰蓝色的牛仔布
fleece 羊毛织物
nylon 尼龙
Keith Haring 凯斯·哈林（美国涂鸦艺术家）
Rubik's Cube 魔方
quilting 绗缝
drawstring athletic waist 腰部运动束带
key item 重要单品
pencil skirt 铅笔裙
snap 纽扣
anorak 短夹克
outerwear 外衣
puffer coat/jacket 羽绒服
sweater dress 毛衣连衣裙；针织裙
baggy pants 袋形裤
cropped top 短款露脐上衣
sheath dress 修身/紧身连衣裙
collection 系列时装

young casual women's wear 年轻休闲女装

Fashion Snoops 一家全球性的时尚潮流趋势预测机构和专业资讯供应商

3. 演讲文本

00：00—01：55

The next theme for your young casual market is something a lot brighter and a lot bolder. It's very much related to that the Artisan Journey theme that we have in contemporary womenswear that we basically set in the 1920s that we did before. This is very very similar, but instead of setting in the 1920s, for the young casual market, we really set in the 70s and 80s. So it's very bold and bright. It's really about that girl who wants to stand away from the crowd in the boldest way possible. Ironica is a theme that embodies everything brilliant about Andy Warhol's Pop Art, bringing in that 70s element by referencing sort of Andy Warhol and about the kitsch elements of his design into a daily wardrobe. We use a lot of licensed products designs as you see here with Campbell Soup because those are iconic Andy Warhol prints. But we bring in these logos or these incorporated design like Pepsi or McDonald's or even Kellogg's Frosted Flakes for those of you who remember the 80s, the sugar rush of a Kellogg's Frosted Flakes breakfast. We bring them in but we use it in a very very ironic way. We are not trying to be selling merchandise. We are really trying to be ironic in the way that we approach this aesthetic for this particular look. But really it's a bright bold color palette from the contemporary market but now moved into the young casual market for the girl who really wants to stand out from the crowd.

年轻休闲市场的下一个主题更明亮、更大胆。这与当代女装"工艺之旅"的主题非常相关，这一主题的背景是在20世纪20年代。非常相似，但没有设定在20世纪20年代，对于年轻休闲女装市场，我们设定在70年代和80年代，所以它非常大胆和明亮。其实就是关于女孩们想要以最大胆的方式显得与众不同。"嘲弄艺术"这个主题体现了安迪·沃霍尔波普艺术的精髓，引入了70年代的元素，参考了安迪·沃霍尔和他的设计中的通俗元素，并将这些元素纳入日常穿着之中。我们使用了许多商品的设计，比如这里你们看到的是金宝汤，因为这些是安迪·沃霍尔的标志性图案。但是我们引入这些商标或者这些公司的设计，比如百事可乐，麦当劳，甚至家乐氏甜麦片，这些都是为了那些记得80年代的人，那时家乐氏甜麦片掀起过一阵早餐风潮。我们加入这些元素，不过是以一种非常讽刺的方式。不是为了售卖商品，我们实际是想表达我们的讽刺理念，这种审美观通过这种特殊的造型来表达。但这个色彩明亮大胆的色系来自当代市场，现在却进入了年轻休闲女装市场，让那些想与众不同的女孩从人群中脱颖而出。

01: 55—02: 42

So here is your colour palette, and again really about your loud brights, so your highlights here would be your scarlet red, your cobalt blue, your golden yellows as well as your clementine orange. But again balanced out with your softs, which adds really a little bit of newness to this particular theme, so your softs would be your sky blue as well as your lavender. Here is your combination. Again what we are trying to do is make the colors pop and make the colors stand out. Again so going back to color theory, you are really looking at colors from the opposite side of your color wheel to make the colors really pop.

接下来介绍色系，大胆强烈的色彩，所以亮点有可能是猩红色、钴蓝、金黄色，或者是甜橘色。然后用柔和的颜色加以平衡，给这个主题加入一点新奇的元素，那么柔和的颜色可以是天蓝色或是薰衣草紫。颜色组合起来就是这样的。然后，我们还想让这些颜色更流行，让这些色彩脱颖而出。再回到色彩理论，我们使用颜色的时候可以不遵循色轮规律，让自己的色彩更加突出。

02: 42—03: 11

That's really the Look that we're going for with Ironica. Obviously with the casual market, you are always gonna have some element of baggy happening in your tops or your bottoms. But really bring in that sports element that is all pervasive this season, so we bring that in here with Leggings. Here really you can see that sort of graphics or Pop Patterns that are essential to this particular theme.

这就是我们"嘲弄艺术"系列的造型。当然在休闲服装市场，总是需要一点宽松休闲的元素，不管是上装还是下装。此外还要加入本季无处不在的运动元素，所以我们在这里使用了打底裤设计。所以现在可以看到这些图案或流行式样对这个主题来说十分关键。

03: 11—04: 33

The materials that we're looking at here, really have, well, it's really in 70s and 80s theme in terms of your prints and patterns. We bring in the 90s with your materials, and it comes through especially in your denim. This is very much a denim theme here with your acid wash or your Ice Blue denim. But then also looking at some lighter materials such as your Fleece, your Mesh and your Nylon. But really this theme is about how you really execute your prints and patterns. So it's very artist-centered theme. So we bring in, you know, obviously the big reference point here would be your Andy Warhol inspired arts, your Pop-Art prints, your Keith Haring graffiti, and then obviously sort of very ironic take on corporate logos, and corporate branding. The one piece that I always thought should be in this slide that was not used by our design theme, but I think it fits naturally into this. Going back to the 80s, it's the Rubik's Cube. If you remember the Rubik's Cube with its really bright primary colors are graphic featuring that would be awesome in this particular theme.

我们在这里所寻找的材料，其实就在70年代和80年代的主题里，有我们想要的印花图案。我们在90年代找到了材料，特别是牛仔布。这是主打牛仔布的主题，包括酸洗牛仔布和冰蓝牛仔布。此外您一定还会想要加入一些轻柔面料，比如羊毛、网眼布、尼龙布。但这个主题主要是想展示印花图案，所以是一个以艺术家为中心的主题。所以我们在这里加入的，如您所见，我们最大的参考对象就是以安迪·沃霍尔为灵感的艺术，流行艺术的印花，凯斯·哈林的涂鸦，更明显的还有讽刺性借用的企业商标和品牌。有个点子是我认为应当放在这个幻灯片里，但没有收入这个主题，我觉得应该比较搭配的，那就是来自80年代的魔方。回想一下，魔方的鲜艳原色和图形特征，在这个主题里一定棒极了。

04：33—05：14

So looking at your design details, again some of the reference points would be suspender straps, quilting, rips on jeans, embroidery. Then there's also that sort of active influence which definitely should be in play. So at No. 7, you see your drawstring athletic waists. So that really brings in that active wear element as well. So you can see certainly in the middle that sort of bling as well as very very important that bling of the hip-hop era that in late 80s and early 90s.

看看这些设计细节，其中一些参考的点包括吊带、绗缝、破洞牛仔、刺绣。还有一些运动元素，也可以应用到设计中。看一下7号，您会看见腰部运动束带。也加入了运动服饰元素。当然中间这些珠宝元素也很重要，很像80年代后期和90年代早期嘻哈爱好者的珠宝装饰。

05：14—06：21

Here are your key items. Looking at things such as your Pencil Skirt, which has snaps down the front and is definitely a much more fitted body conscious style. The Matched Set which is usually done in a sweatshirt style particularly always a sweat shirt in the young casual market. The key Outerwear piece, rather than anything else, we believe is the Anorak this particular season, rather than your wind sweater or whatever. The Anorak sort of goes half-way down, so the Anorak as the key Outerwear piece and your Sweater Dress again, which I talked about many times before. Your baggy pants again something very natural for your young casual girl's market, your cropped top again the same, again to bring in that sense of sports as well. Your sheath dress and your

第九单元　时尚潮流 Fashion Trend

Puffer Jacket. So here is your Style Guide for Ironica.

　　这些是重要单品,比如铅笔裙,前面有纽扣设计,属于一种更紧身的风格。套装通常是运动衫风格,年轻休闲服装市场上几乎总是运动衫。最关键的外衣,我们相信本季是带风帽的厚夹克,而不是防风毛衣或者其他什么。厚夹克延续到中间部位,所以厚夹克作为关键的外衣单品和毛衣裙一起,我之前就反复提过。宽松的袋形裤再一次在年轻女孩服装市场上流行,还有短款露脐上衣,一起营造运动风格,还有紧身连衣裙和羽绒服。这就是"嘲弄艺术"的款式指南。

06:21—06:54

　　Now I have one more theme which is very related to Indigenous Territory, which is called Arctica. So I am just gonna go by that because really running out of time. The only real difference to this theme and Indigenous Territory is really much more earthy, inspired by ice and the Arctic Circle rather than the cultures of the Arctic Circle's. So it's really the only difference between this one and that one. So we can skip part by this one.

　　还有一个主题与"土著风情"有关,就是"北极冰雪"。只能直接跳过,因为时间关系。这个主题和"土著风情"最大的区别就是有更多的大地元素,主要是受冰雪和北极圈的灵感启发,而非北极大陆的文化。这就是两者之间的区别,我们可以跳过这部分。

06:54—08:50

　　I just wanna to finish on this particular slide. Because mixed in to our entire presentation of autumn/winter 2015—2016, we have 5 themes for contemporary women's and 5 themes for young casual women's. These days nobody does one collection or one delivery a season. We, at the very minimum, do 3 deliveries into our store over the course of the season. So by doing so many themes, we allow our clients to position different themes for different deliveries. So what you saw today, we felt, we split the season into pre-fall, which is a little bit transitional, from summer into fall, the main fall delivery and a winter delivery. So from the theme that you saw today, City Slicker, Delinquent and Ironica are themes that we feel should be used in that pre-fall or that transitional season or delivery. The main fall themes would be Artisan Journey and Indigenous Territory. There are others of course on the site that you can see during your free trial. For winter, the two themes Inner Calm which you saw and the Arctica which I flew pass are the key themes for your main winter deliveries. How we split those different themes, obviously it could be the color palette. It could be the material choice. The choices that we suggested for winter delivery are going to be obviously featuring heavier materials, you know, your pockets, whatever. You can obviously change it up.

But if you do change it up, we would certainly ask you to be a little more careful and to, you know, take into consideration you might need to change up some of your colors or change up some of your materials.

幻灯片马上就播放完毕。在2015—2016年秋冬服装潮流预测的演讲中，我们呈现了5个现代女性服装主题和5个年轻女性休闲服装主题。如今人们不会在一个时装季里只展示一个服装系列或交付一种风格的成衣。我们会在一个时装季里至少交付3种风格的成衣。通过呈现不同的主题，我们可以向客户交付不同风格的成衣。所以正如你们今天看见的，我们把时装季分为秋季前夕，这是换季的服饰，从夏到秋，主要是秋季交货，加上冬季。因此，今天看到的主题"都市丽影""叛逆少女"和"嘲弄艺术"是我们认为应该在秋季或过渡季节或交付时使用。主要的秋季主题会是"工艺之旅"和"土著风情"。网站上还可以看到其他主题，免费试用的时候能看到。在冬季，有两个关键主题，一个是"平静之心"，一个是我刚刚略过的"北极冰雪"。至于我们如何分割这些主题，当然是可以按色系来分，也可以按面料来分。我们建议冬季款使用一些比较有特色的厚重材料，比如说口袋部分等。您也可以做些改变。不过如果您确实要做调整，我们肯定会提醒您要考虑是否要换颜色或面料。

08：50—09：32

Now that's a really quick run-through. One of the sub-directories on Fashion Snoops which is a forecasting directory, our site contains so much more information than that. We have analysis of what's happening on a weekly basis of retail around the world, of trade shows happening around the world. We are updating hourly during the catwalk season. So I would really encourage you, if you like to take the free trial that we are offering everyone here today. So you can go on our site, take a look at it, see whether it will help you in your product development which of course is all important now, because the manufacturers as well as brands, everyone is developing collections.

我们快速过了一遍。Fashion Snoops公司的一个子目录就是时尚潮流预测，我们的网站则包含了更为丰富的信息。我们会分析世界各地的服装零售每周发生的事情，以及世界各地的服装展。我们的网站在时装季会每小时更新一次。所以我衷心推荐大家试用一下我们今天在这里为大家提供的免费试用版，可以去我们的网站逛一逛，看是否有助于您进行产品开发，产品开发显然非常重要，因为现在不管是制造商还是品牌方，每个人都在开发新系列的时装。

09：32—09：50

But really, we hope you enjoy the seminar today. We hope you found it useful. If you are interested in menswear, we are doing it all again tomorrow, but with menswear at 2 o'clock. Thank you all for your time. I really appreciate it. Have a good day.

我们衷心希望大家享受今天的研讨会。希望能对大家有所启发。如果对男装感兴趣，我们明天会再做一次展示，2点钟左右开始。谢谢大家，非常感谢！祝您过得愉快！

第十单元 建筑和城市规划
Building and Urban Planning

I. 实战练习一

1. 演讲背景

贝诺建筑事务所全球设计总监应邀参加"中英建筑论坛（珠海站）",并发表主旨演讲。他在演讲中分享了事务所开展的几个开发项目，包括苏州中心、伦敦西部的项目、九龙圆方购物中心项目、上海的城市娱乐村、深圳来福士广场、广州天环广场等。所有的项目开发都遵循以下原则：城市是一个生命有机体，新开发的项目应当与城市大环境无缝衔接，连接水域和现有景观，创造城市纹理，路网设计应当有利于步行。

2. 预习词汇

Global Design Director 全球设计总监
mixed-use 混合使用
living organism 生命有机体
CBD/Central Business District 中央商务区
ground-level 地面
waterfront 滨水区
hardscape 硬质风景；人造风景
softscape 软质风景；自然风景
Longines 浪琴（瑞士手表品牌）
urban grain/city grain 城市纹理
energy conservation 节能
Elements Shopping Center（香港西九龙）圆方购物中心
Kowloon 九龙
roof deck 屋顶平台
demolish 拆毁，拆除
externalization 外部化
Parc Central 天环广场

MTR 地铁

3. 演讲文本

00：00—01：12

Good morning everyone. Good to be here, my name is Simon Bee, Global Design Director with Benoy. I am based in HK, which is our largest studio. But I have responsibilities around the world, which means I travel a lot. I've been in Hong Kong now 18 months. I have to say it's been a very exciting time in my career. It's good to be here. As well as our western offices and studios in Hong Kong and elsewhere in Asia, we have 3 offices in China. We are doing some fairly major mixed-use schemes in China at the moment. So what I would like to talk to you a little bit about today is sustainable urban design, particularly in terms of creating what I would call connected cities, because I think it is an extremely important part of what we do. I would see a city as a living organism. If those parts of that organism don't work together and aren't connected properly, then the organism will not function correctly. And this is really important. So see every new development, if you like, as an organ within the body of the city, and it has to work and it has to be connected in a right kind of way.

大家早上好！很高兴来到这里，我叫 Simon Bee，是贝诺的全球设计总监。我在香港工作，那里有我们最大的工作室。我负责全球的业务，也就是说我经常出差。我在香港已经呆了一年半，不得不说，这是我职业生涯中非常激动人心的时刻。很高兴来到这里。我们在西方国家有工作室，在香港和亚洲其他地方都有工作室，我们在中国有三个工作室。目前我们在中国做非常大型的混合使用的项目，所以今天我想和大家讲一些关于可持续城市设计的内容，尤其是创造出我提到的连接型城市，因为我认为这是我们做的事情中非常重要的一部分。我会将城市看作一个生命有机体。如果一个有机体的各个部分无法协调运作、恰当地连接起来，那么这个有机体就无法正常运转，这一点非常重要。所以将每个新项目看作是城市身体的一个器官，它必须发挥作用，并以正确的方式和其他器官联系在一起。

01：12—02：41

So with that in mind, I'd just like to start with this project that we are working on in Suzhou to the west of Shanghai. It's called the Suzhou Center. It's part of a much bigger master plan, which actually engages with a lake, called Jinji lake. And the part I really want to dwell on is what you are looking at now, which is the heart of the CBD, which faces on to the lake and how the whole area connects together, because I think this is quite unique in a sense. And that I believe many projects in China seem to dwell to me as a new comer just on single sites. And they tend to be rather separated by some fairly major roads in my experience. And yet, this one seems to break the mode slightly in making a great effort to make sure that it is connected with its neighbors. And a lot of expenses have gone into this to make sure that this is the case. So here is Jinji lake. Here is the body of the master plan, not done by us, done by others. But the part that we've been involved in is the section through here, particularly the ground-level shopping and entertainment and dining in mixed use, which really animate the streets and then allow the engagement with the waterfront. And you can see the amount of landscapes that our landscaping colleagues have brought about on the project as well, which actually starts on the roof of the project. Just flicking through these a little bit too quickly. So let's go back to that.

所以，我想从这个项目开始讲，这是我们在苏州，即上海西边正在做的项目，叫做苏州中心。它是总体规划里的一部分，与一个湖有关，叫金鸡湖。我想仔细讲的部分就是你们现在看到的，位于中央商务区的中心地带，面向金鸡湖，看看整个区是怎么连接在一起的，因为我觉得在某种意义上来说非常独特。我觉得中国很多新项目看起来像某个地方的外来物，它们似乎彼此分离，被一些大道隔离开来，这也是根据我丰富的经验总结出来的。但是这个项目似乎打破了这种模式，非常努力地尝试与"邻居们"保持联系。投入了大量的资金到这个项目中来，只为实现这一点。这里就是金鸡湖，也是总体规划的主体，总体规划不是我们做的，是其他人做的。我们参与的部分就是从这里开始，尤其是地面购物、娱乐和餐饮的混合使用功能区，这些真正给街道增添了活力，也增加了与滨水区的联系。大家可以看看这里的风景，这也是我们项目负责景观美化的同事设计的，事实上这是从项目的屋顶部分开始的。快速地浏览一下就行，我们又回到刚才那个主题。

02：41—03：53

So starting at the roof, the whole of the roof is animated by landscape. In fact, 50% of the roof is soft landscaping, giving out onto these arms of, if you like, land bridges, which connect with this active waterfront. I think it is such a great lesson to connect properly with water and not separate your development or separate what you are doing from the waterfront. There are many cities in the world which have suffered in this way. I have to say Hong Kong is one of them. And it's only just if you like breaking the chain of the road system to actually allow the people to connect with the water properly. This is looking in the other way. Then so the heart of the scheme is a transporting to change as there are two-line metro stations underneath the development of these three towers. And they overload a lot of public roads. Hardscape as well as softscape, leading down to the waterfront, lots of taller buildings which are not by us as well. And this gives you the bare bones of some of those connections. And you can see the effort that is being made to break the car load of the road system and make sure this will connect through to the water.

从屋顶部分开始，整个屋顶因风景而变得有活力，其实50%的屋顶都是软质景观，延伸到大陆桥的狭长地带，而大陆桥连接着生机勃勃的滨水区。我认为这是一个非常好的经验，恰当地和水域连接在一起，不会将您的开发项目或者您正在做的事情与滨水区分离，世界上很多城市都出现了这个问题。不得不说，香港也是其中之一。除非您想打破道路系统的连接，只为让人们和水域恰当地连接在一起。这是从另一个角度看到的，所以计划的核心就是改变交通，因为这里是两条地铁线经过的地铁站，地铁站就在这三个塔楼开发项目的地下。上面承载着多条公共道路，包括硬质景观和软质景观，通向滨水区，很多高层建筑也不是由我们负责的。这里给出了这些连接的基本框架。大家可以看到，项目努力打散道路系统的车流，确保能和水域连接起来。

03：53—04：29

In giving places for people, places for people to really enjoy the water, and engage and be able to walk the city, and to be able to get from A to B without having to resort to getting into your car. And then when you get down to the micro scale, how you really engage with… untouch the landscape and those natural features and there's a lot of effort have gone into that as well. And on site, I mean it's just the major, major site, as you can see these are a little old now. It's for the Longines, but I just thought you'll be able to see the scale of that site.

我们想为人们打造这样的地方：能欣赏水域风景，在城市中散步，不需要开车就可以从甲地去往乙地。接着，当您开始做微观设计时，您怎么真正保留原来的景观和自然特色？这方面也需要很多努力。在现场，也就是主场地，您可以看到这些都有点陈旧了。这里是为浪琴设计的，但我只想您看看这个场地的规模。

04：29—05：40

But just turning back the clock a little bit to some of the work I was doing back in London, which I think really inform this whole debate. I think that Asia is so confident in terms of the ambition of this development. It's been really great to see the ambition of the mixed use here, what developers are prepared to do because back in the west it was a different story for a long time, there were many barriers in the way of… really complex sophisticated mixed use. I think that's been broken now with new ways of financing projects in particular. But I do think that in the west there's a long history and a pedigree of urban design, which means that new development is very well integrated into existing city scapes. I think the previous speaker mentioned that in terms of developing an urban grain on the project which sits within its context, in a rather seamless fashion, to look at there is so much developed from that. A part of that is really studying the place that you're working in, understanding the history, and what that's all about.

再回头看看我在伦敦做的项目，我认为可以为我们稍后的讨论抛砖引玉。我觉得亚洲对这方面的项目开发非常有自信。也很高兴在这里能看到你们有进行混合使用的追求。长久以来开发商们要做的事，对西方来说是非常不同的，所以进行非常复杂、精细的混合使用存在很多障碍。我认为这已经有了突破，得益于很多新融资项目的开展方式。但是西方城市设计历史悠久，经验丰富，也就是说新开发项目已经很好地融入了现有的城市景观中。上一位发言人提到：关于项目中的城市纹理开发，如果要与城市大环境实现无缝衔接，这里的发展看上去比那里要好得多。其中一点就是要研究项目所在地，理解它的历史，透彻了解这个地方。

05：40—07：20

In fact, this project in west London in a place called Trott, we even look as far as naming the streets based on the history of the place and that plan that you see there is based on all those new street names which came to there within the project. So there are many sustainable layers in this project, in a right through from social issue, like create the great housing, you know you wouldn't need to leave this place if you didn't want to, you enjoy living there. Right through to low carbon issues, energy conservation and so forth. And really, it depends on how the local authority and the clients are working together, as how many of those tactics you input, but overriding all that to my mind, it's this notion of the urban grain creating the street networks and city grain that allow this to be an integrated walkable place. London is such an interesting city of contrast, which is so close together. In fact, you get the busy places, the heart square, and it almost seems to me that one block back in many cases, you get some quiet reflective garden squares, which are structured in a fantastic way, punctuate the city in the way they do. Of course, we know there are many ways of applying green to these developments, green on roofs, massively important, never waste the roof space if you can help it. Green walls, green squares, in every balcony. And I think, you know, travelling around the world as I do, I think Singapore gives a great lesson in terms of greening development.

其实，在伦敦西部Trott这个地方的项目，我们甚至根据地方的历史来给街道命名，这个计划中，这里全是立足于那些新街道的名字，并成为项目的一部分。所以很多可持续发展的层面存在于这个项目中，包括社会问题，如提供优质住房，您可以住在这儿，如果您不想离开这儿，如果您喜欢这儿的生活。还包括低碳问题、节能等。所以真的取决于地方政府和客户如何合作，以及您采取的策略，但我觉得最好的就是城市纹理理念，它创造了街道网络和城市纹理，让这里成为完整统一、

第十单元 建筑和城市规划 Building and Urban Planning

适合步行的地方。相比之下,伦敦就是趣味盎然、对比鲜明、联系非常紧密的城市。其实你们可以看到繁华的地方,中心广场,对我来说只是在后面一个街区的距离,就可以看到静谧、适合沉思的花园广场,其结构非常巧妙,给这个城市增色添彩。当然,有很多方式来将绿色应用到这些开发项目中,绿色的屋顶非常重要,尽量不要浪费屋顶的空间。绿色的墙壁、绿色的广场,每个阳台都是绿色的。我去世界各地旅行,我觉得新加坡在绿色发展上给我们很大的启示。

07:20—08:08

So patterns of movement, making sure you don't need to use your car more than you really do need to, and there are other ways of getting around. And then crafting great places, really think inside the details of the squares and what you are hoping to provide, make sure that streets and squares are animated in the right kind of way. You know, retail is a great animator. Cultural uses, entertainment, dining are great animators of streets. Never leave a black street if you can help is my philosophy. It makes them safe, and also think about prototyping new forms of residential. I mean this was a very interesting idea we have for actually stacking 10 houses within a tall building within that development.

出行方式,确保开车的次数尽量减少,也有其他的出行方式。精心打造最好的地方,深入考虑广场的细节部分,以及您希望提供什么,确保街道和广场具有活力,协调统一。零售业非常有活力,文化、娱乐和餐饮也会给街道增添活力。尽量不要让街道昏暗,这就是我的原则。这样街道会比较安全,同时也可以想想住宅的新形式。我觉得非常有趣的想法就是我们的开发项目中的一栋高楼容纳10个房子。

08:08—09:25

So again taking those messages from London back into Asia, what do we learn and how do we apply them? First, major project, we have to collaborate with our friends of Aedas on this one, was the Elements Shopping Center in Kowloon, where we covered the entire roof deck with the garden, with restaurant space, to create it like a plaza in the sky that connected all the towers together. And this has not been done in this scale before. And then up into Shanghai, this is what I describe as an urban entertainment village. So this is an open street scheme. It's more about the places than it's actually about the buildings, but what really brings this to life in terms of memories of the place in particular is the creatively use of many old industrial buildings on the site which people will know. So here are some cement silos and old warehouses that we not just demolished, throwing away. They were reused as art spaces, so the big one on the right is a theatre, the one in the center is an art gallery and so on. They are reused and people remember those buildings as working buildings, and yet now they become, they take on a new leads of life.

了解了这些信息之后，让我们把目光从伦敦转回到亚洲，我们学到了什么？我们如何应用？首先这是大项目，我们必须和凯达集团的朋友们合作，也就是九龙圆方购物中心项目，我们在屋顶平台上设花园和餐厅，将其打造成空中购物中心，连接所有的塔楼。如此大规模的项目之前还没有做过。我们看看上海，这就是我描述的城市娱乐村，这是一个开放的街道计划。这个计划更加关注地点，而不是建筑，然而真正使这个计划生动有趣的是对这个地方的记忆，也就是对一些古老工业建筑的创造性使用，将来你们会知道的。这里是一些水泥筒仓和陈旧的仓库，我们没有拆除或丢弃，而是重新用作艺术空间，右边大一点的是一个剧院，中间是画廊等。这些都得到重复利用，人们记得这些建筑都是工业建筑，现在会呈现崭新的生活面貌。

09：25—10：08

Locally here in Shenzhen, we have a project which is all about externalization. It's about the buildings having a communication, if you like a conversation with the landscape. So this is not just the big internalized podium that has no interest in the outside. It is all about activity. As this one showed also Shenzhen, the capital round steel in the Raffles City, all about engagement with a public park. For me, it is so important to get this conversation between your buildings and the outside of the streets, softscape, park or whatever.

在深圳我们有个项目，是关于外部化的，即建筑之间是有交流的，只要您想和景观对话。所以，这不是个大型内部化的平台，并不是与外界毫无联系，而是一个展示活力的平台，它也表明，作为深圳来福士广场中被钢铁围起来的中心，这里也是个公园。对于我而言，重要的是让您的建筑与外界的街道、软质景观、公园等有交流。

10：08—11：02

And then another one, not too far away, that we are doing for Sun Hung Kai, which is the project in Guangzhou called Parc Central, where actually taking the landscape deep inside the building. Now this has many ground plans, because it plunges through the ground all the way down to the MTR. The train link is at the bottom, but every level is a landscape courtyard, and I have been on site and seen this, and the greenery is coming along really well. Green walls everywhere, huge trees being planted, I think this is going to be quite spectacular. It almost feels like a stadium. The way the building laps it on itself and all those landscapes, you can see the complexity and what

第十单元 建筑和城市规划 Building and Urban Planning

happens on the ground with this one. That's a side view a little while ago from my friend, Wang Lu, who was working with us on this one.

另一个也不太远,是我们为新鸿基做的一个项目,这个项目在广州叫天环广场,它将风景深深地融入建筑之中。这个项目有很多地面规划,因为地面骤降,一直降到地铁站。地铁在底部连接,但是每一层都是风景庭院,我去过现场,也看到过这个,绿色用得恰到好处。到处都是绿色墙壁,也种满了大树,我觉得这会非常壮观,感觉就像一个体育场。从建筑交错的方式以及所有那些景观,您可以看到这其中的复杂之处,以及这个建筑给地面带来了什么变化。这是一个侧面图,刚刚我朋友王露给我的,她和我们一起负责这个项目。

11: 02—11: 47

And just a real final thought really. This is a very early sketch on a project we're working on right now in Shanghai, which are actually eight different plots. But our client there has realized the power, the wealth creation of connections, and he is encouraging us now to make sure this is properly joined up. So again you know you can go from A to B without necessary having to use your car, I think it is a very strong thing, the landscapes there are equally important. I think urban design has a huge amount to play in employing, say, new development in China. So thank you very much for listening!

最后一点,这是一个项目的早期设计图,是我们现在在上海开发的一个项目,占了八块不同的地皮。我们上海的客户意识到了连接的力量,认为连接可以创造财富,于是鼓励我们让这个建筑与周围环境很好地融合在一起。这下您总该知道您从甲地去往乙地不一定得开车了吧!这点很厉害!当然,那里的景观同样重要。我认为城市设计作用非常大,影响了中国新项目开发。非常感谢大家的聆听!

II. 实战练习二

1. 演讲背景

英国维尔金森·艾尔建筑事务所的亚太总监应邀参加"中英建筑论坛(珠海站)",并发表主旨演讲。他在演讲中分享了事务所开展的几个开发项目,包括广州国际金融中心、位于多伦多市中心的一座铂金级绿色建筑塔楼、伦敦的西门子建筑项目、新加坡的滨海湾花园、纽卡斯尔重建项目、伦敦东部的临时篮球场、伦敦国王十字车站改造项目。

2. 预习词汇

Wilkinson Eyre 维尔金森·艾尔建筑事务所

International Finance Center 国际金融中心
Arup 英国奥雅纳工程顾问公司
LEED platinum 铂金级绿色建筑
regeneration project 重建项目
Benoy 贝诺设计有限公司
wind excitation 风振
atrium 中庭
Union Station 联合车站
onerous 繁重的，麻烦的
façade 幕墙
amenity 舒适；便利措施
down draft 下冲气流
canopy 天蓬，华盖
Green Mark Platinum 绿色建筑标志铂金奖
International WELL Building Standard 国际建筑标准
Toronto Green standard 多伦多绿色建筑标准
DLR/Deutsches Zentrum für Luft-und Raumfahrt 德国宇航中心
Emirates cable car 阿联酋航空空中缆车
SIEMENS 西门子
BREE-AM/Building Research Establishment Environmental Assessment Method 英国建筑研究院环境评估方法
photovoltaic 光伏的，光电的
grid 电网
Gardens by the Bay 新加坡滨海湾花园
lux 勒克斯（照明单位）
desiccant system 干燥系统
puddle 水坑
biomass boiler 生物质锅炉
New Castle 纽卡斯尔
Stratford n. 斯特拉特福德
stripped foundation 条形地基
King's Cross（英国）国王十字车站
refurbish 修缮，翻新
bolt 螺栓；螺钉
gasholder 储气罐
iconic building 标志性建筑

Thames 泰晤士河
turbine hole 涡轮机孔
retail podium 商业裙楼
residential flank 居住侧翼

3. 演讲文本

00:00—00:33

Thank you very much! Good morning. It's a pleasure to be here. My name is Mathew Porter. I run the Hong Kong office Wilkinson Eyre. It's been a fantastic morning, extremely informative projects and what I thought I might try and do is just add into the lessons that we've learned with some of the projects that we've delivered around the world where we have sought to work as part of a very integrated team. We work very closely with our engineers and we consider that to be increasingly important as we seek to deliver low-carbon design.

谢谢大家！早上好，非常高兴来到这里。我叫 Mathew Porter，负责维尔金森·艾尔建筑事务所香港分部。这是一个美妙的早晨，听到了介绍非常详实的项目，我想我会努力加入一些有意义的内容，之前我们已经借鉴了世界各地的项目，并努力造就一个有凝聚力的团队。我们与工程师紧密合作，这对于达成低碳设计来说越来越重要。

00:33—01:23

So I'll start with a project just up the road in Guangzhou, the International Finance Center, where we've worked very closely with Arup to generate a structure that was particularly effective to reduce material usage. I'm then gonna go through three projects which are our latest highly sustainable project such as LEED platinum that work to achieve the goals of all future cities which needs to provide high-quality livable spaces. They need to be economically competitive, excuse me, and they need to protect the environment. And then my last section is just to run through some of our regeneration projects. Mr. Bee from Benoy mentioned the importance of using the buildings that we've already got to regenerate areas and to use the building stock in a new and exciting way.

因此首先我先讲一个项目，就在广州这条路的前面，那就是国际金融中心，在这里我们和英国奥雅纳工程顾问公司合作设计了一个架构，非常节约建筑材料。接下来我要讲讲三个项目，都是我们最新的、可持续性很高的项目，比如铂金级绿色建筑，能帮助我们实现未来城市的目标，包括提供优质的宜居空间。这些项目需要具备高性价比，抱歉，应该是能保护环境。最后我将大致谈谈重建项目。贝诺设计有限公司的 Bee 先生曾提到非常关键的做法,即利用已有建筑重建区域,并以一种全新的、令人振奋的方式利用建筑群。

01:23—02:50

So Guangzhou [IFC] is a 438-meters' super high-rise tower, deliver this part of the new masterplan and completed in 2011 [2010]. It is split into two major usages obviously the office component for some 69 floors, the base of the building, and then a 33-storey, five-star hotel at the top. And that've been a long morning, so I'm gonna go through this quite quickly. And I will be happy to talk about them in detail after. But the main feature of the building is the dialgrade structure, which expands the four heights with a dialgrade. A 54-meter tall unit there are eight of these diamonds of the building, and it provides an extremely stable structure. Combined with the form of the building, we are able to reduce the wind loading by some 30%, and the dialgrade structure ties back to the core, an extremely efficient way through floor plates, avoiding the need for transporting. It also in combination with form reduces what our engineering friends called wind excitations, which is a good thing to avoid. Looking at the top, the structure then sends itself inside out, and we create a super high atrium, which looks something like that with the hotel arranged around it, providing a delightful, exciting space to arrive at at the top of the building.

广州塔(编者注:翻译口误,此处应为[广州国际金融中心])是一座 438 米的超级高塔,体现了这一部分的总体规划设计,于(编者注:经核实,应为 2010)年竣工。塔身分为两大用途,一是办公区共 69 层,属塔楼的底座部分;二是 33 层的五星级酒店,在塔顶。由于今早日程较满,所以我只简单叙述一下。我也很愿意稍后详谈。但建筑的主要特点是斜盘式轴向柱结构,以此将建筑的四脚加高。有一个 54 米高的部位,包含 8 组菱形结构,令塔身稳固无比。结合塔楼的外形,能够减少 30% 来自大风的影响,且斜盘式轴向柱结构和塔心紧密结合,能很快地到达地面,减少运输负担。这种结合还能减少工程人员所称的"风振",我们要避免风振。再看塔顶,直入云霄,有一个非常高的中庭,看起来好像酒店就环绕四周一般,创造了一个让人心情愉悦、振奋人心的地方,可以直达塔顶。

02:50—03:55

Another project that we're currently working on is in detailed design stage. It's a LEED platinum tower in Toronto, right into the centre, spanning the Union Station with extraordinary transforming and a very very onerous environment to contend with. So the temperatures in Toronto drop down to less than 20 degrees centigrade in winter and can get above 30 degree in the summer. One of the things that's particular to Toronto is the

第十单元 建筑和城市规划 Building and Urban Planning

ice storms we need to contend with, so the façade needs to be extremely smooth because in the winter, you can get ice built up on the outside of the façade which tends to rip things off the building. What we produce is a highly transparent facade giving good day lighting, great views out of the extraordinary location, and actually allowing a little bit of heat loss through the façade is a high performance façade. We allow a little bit of heat loss to keep the ice away. We also have used a product which ensures that birds can see the building and there's no risk of them flying into the glass.

我们的另一个项目正处于具体设计阶段,是一座铂金级绿色建筑塔楼,位于多伦多市中心,一直延伸到联合车站,那里交通便利,环境复杂。多伦多冬天低于零下20摄氏度,夏天又能超过30摄氏度。需要特别注意的是多伦多的暴风雪,因此塔楼幕墙需要格外光滑。因为在冬天,冰雪会挂壁,还会脱落。我们设计的是高透明度的幕墙,便于获得日光,视野极佳,地理位置好,而且热量散失很少,塔楼幕墙性能很高,这样幕墙就不会结冰。此外,我们还使用了一款产品能确保鸟类能够看到建筑,而不会撞到玻璃上。

03:55—05:32

Something that we as designers are able to do is to really consider the spaces between the buildings and we have worked very hard to ensure that all surfaces that we can plant on are planted. We create great visual amenity and great public amenity, spaces between our towers which are well-planted with local species. And we create the space which people can come down from the towers. They can have their lunch and they can use the public space. This collectivity is extremely important. Previous speakers have already talked about how important this is in terms of creating effective and livable cities. And we work very hard to ensure that not only were the towers comfortable to occupy, but the spaces beside them. So it's to avoid down draft, protecting the people that move around the buildings from the sun, from the wind, from the rain, and from the risk of falling ice. We create a very simple canopy which we subject it to the usual day lighting analysis to ensure that we are providing the right amount of light at the right time of the year to create an exciting and pleasant space to live and work. It's achieved Green Mark Platinum or it's on target to achieve Green Mark Platinum with the potential of somewhere between 84 and 90 points out of the possible 110. We're also targeting the International WELL Building Standard, which looks to talk about livable spaces, comfortable spaces for people to live in and we're also meeting the Toronto Green Standard, which is a spectacularly high standard. And there it is from the view from over the bay.

我们在设计时还要考虑建筑物的楼距,并尽可能地增加绿化,带来绝佳的视觉效果和公共便利设施，塔楼之间的空间都栽种了本土绿植。我们还设计了塔内穿行的空间。人们可以在这吃午餐，使用公共空间。这种集合性非常重要。之前的演讲嘉宾已经谈到创造高效和宜居城市的重要性。我们也在尽力确保不仅塔楼本身很舒适，周围的环境也能如此。因此要避免下冲气流，确保周围经过的人不受阳光、大风、雨水和落冰的影响。我们设计了一个简约的华盖，用以分析日常光照，以确保建筑物能提供合适的光照，能够随时节调整，营造美妙舒适的生活和工作环境。我们希望此塔楼能获绿色建筑标志铂金奖，或争取评比时得到84—90分，110分满分。另外，我们旨在达到国际建筑标准，此标准主要涉及宜居、舒适的居住空间。我们也已达到多伦多绿色建筑标准，此标准尤为严格。这是从海湾看过来的风景。

05：32—07：21

Moving on now this building in London, it is conceived very much to consider low-carbon cities. It creates a hub, a place in which people can learn about the future cities, how they need to respond to the demands. And ideas can be exchanged. It is open to the public as it is open to specialists. It's located in east London, which has been a very deprived part of London. And it's now being subject to huge regeneration. It's next to the city airport, has connections to the DLR, and to the Emirates cable car, which we are fortunate enough to help and then design of. It's a SIEMENS project and they set a very particular brief that it needed to create the opportunity to discuss the future cities, how buildings can be improved in their design, and to be a landmark project at itself. They wanted it to be highly sustainable and they ask us to meet the highest standards in two environmental assessment strategies. It needed to be BREE-AM outstanding, and LEED platinum. And because it's a SIEMENS project, they were keen to its showcase, or the extraordinary technologies that SIEMENS produced to make these buildings highly sustainable. So it really is a kit of parts. There are some very very developed technologies here from the performance of the glass to the photovoltaic to the ball piles that we use. Every opportunity to maximize the free energy, the passive design so that we can gather wind, we can gather light, and we waste as little as possible before then we were relying on highly sophisticated active systems.

下面我们谈谈这幢位于伦敦的建筑，伦敦被广泛誉为低碳城市。这幢建筑创造了一个中心，人们能在这里了解未来城市和如何应对各种需求，还能交换意见。它向公众开放，正如同向专家开放一样。这个中心位于伦敦东部，一直都很偏僻，现在又得到重建：紧邻机场，与德国宇航中心和阿联酋航空空中缆车都有联系，我们有幸能参与设计。这是西门子的项目，他们在设计任务书中具体提到，该项目需要创造机会来探讨未来城市、如何改进建筑设计使其成为地标性建筑物。他们想建设可持续性极高的建筑，并要求我们达到最高的两项环境评估标准，即英国建筑研究院环境评估方法和铂金级绿色建筑评估标准。因为是西门子公司的项目,他们要求能够展示西门子绝伦的技术,令建筑具有高度可持续性的技术。因此这的确是个大项目。这里有一些非常成熟的技术,从玻璃性能,到光伏设备,到我们使用的堆球结构。抓住每个机会最大化自由能源,被动设计,以收集风能和光能,尽可能减少浪费,这一切都依靠高度精密的主动系统。

07:21—08:21

There is an exhibition within the building that talks about the challenges of designing low-carbon cities. And we use a very light recycled steel frame as a module and at early stages where may be, would be a one-crystal building, a two-crystal building, or it could be expanded to a three-crystal building. It ends up being a two crystal building, and then this started to inform how the façades might be shaped, how they might be implied to ensure that the spaces that didn't need additional heating were self-shading, where the spaces that could benefit from a little bit of warmth, the café for instance, the façade leans out to capture the sun. We created a well-ventilated central atrium and then the exhibition space itself is mixed-mode with good natural daylight and maximizing the use of good ventilation. So they can start to see the fracture form of the building. This is supposed to be a landmark project. They wanted it to look different.

建筑内有一个展示区,讲述设计低碳城市的挑战。我们以轻质循环利用的钢架为模块,早期设计成一层和两层晶体结构,最后也可以扩展到三层晶体结构。最终设计成了两层晶体结构,然后开始展现建筑幕墙的塑造方式、如何确保空间不需要额外供热并能自遮荫,只需要很少的供暖空间,比如咖啡厅,这里的空间延伸出去能接受阳光照射。我们设计了一个通风良好的中庭,展示区本身是混合使用模式的,有良好的自然光照,并最大化实现良好通风,这样人们还能看到建筑的结构。这是一个地标式工程,旨在与众不同。

08:21—09:51

And then we would like to talk about on the active systems how we can start to draw energy from the site and to very very gently condition the space within. Something that is really extraordinary about this project is the use of water, very very little water from the main that's delivered to the project. It captures most of its rain, so it can capture most of its water from rainfall, which and then process it and it also has black water recycling on site which is then used to irrigate the community gardens that are set around the project. And all of the energy, all of the electricity is generated through on array of some 1,500 square meters of photovoltaic cells on the rooftop, which then feed into systems. We also are connected to offsite energy generation with the proposal that this building will be ready for the decarbonization of the grid. It's that we will be able to generate energy and release energy back to the grid when the building itself does not need it. It has achieved GREEN MARK, I'm sorry, LEED platinum and BREE-AM outstanding with the score of 89 points. The view at night really gives a sense of how the façades are working in different ways and different places to create an exciting impression.

然后我们再来谈谈主动系统，如何开始从周围环境中获得能源，并利用能源精心维护建筑内部的环境。这个项目最了不起的一点是用水，它仅使用很少的水，大部分水是收集的雨水，然后处理；还能将黑水在现场处理，然后灌溉项目周边的绿地。所有能源和电力都是从一片1,500平方米的光伏电池板上得来的，电池板安装在屋顶，电力接入整个系统。我们还与社区外的发电厂相连，希望此建筑能为电网低碳化作出贡献。这样我们就能发电，并在电力盈余时将其输送回电网。这个工程已取得绿色建筑标志铂金奖，抱歉，是铂金级绿色建筑和英国建筑研究院环境评估方法的89分。晚上看它，就能知道建筑幕墙如何在不同角度和地方产生美妙的效果。

09：51—11：19

The third project is a project we delivered in Singapore, the Gardens by the Bay, very challenging brief to air-conditioned glass houses. The thing that's interesting about the project in terms of the city design and other speakers have mentioned how Singapore really is leading the way in terms of turning their city into an extremely green, planted landscape. The concept is the city in a garden. And this is to create a large public park that will then have the city develop around it to create an amenity space for the future residents. We were very very keen that the landscape speaks to the building and the building be connected to the garden with a whole series of virtual cycles where waste from one can benefit the other. And we display plants from around the world that are most exposed to global warming. Because of the plants, we have very very high light requirement. Some 45,000 lux. Above that point, the light starts to become a risk in terms of heat gain, and so we kept the amount of light that came in at the minimum requirement for the plants, 45,000 lux. And the extra light we cut out, using the deployable shades, reducing the cooling load significantly. We're also creating a spectacle for the building.

我们的第三个项目是新加坡的滨海湾花园，任务书极具挑战性，要在玻璃房里安装空调系统。有趣的是，在城市设计方面和其他演讲嘉宾提到的，新加坡如何引领潮流建设绿色城市，这一概念即花园城市，即创造一个大型公园，城市围绕公园而建，为未来居民创造舒适空间。我们致力于营造能与建筑相得益彰的景观，建筑与周围的绿地花园相连，彼此形成一个良性循环系统，这里的废弃物能够再次利用。我们展示了世界各地的植物，它们最容易受全球变暖的影响。植物需要大量光照，大约45,000勒克斯。超过这一界限，植物会有热量过剩的危险，因此我们使光照保持在植物所需的最低限度，即45,000勒克斯。多余的光照我们会使用可调节遮光罩挡住，大量减少冷却载荷。我们还营造了绝美的景观。

11：19—12：34

We only cool the spaces that the plants live or that people live and allow the air to get really hot at the top, which is then collected and used to regenerate a desiccant system which drive the air which makes it easier to cool. The coolth collected in little spaces in the garden, so we created these landscape zones where the coolth could collect almost like water in puddles. And we cool the ground, cool the floor that you walk on, using an energy center, which turn a waste problem the city had. Too much biomass that was being shipped to Malaysia and put into landfill, we turned that into an energy source by having a biomass boiler on site, which generates all of the energy that the building needs and ensures that the cooling of the conservatory is entirely carbon neutral. In fact, our challenge was to originally be no worse than a typical office. The target that we've achieved by some 3 or 4 times and actually are managing to generate enough energy on site to be carbon negative. We are actually producing more energy than we require.

我们只冷却植物生长和人们生活的空间，并让热空气上升至顶部，将其收集并用于更新干燥系统，促进空气流通，方便降温。冷气聚集在花园绿地这块小空间里，所以我们创造了这些景观区域，冷气就像水坑里的水一样收集起来。我们还给地面降温，这是能源中心的功劳，它能减少城市的浪费。大量生物质被运送到马来西亚填埋，我们将其转化为能量来源，在现场建造生物质锅炉，产生建筑所需的各种能量，并确保玻璃暖房里的制冷系统完全是碳中和的。事实上，我们最初的挑战是确保这个玻璃房子的碳排放不要超过一个典型的办公室。实际上我们的成绩是这个目标的3～4倍，并努力产生足够的能源，保证碳排放是负值。我们产生的能源供大于求。

12：34—12：54

The other very important part of this building is the story that it tells. All the visitors that come through, there are now being 20 million visitors to Gardens by the Bay. We explain that technologies that are used in the building to make it truly sustainable. Fortunately, people share this using their social media and the word we hope to gets out.

另一个重要的部分是这个建筑背后的故事。共计已有2,000万游客造访海滨湾花园。我们向大家讲解那些让建筑物变得真正可持续的技术。幸运的是，大家在社交媒体上分享所见所闻，我们也希望这些话能被更多人看到。

12：54—13：45

I'm gonna keep talking very very quickly. This is the final section. I just wanted to talk about the possibility of regeneration, and I think this can be an extremely effective way of bringing new life to city. I'm just simply placing an effective piece. That doesn't need to be a building. In this case we are fortunate to be involved in the regeneration of New Castle. A City in North England that has been in really deprived but it's really really started to pick up momentum and become an exciting place and this was to introduce a pedestrian bridge across the river. The move to allow ship to under beneath it and what it means is that you can now walk all the way around New Castle. People can get from one side of the river very easily to the other. And that's a great exchange, also, being the subject of art installations. I assure you that's not what New Castle looks like every day.

我要说得很快才行了。现在是最后一个部分，我想谈谈重建的可能性，我认为这会成为极为有效的方式，赋予城市新生。我简单说一下有效的一面。这不一定要是一幢建筑。在这方面，我们有幸参与到纽卡斯尔的重建中。这座英格兰北部的城市，已经非常落后，但情况还是逐渐好转，并已经成为一个令人激动的地方，要建一座人行天桥跨越河流，桥下的河流里有船驶过，也就意味着您可以步行游览整个纽卡斯尔。有了这座桥，人们能轻松地走到河对岸。这座桥是一个非常棒的活动场所，也成为了一个艺术景观。可以说，纽卡斯尔已经焕然一新。

13：45—14：27

Another project that we're involved in is again in the east London, Stratford. The London 2012 we provided a facility for the basketball events, which look like that on the inside. It's a temporary building. The thing that is interesting about this as a sustainable model is that only the envelope is the supposed piece of structure. Everything else was essentially leased, hired, and after the event, was released back to the owners, reused, recycled. Nothing left on site. Very very small stripped foundations and by simply adjusting the framing of the PBC enclosure we're able to create an exciting, temporary and memorable building.

我们参与的另一个工程也在伦敦东部，在斯特拉特福德。在2012年伦敦奥运会上，我们提供了篮球场的设施，和这个工程的内部很像。这是个临时建筑。有趣的是，作为一个可持续的模式，只有围护结构是按原本的设计建造的。其他地方都通过租赁和雇佣完成，比赛后归还给所有者，或重新使用或回收。没有任何遗留。只用了很小的条形地基，仅将建筑框架调整为PBC围墙，我们就建造了一个特别的、临时性的却让人回味的建筑。

14:27—15:56

We're working on the King's Cross development in London, an area, an old railway area that was extremely deprived and unpleasant to be in. Not quite sure why the columns look green, they are meant to be white, but we're reusing the old gasholder structures which are really high-end Victorian engineering in fact. Some of the difficulties that we've had in refurbishing these columns is they used to drop small children down them to tighten the bolts so you can't get people down there any more to manufacture them. So we're really simultaneous. We are heritage to projects where we're reusing the old structures of the gasholders to create a high grade residential building. And then finally, back to see power station and extraordinary iconic building on the bank of the Thames, which is falling in disrepair. Extraordinary control room that they used to have, these beautiful turbine holes and we are turning it to mixed-use development with a large retail podium, residential flanks, offices and an exciting viewing platform in one of the chimneys. The retail tries to maintain the extraordinary history of the building, the residential spaces on top all get a good view of the extraordinary chimneys, and we hope it will be a very great success. Thank you very much for listening!

我们现在致力于伦敦国王十字车站的改造，这是个老铁路区，非常落后，环境很差。我们不清楚为何柱子是绿色，它们本应是白色，但我们重新使用这些老式的储气罐，其实它们蕴含着维多利亚时期的顶级工程技术。我们遇到一些难题，翻新柱子时，我们发现过去常常需要小孩子从上面滑下来加固螺钉，所以现在不能让人这样进行维护。所以我们同步进行多项改造。我们遇到了瓶颈，主要在重新利用这些老式储气罐来创造高级居民楼。最终，我们回过头审视泰晤士河边的发电站和绝伦的标志性建筑，它们都已年久失修。里面曾有极好的控制室和涡轮机孔，我们将其变成混合使用的开发项目，有大型零售楼层，侧面用来居住，还有办公室和视野极佳的观景平台，建在其中一个烟囱里。零售方试着保护这栋建筑的卓越历史，顶部的居住空间能看到包括烟囱在内的绝佳视野。我们希望这个项目能取得巨大的成功。非常感谢大家的聆听。

第十一单元 知识产权
Intellectual Property Rights

I. 实战练习一

1. 演讲背景

美国联邦巡回上诉法院前首席法官、清华大学法学教授应邀参加在深圳举行的"企业涉外知识产权讲座",讲解标准必要专利。他在演讲的第一部分详细介绍了标准的重要性,标准必要专利必须要履行 FRAND 义务,即遵循"公平、合理、无歧视"原则。由于专利被纳入了标准,因此需要设定合理的专利使用费。标准组织规定,企业必须披露自己的专利才能参加标准制定,否则将受到处罚。由此就引发出"专利套牢"和"使用费累加"的情况。

2. 预习词汇

most prized title 最引以为傲的头衔
intellectual property 知识产权
intellectual property law 知识产权法
receiver 接收器
transmitter 发射器
patent 专利
director 局长
be incorporated into 纳入
reasonable rate 合理使用费
override 否定,颠覆
patented technology 专利技术
SSO/Standard Setting Organization 标准制定组织
breach 违背,违犯
penalize 惩罚,处罚
antitrust law 反托拉斯法
contract law 合同法
doctrine 信条,学说

reasonable royalty 合理使用费
patent hold-up 专利劫持
royalty stacking 使用费累加
port 端口
mediation 调解

3. 演讲文本

00∶00—00∶49

你好！I am very happy to be with you today. I heard so many nice things said about me. I almost did not recognize myself. Actually, my most prized title now is that I am a professor of law at Tsinghua University in Beijing. I teach intellectual property there and I am very proud to be a part of such a fine Chinese university.

你好！今天很高兴和大家见面，我听到了许多赞美我的话，我几乎都没意识到这是在说我。其实，现在最让我引以为傲的头衔就是清华大学法学教授。我在清华教知识产权课程，非常自豪能够成为中国知名高等学府中的一员。

00∶49—02∶48

Today, along with many of my close friends, we are going to talk about the importance of intellectual property in the Chinese market. I just wish to say one word at the beginning, and that is that China is now a leader in the world. This is just a fact. You are the second largest economy in the world and you are a leader. But leadership requires also responsibility. And you have a responsibility as leaders to help the rest of the world understand the value of the rule of law and how it can help their nations to become strong economic forces like China, so it becomes your obligation to not only learn intellectual property law, but to teach it to other nations, to other economies. I think as you recognize this leadership role, you will feel the responsibility that it also places on you.

今天，我和许多好朋友一起，讲讲知识产权在中国市场上的重要性。我希望开始时我能说一句话，就是中国现在是世界的领袖。这是事实。中国是世界上第二大经济体，也是领袖。但是领袖同时也意味着责任，作为领袖你们有责任帮助其他国家理解法治的价值，理解法治又是如何帮助他们的国家成为像中国一样的经济强国，所以你们的责任不仅是学习知识产权法，也包括教会其他国家和其他经济体。我想，当您承认这一领导角色，同时您也会感受到它带来的责任。

02∶48—04∶54

Now today, I am going to discuss a topic which gets a lot of attention in the current intellectual property field. I sometimes think it gets too much attention. It is an important topic, but it's a topic that the law handles or can't handle well. Let's talk about standards and patents. We all know the value of standards in our economy because we have standards, our phones will work anywhere in the world, because there are now standard receivers and transmitters. Because of standards, we can buy a mouse that attaches to any computer, so it allows Chinese manufacturers to make components that will fit in any computer and allows them to compete in the market place, so standards bring great values to our economies. They make our technology more available; they also provide competition throughout the world and thus reduce prices and improve access to technology. Standards are important.

今天，我想谈一个话题，这个话题在当今知识产权领域引起了很多关注。有时我觉得它受到了过多的关注。这个话题很重要，但是法律有时候处理得很好，有时候处理得不好。我们讲讲标准和专利吧。我们都知道经济中标准的价值，这是因为我们有标准，我们的手机在全世界都可以用，因为我们有标准的接收器和发射器。因为有标准，我们可以买到连接到任何电脑上的鼠标，让中国制造商能够生产适合任何电脑的零件，让他们能够参与市场竞争，因此标准给我们的经济体带来了巨大的价值。它们让我们更容易获得技术，也给全世界带来了竞争，因此，这不仅降低了价格，还增加了获得技术的机会。标准很重要。

04:54—05:54

Patents are also important. They provide the incentive to advance our technology. Specifically, they protect the research and development investments of companies and nations. I would like to give you a whole speech about the value of patent law, but I think, as the Director has pointed out, you understand this well. You have been getting more patents than almost any region in the world for many years.

专利也很重要，专利能鼓励技术进步，具体来说，专利保护公司和国家的研发投资。我想给大家做一个全面的演讲，谈谈专利法的价值，但我认为，就像局长所说的，你们已经很好地理解了这一点，你们的专利数量很多，比世界上任何地区都要多，多年来都是如此。

05:54—07:52

I will tell you a little secret. When I said I would come to Shenzhen, it was very easy for me to find my American colleagues to come with me, because they all know Shenzhen very well. In fact, here has been Doctor Beckham, has been here many times. They know that Shenzhen is one of the hot places in the world for intellectual property. Now we need to understand how standards and patent law work together, because you

第十一单元 知识产权 Intellectual Property Rights

see, when you get a patent, that patent can be incorporated into a standard. Now, what does that mean? That means that of course, everyone must use the standard in their technology. See, I held up one of my phones, but I have two. Here in China, I always use my Huawei phone. But a patent, of course, gives the owner of that patent a right to exclude everyone else from using it. That is the power that encourages people to make new technology.

我会告诉您一个小秘密。当我说我会来深圳，我很容易找到美国同事和我一起过来，因为他们都很了解深圳。事实上，Beckham博士来过深圳很多次。他们知道深圳是一大热门地区，在世界上因知识产权而闻名。现在我们需要理解标准和专利法如何才能相得益彰，因为，当您获得一项专利，专利可以纳入一项标准里。这意味着什么？这意味着，当然，每个人必须使用技术中的标准。大家看，我拿着一个手机，但是我有两台手机，在中国，我经常用我的华为手机。但是专利给了专利权人权利，防止其他人使用它。就是这种力量鼓励着人们去创新技术。

07：52—08：49

But what happens when that new technology is important as a part of a standard? Well, the standard will adopt that technology and then the patent owner has the power to require everyone who uses the standard to pay them royalties for the use of their technology. You can quickly see that this could be unfair. People could be required to pay for technology in order to get the standard and the benefits of the standard.

但是，当那项新技术成为标准的重要部分时会发生什么？这个标准会采用那项技术，专利权人有权利要求使用这项标准的所有人支付使用费，因为用了他们的技术。很快您就知道这是不公平的。人们会被要求为技术买单，才能获得这项标准、享受这项标准带来的好处。

08：49—11：06

So, the key is we must have some way to ensure that the benefits of the standard and the benefits of patent law both work together. There are several ways this happens. The most important way is that the standard setting organization. These are the correlations of business around the world corporations that meet together to decide what new standards they should adopt. These businesses in the standard setting organization adopt a requirement that any patent in a standard must also come with a FRAND obligation. Let me explain what FRAND means. FRAND is an abbreviation that means "fair", that's the "F", "reasonable", "R", and a "non-discriminatory" licensing. So fair, reasonable, and universal licensing. A patent owner, if they are in a standard organization must promise to give all users of that standard a very reasonable license rate so that they can't charge unreasonable rates for use of their technology in the standard.

所以，关键是我们必须有办法确保标准和专利法的好处能够相得益彰。有很多方法来实现这一点。最重要的方法就是标准制定组织，也就是全世界相关的企业聚在一起，共同决定应该采用什么新标准。在标准制定组织中的企业规定，标准中的任何专利都必须履行"FRAND"义务，我会解释一下"FRAND"的意思。FRAND是一个缩略词，F代表"公平"，R代表"合理"，以及"无歧视性授权许可"。意思是公平、合理及通用许可。如果专利权人是标准组织中的一员，它必须承诺给予这项标准的所有使用人非常合理的许可使用费，这样专利权人就无法对标准中技术的使用征收不合理的使用费。

11：06—13：42

Now of course, this leads to the important question, what is a reasonable rate? Of course, manufacturers who build products incorporating the standard, they all want the reasonable rate to be incredibly low. They don't want to have to pay to use others' technology. But of course, the patent law will only work, will only protect innovation policies, if there is some reasonable charge for the use of that new technology. That leads to the series of cases (I am) from around the world that I am going to discuss with you today. And you will see that the big issue in all of these cases is what is a reasonable rate? It's not an easy thing to decide what is a reasonable rate, particularly in a standard setting. Because everyone must use the standard, so they are kind of forced to use the technology. Thus, they are forced to pay the rate, the reasonable rate for the patents that are included in their standard. We will see in a moment that for this reason, corps have tended to discount the value of the technology. The key is what if they discount it too much, so that they override the value of the technology itself.

当然，这会导致一个重大问题，合理使用费是多少？当然，产品中包含这个标准的生产商们都希望合理使用费越低越好。他们不想为使用别人的技术买单。但是专利法要生效，要保护创新政策，必须对新技术的使用收取合理使用费，这就会导致一系列的案件，这些案件发生在全世界各地，这也是我今天想和你们讨论的。你们可以看到，所有这些案件中的关键问题就是设定合理使用费。制定合理使用费是不容易的，尤其是在标准设定中，因为每个人都必须使用这项标准，所以他们被迫去使用这项技术。因此，他们不得不交使用费，该使用费是专利的合理使用费，是包含在标准中的。我们马上可以看到，由于这个原因，企业开始贬低技术的价值。关键在于如果他们打的折扣过多，就会否定了技术本身的价值。

13：42—14：20

Let me, how do I make this work here? Here we go, boom, boom, there we go. I am not going to cover everything in this presentation. I use this to teach my class at Tsinghua and the class goes for about four hours. Do you want to spend four hours talking about standards? No, I don't think so. So, I will go more quickly through some of the important cases.

PPT怎么播放呢？好了，开始吧！我不会讲PPT里的所有内容。我用这个PPT给清华大学的学生上课，整堂课用了4小时。你们希望我花4个小时讲标准吗？我猜你们不想。所以，我会讲快一点，快速过一下其中的一些重要案例。

14：20—16：44

Let me first kind of discuss briefly the theory of this. The problem we have in this area is that patented technology does have value and it's actually chosen for the standard, usually because it's the best technology. So, we can't completely eliminate that technology from our standards. We also must give compensation for it or the owners of that technology will not participate in the standard setting, and then we will have a great difficulty in incorporating important technology into standards, so it all really comes down to getting the proper, reasonable rate for technology that has put into the standard. Let me tell you as well that within standard setting organizations, there are often significant questions as to the fairness of companies sitting in those committees that are making the standards, when they know that they have patents on that technology that will allow them to profit from this standard. Because of this, all of the standard organizations have a rule that corporations must disclose their patents before they participate in standard setting and if they fail to do that, there are can be significant penalties placed on them.

首先我们简单讨论一下理论知识。在这个领域里，我们的问题就是专利技术的确是有价值的，技术被选作标准通常是因为这项技术是最好的。所以，我们不能完全将技术从我们的专利中排除。我们必须对它作出补偿，否则这项技术的所有人不会参与标准制定，然后，将重要的技术纳入标准中也很困难，因此，所有问题都可以归结为：如何为纳入我们标准中的技术设定合适、合理的使用费。我想告诉你们的是，在标准制定组织中，也有重大问题，如怎么确保委员会中公司之间的公平性，因为它们是制定标准的人，尤其是当它们知道它们在这项技术上的专利可以让它们从标准中获益时怎么确保公平。鉴于此，所有的标准组织规定，企业必须披露自己的专利才能参加标准制定，如果它们做不到，它们会面临重大处罚。

16：44—18：11

I am not going to spend much time (going the wrong way,) not going to spend much time telling you about that procedure of the standard setting organizations. That's what SSO means. Let me just show you very quickly that there are rules that govern the standard setting organizations and if those rules are breached, you will see many cases here involving companies that breached those rules. If they are breached, there are ways to penalize them. We have antitrust laws, we have contract laws, and we have other doctrines that will prevent companies from exploiting the standard setting process to make profits.

我不会花很多时间（PPT 翻页顺序反了），我不会花很多时间告诉您标准制定的程序，这就是 SSO 的含义。我想快速地向您展示一下，有很多规则用来管理标准制定组织，如果违背了那些规则，您可以看到这里有很多公司违背了那些规则。一旦违背，会有办法来惩罚它们。我们有反托拉斯法，合同法和其他原则来防止企业用标准制定过程来谋取私利。

18: 11—23: 36

Let me address one other thing before we go. Here. This is an area with a lot of faults vandalic, by faults vandalic I mean there are a lot of people who accuse others of abusing the process. Manufacturers, remember, often want low reasonable royalties and so they will accuse patent owners of patent hold-up, that means they are using their patent to get more value than it deserves. They are kind of stealing some of the value that the standard creates for their own personal enrichment. Usually, the argument they make is that patent owners engaging royalty stacking. What does royalty stacking mean? Let me give you one quick example. This is my computer. You all have a similar computer. Right there is a little opening, we call it a port. We use sticking memory device, a USB. You are familiar with this minor part of a computer. How many patents do you think cover that small opening which accepts memory devices? How many would say, 50 patents on that? How many would say 100? How many would say 150? 300? 356! That's the right answer. And actually, that was the right answer about a year ago when I dealt with a mediation amongst the major companies who owns the patents on this technology feature. And of course, it's governed by standard. All USB devices are standard-sized that fit a standard opening, but there are 356 patents on that. Imagine if each owner of a patent waited till the end of negotiations over reasonable royalties and they tried to get more money for each successive piece of technology, each of the patents in this technology needs to be licensed to a reasonable rate. And so, in theory, each owner of a patent could stack their royalty on top of the next and the next and trying to get more and more value out of that one little feature. This is called royalty stacking. Now I will tell you quite honestly that there is no empirical evidence that this happens. It is only a theory. Why doesn't it happen? By the way, you know as a consumer that it does not happen. How do you know that? Well, because how many patents are there on this?

第十一单元 知识产权 Intellectual Property Rights

Thousands, right? And if each patent owner demanded a little more than the last one, stacking one royalty requirement on top of the next. This would soon cause so much money that we could not afford them.

在我们讲下一点之前我想再讲一点。这里，这是一个领域，有人专门负责纠正错误的，这里的"纠正错误"是指很多人指控其他人滥用标准制定过程。记住，生产商总是想得到非常低的合理使用费，所以他们会指控专利权人进行了专利劫持，意思是专利权人用专利获得更多价值，比应得的要多得多。他们就像盗取了一些价值，也就是标准为他们带来了不当得利。通常他们用的论点就是专利权人涉嫌使用费累加。什么是使用费累加？我们快速地看一个例子。这是我的电脑，你们都有类似的电脑。这里有个小的开口，我们叫它端口，用来插入 USB 存储设备。你们对电脑的这个小部位非常熟悉，你们觉得这个小小的端口有多少个专利？多少人说为 50 个专利，多少人说有 100 个专利，150 个？300 个？356 个是正确答案。其实，这个答案是一年前的，那时我正在进行调解，对拥有这项技术特征专利的大公司进行调解。当然，这是用标准进行管理的。所有 USB 存储设备都是标准尺寸，使用标准端口，但是这里面有 356 项专利。想象一下，如果专利权人就合理使用费等到了谈判的最后，他们试图从这项技术中每一个连续的技术得到更多钱。这项技术中的每一项专利都需要给出一个许可的合理使用费。这样，理论上，一项专利的每位所有者都可以在下一个专利上不断累加，只为从那个小小的特征上得到更多的价值。这就是使用费累加。老实告诉您，现在还没有实证表明这个发生了。这只是一个理论。为什么它没有发生呢？顺便说一句，作为消费者，你们知道这个没有发生。您怎么知道的呢？因为这个有多少专利吗？几千种，对吗？如果每个专利权人比上一个所有人要的钱多一点，在下一个专利上累加使用费，很快这就会导致电脑价格很高，我们就买不起了。

23：36—25：01

But what do you know as a consumer? You know that you can walk into any store and buy 50 or 100 different varieties of this, and you also know that the prices are going down, not up. So, as a matter of fact, you can get these for free if you sign up for a lengthy service contract, of course. But you know, for that reason that royalty stacking really doesn't happen. The reason it doesn't happen is simple. The way that patent owners get value from their technology is by keeping the price low so that everyone can use it. If everyone can use it, they get a little tiny bit from each device and that gives them in the market more return on their investment than they would otherwise get. So, the royalty stacking is really a myth.

但是作为一个消费者你们知道吗？你们知道你们可以走进任何一家商店，买 50 或者 100 种 USB 存储设备，您也知道价格会便宜点，而不是更贵。所以，事实上，

171

您可以免费得到这些,只要您签署了长期服务合同。但是您知道,由于这个原因,不会出现使用费累加,不会发生的原因很简单:专利权人从技术中获取价值的方法就是让他们的价格保持在较低水平,这样每个人都可以使用。如果人人都可以用,他们可以从每个设备中获取一点点利润,这会让他们在市场中的投资得到更多的回报,比他们原本可以获得的回报要多得多。所以,使用费累加只是虚构的。

II. 实战练习二

1. 演讲背景

下文也同样摘自美国联邦巡回上诉法院前首席法官、清华大学法学教授在深圳举行的"企业涉外知识产权讲座"上所做的主题为"标准必要专利"的演讲。他在演讲的第二部分详细介绍了"反向专利劫持",并分享了许多现代"FRAND"诉讼案例,例如微软诉摩托罗拉案、苹果诉三星案,说明法院倾向于在制定合理使用费时低估技术的价值。接下来还分享了爱立信诉友讯科技案和联邦科学与工业研究组织诉思科公司案。在演讲的最后他还分析了德国、美国、日本和中国在标准必要专利方面的最新进展。

2. 预习词汇

patent hold-out 反向专利劫持

patent hold-up 专利劫持,专利套牢

to reach a license agreement 达成许可协议

FRAND/Fair, Reasonable and Non-discriminatory 公平、合理、无歧视(原则)

litigation 诉讼

reasonable rate 合理使用费

Microsoft 微软

Motorola 摩托罗拉

procedural exception 例外程序

the 9th Circuit/the 9th Circuit Court of Appeals 第九巡回法院;第九巡回上诉法院

Apple 苹果公司

Samsung 三星集团

ITC/International Trade Commission 国际贸易委员会

sue 控诉,指控

infringe 侵犯,侵权

reasonable royalty 合理使用费

第十一单元　知识产权 Intellectual Property Rights

administrative trade remedy 政府贸易救济机构
overturn 推翻
jurisprudence 法学；法理学
methodology 做法，方法
Ericsson 爱立信集团
D-Link 友讯科技
Federal Circuit/CAFC/the United States Court of Appeals for the Federal Circuit 联邦巡回法院；美国联邦巡回上诉法院
allege 声称
royalty stacking 使用费累加
CSIRO 联邦科学与工业研究组织
CISCO 思科公司
wireless signal processing 无线信号处理
apportionment 分摊，分配，分派
injunction（法院的）禁令，强制令
escrow account 第三方交付账户
European Commission 欧盟委员会
validity 合法性
restore 恢复
grant（尤指正式地或法律上）同意，准予，允许
reasonable license 合理许可
IP high court 知识产权高等法院
NDRC/National Development and Reform Commission 国家发展和改革委员会；国家发改委
State Council of Industry and Commerce 国务院工商行政管理委员会

3. 演讲文本

00：00—01：59

There is also another side to this, however. And that is patent hold-out. Hold-out means that when a manufacturer refuses to pay anything for the technology. They want to use the technology to make their products without paying the owners for using their technology. This happens also. I could spend a long time on the theory of this. But let me give you my basic experience and that is that patent hold-up where the patent owner tries to get more money than they deserve from their technology, and patent hold-out where the manufacturer refuses to pay anything for the use of others' technology. Those two forces are really equal. In every case I've seen, and I've seen many, the patent

173

owners are often exaggerating the value of their technology—hold-up. And the manufacturers, on the other side of the case, are undervaluing the technology—hold-out. And therefore, they refuse to reach a license agreement and they come to the court to resolve that.

　　然而，这也有另外一面。也就是反向专利劫持。反向专利劫持是指生产商拒绝为这个技术付费，他们想使用这项技术来生产产品，不向专利权人付费。这也会发生。我可以花很长时间讲讲这个理论。我想讲讲我的一个基本经历，在专利劫持中，专利权人试图得到更多的钱，比他们从技术中应得的钱要多，而在反向专利劫持中生产商拒绝为使用别人的技术付费。这两股力量是旗鼓相当的。我见到的每个案例中都有，我见过很多。专利权人经常夸大他们技术的价值，形成专利劫持，而另一方面，生产商贬低技术，进行反向专利劫持。因此，他们拒绝达成许可协议，然后在法庭上解决这个问题。

　　01:59—08:42

　　Let's go now to cases where courts had to be involved in setting a reasonable royalty. Boom, we've gone through this procedure cases already. Let's go quickly to the modern FRAND litigation. These are cases where a court has to step in and say what is the reasonable rate of the technology. And I would tell you in advance that courts generally have not done a very good job with this question. Let me show you the first and probably most important case, it's Microsoft vs Motorola. It happened in the State of Washington. Judge Robert, a good friend of mine, was the judge who handled this case. He was asked to determine the value of Motorola patents on important standards for Wi-Fi and video compression. This was a very important ruling just a few years ago. Judge Robert issued a 207-page opinion. I would love to tell you all the details about it, but I will go kind of to the major point of this case. The major point of the case was that the judge ultimately undervalued the technology. Motorola, after it had been in the case for a period of time, made an offer to license its technology at these rates. This was the Wi-Fi technology. It was going to license its Wi-Fi technology for eleven dollars per device that used it, and its video technology for four dollars. That was probably too high. I know this area of technology. Motorola does have some important technology in this area. But these rates were probably too high. Judge Robert eventually gave a half a cent for the Wi-Fi and three cents for the video. Now I must also tell you that's far too low, that's far too low. The problem with Judge Robert's opinion, and once again I always have to say how much I really respect and admire judge Robert. He is a wonderful judge. I just don't agree with him on this decision. The problem with his decision is that he analyzed the fifteen factors that you typically use to set the reasonable royalty and in each one of them he discounted those factors significantly because they were used in the standard. He said because they are in the standard, I am going to discount them. He said I am going to discount them because there is this chance of hold-up and there is this chance of royalty stacking. So, he analyzed hold-up and royalty stacking but he ignored the other side of the equation that the technology users were also refusing to pay reasonable rates for the technology. By only focusing on one side of the equation, I think he made the mistake of grossly undervaluing the technology. You see, however, that this case became very influential on the courts. The 9th Circuit heard the appeal in that case. Usually it would have come to my court at the Federal Circuit. But there was a procedural exception which took it to the 9th circuit. And the 9th circuit affirmed the case really without much analysis. Just saying Judge Robert had done as well as he could do. And so, this case became an important precedent in our system on how you evaluate standard technology which has patents.

接下来我们来看一些案例，其中法院不得不涉及到合理使用费的制定问题。好了，我们已经了解了程序案例，我们再快速地看一下现代"FRAND"诉讼吧。这些案例法院都必须参与其中，并说明什么是技术的合理使用费。我会提前告诉您，法院通常在这个问题上没有给出很好的答案。我想让你们看看第一个、也是最重要的一个案例，就是微软诉摩托罗拉案。这个案例发生在华盛顿州。Robert 是我的好朋友，他是当时的法官，负责处理这起案件，他要定夺摩托罗拉专利对 Wi-Fi（无线传输系统）和视频压缩重要标准的价值。这在几年前是个非常重要的判决。Robert 法官公布了自己长达 207 页的判决观点。我很想告诉您所有相关细节，但是我只能讲讲这起案件的重点。这起案件的重点在于法官最终低估了技术的价值。摩托罗拉涉案一段时间后，提议以这些使用费授权它的技术，即 Wi-Fi 技术。它会授权每个设备以 11 美元的使用费使用 Wi-Fi 技术，以 4 美元的使用费使用视频技术，这也许太高了。我了解这个技术领域。摩托罗拉确实在这个领域有一些重要的技术，但是这些使用费也许太高了点。Robert 法官提议 Wi-Fi 技术的使用费为 0.5 美分，视频技术的使用费为 3 美分。现在我必须告诉您这个价格实在是太低了。Robert 法官的观点存在问题。我想再一次表明我有多么钦佩 Robert 法官，他是位了不起的法官，我只是在这个判决上不同意他的观点。这个判决的问题在于他分析了 15 个通常用来制定合理使用费的因素，对于每个因素他极大地贬低了这些因素只因为标准中用到了它们。他说就是因为它们是标准的一部分所以我会贬低它们的价值。他还说我会贬低它们因为存在专利劫持的风险，但也存在使用费累加的风险。因此，他分析了专利劫持和使用费累加，却忽略了天平的另一端，即使用技术的用户也会拒绝支付技术的合理使用费。他只关注了天平的一端，所以我认为他犯了过度贬低技术价值的错误。然而，您看这个案例在法庭上变得非常有影响力。这个案件上诉到了第九巡回法院。通常这起案件会来到我的法院审理，也就是联邦巡回法院。但是一个例外程序让它直接进入了第九巡回法院,第九巡回法院维持原判,没有进行过多的分析,于是宣布 Robert 法官一如既往地作出了很好的判决。所以,这起案件成为我们体系中一个重要的先例,指导你们如何评估拥有专利的标准技术。

08:42—12:19

Let's look at the next important case. I am going to check my time. How am I doing with my time? OK. I have to move quicker. This is Apple vs Samsung. Quite a famous case which these two companies sued each other around the world. But this particular case occurred in the International Trade Commission, where Samsung sued Apple for using its patents in the standard and Apple did use its patents. And the International Trade Commission examined closely the entire record of the case and found that Apple infringed those patents. They found that the public interest favored protecting the patented innovations. They determined that Samsung had offered a reasonable royalty that Apple refused to accept. It had held out and refused to take the rate. This case, however, has a sad ending. Because the ITC is not a traditional court. It is an administrative trade remedy. Because it is part of the government, our President intervened and overturned this case in favor of Apple, and said, "I am going to prevent the enforcement of the patents and prevent Samsung who have won the case from obtaining any remedy." He recommended that in the future the ITC should look at the public interest and the hold-up factors. But of course, the ITC had really already done that. I must say I think this is not the finest hour of American jurisprudence. This is a sad instance when we allowed politics to intervene in the proper administration of the law. I would encourage China to not make this mistake. But it again was another important indication that in standard cases the courts tend to undervalue the technology.

我们来看看下一个重要案例。我想看看我的时间,还有时间吗? 好的,我要讲快一点。这是苹果诉三星案,这是一个很有名的案例,两家公司满世界打官司。但是这个特殊的案例发生在国际贸易委员会上,其中三星控告苹果使用了标准中的专利,而苹果也确实用了它的专利。国际贸易委员会也非常仔细地核查了这个案例的完整记录,发现苹果侵犯了那些专利权。他们发现大众倾向于保护专利创新,所以给出了判决:三星报出了合理使用价格,而苹果拒绝接受这一价格,构成了反向专利劫持,并拒绝缴纳使用费。然而这个案例却以失败告终,因为国际贸易委员会不是传统意义上的法院,它是一个政府贸易救济机构,因为它是属于政府的。我们的总统进行了干预,并推翻了这个案例,支持苹果,还说:"我会阻止这个专利的实施,阻止三星通过法律救济来赢得这个案子。"他建议,未来国际贸易委员会应该考虑公共利益和专利劫持因素。当然,国际贸易委员会确实已经做到了这一点。我必须说，我认为这不是美国法学界最精明的时候，这是一个令人悲哀的时刻，因为我们让政治干预了法律的正当管理程序。我建议中国不要犯这种错误。但是这也是另外一个重要暗示，表明在标准案例中法院会低估技术的价值。

12：19—13：18

This is another case. It followed Judge Robert's methodology in the Microsoft case that we talked about, which means it discounted every factor in setting the value of the technology because it was used in a standard. Once again, the courts undervaluing the technology. Now I [am] going to suggest to you, however, there are some new cases that are beginning to recognize that the technology and standards have great value and must be acknowledged and used according to its value.

这是另一个案例，它效仿了Robert法官在处理微软案例中的做法，这是我们刚刚讲过的案例。这意味着这一案例低估了制定技术价值的每一个因素，只因这个技术已经用在了标准中。法院再一次低估了技术的价值。然而此刻，我想给你们的建议是，有一些新的案例，它们逐渐开始意识到技术和标准是有着重大价值的，必须依据它的价值得到认可和合理使用。

13：18—15：36

Here is the first case, Ericsson vs D-Link. And this is a case that goes to the Federal Circuit. The district judge had found that D-Link had properly shown that its technology was infringed by Ericsson and that it deserved the running royalty. The Federal Circuit ultimately sends the case back for further analysis of the proper royalty rate. But I want to hit one point in that case that's quite important. It says that if Ericsson or anyone else is going to allege that there is patent hold-up that the technology is vastly overvalued or there is royalty stacking that the patent owners are stacking their royalty demands one on top of another to injure the products, productivity. If there are those allegations, they must be proved. Because I think there is no evidence in the marketplace of royalty stacking and hold-up is just as influential as hold-out, those equal forces. This I think will be an important requirement that they must provide evidence on the record, which if they cannot do, we will help ensure that the technology gets its proper value.

这是第一个案例，爱立信诉友讯科技案。这个案例是在联邦巡回法院受审的。地区法官发现友讯科技合理证明了它的技术被爱立信侵权了，它理应征收使用费。联邦巡回法院最终驳回重审，以便进一步分析合适的使用费率。但是这个案例中我想提一个非常重要的点。据说，如果爱立信或者任何人声称存在专利劫持的现象，过度估计这项技术的价值；或者存在使用费累加，专利权人将他们要求的一个使用费累加在另一个专利上,这会损害产品和生产力。如果存在这些说法,必须有证据能够证实。因为我认为市场上不存在使用费累加的证据,专利劫持和反向专利劫持一样具有影响力,它们势均力敌。我认为这个会成为一个重要的要求,也就是他们必须提供记录在案的证据,如果他们找不到,就能确保技术能得到它真正的价值。

15:36—18:07

Here is the most recent case and it continues the trend of recognizing the value of technology, CSIRO vs Cisco. Once again, I am talking about important technology in patents on wireless signal processing. The key is that when you try to set the reasonable rate of the technology, you must, of course, try to find out how much that technology actually contributes to the market value of the entire product. We call that apportionment. The court makes an important recognition. It recognizes that you should first set this value of the technology. If you do that independent of the standard, then see you can tell if there is a hold-up or hold-out. If the royalty is above, the royalty request of the company is above the real value of the technology, that is hold-up. The patent owners are asking for too much. Or if it's below, if the manufacturer, the patent user is refusing to pay a reasonable rate, then we know that's hold-out. So, the court here is moving towards independently valuing that technology which gives us some way to accurately predict whether the FRAND rate is being properly set. Now this is a recent case, then there will be more in the future.

这是最近的一个案例,它也会延续承认技术价值的这一趋势,联邦科学与工业研究组织诉思科公司。同样地,我会讲无线信号处理专利中的重要技术。关键在于,当您试着制定这个技术的合理使用费时,当然您必须试着找出这个技术对整个产品的市场价值做出了多大的实际贡献。我们称为"分摊"。法院也意识到这个的重要性,意识到您首先应该设定这个技术的价值。如果您独立于标准之外来看的话,您就可以分辨是否存在专利劫持或反向专利劫持。如果使用费过高,企业要求的使用费高于技术的实际价值,那么就是专利劫持。专利权人要得太多。若使用费低于技术的实际价值,如果生产商、专利用户拒绝支付合理使用费,那么我们知道这就是反向专利劫持。因此,法院应该独立评估技术的价值,这也给我们提供了方法,去真正预测一下FRAND使用费制定得是否合理。这是最近的一个案例,未来会有更多这样的案例。

18:07—20:39

Let me in my last few minutes quickly show you some things that are happening elsewhere in the world. In Germany, they had the first standard case, and they dealt with it quite differently. They would automatically impose an injunction on the manufacturer who used patented technology even in a standard and the only way the manufacturer could escape that injunction was to be willing to pay into an escrow account, an amount that was a proper royalty for the technology. This kind of reversed in it. In the U.S. the technology was vastly undervalue by the courts. In Germany, it tended to be the other way that the technology was probably overvalued and the process of the courts favored the patent owner where the patent owners appealed to the European Commission. The European Commission cut back on the German court's policy by requiring at least time for the validity of the patent to be fully examined and requiring at least one year of negotiation between the two parties before the courts could enjoy the technology. The bottom line here is that the European Commission has restored a little of the balance to the processes of German standard setting in patents.

在最后的几分钟里，我想向你们展示一下发生在世界各地的一些事情。德国出现了第一个标准案例，他们的处理方式非常不同。他们会自动签发禁令给使用专利技术的生产商，即使这个专利包含在标准中，生产商可以摆脱禁令的唯一方式就是自愿将费用打到第三方交付账户中，费用数额就是这项技术的合理使用费。在美国这恰恰相反，美国的法院会过度低估技术的价值。然而德国的做法截然不同，技术价值也许会被过度估计，法院诉讼程序有利于专利权人，专利权人上诉到欧盟委员会。欧盟委员会不支持德国法院的政策，要求至少有时间全面检查专利的合法性，也要求双方之间至少有一年的谈判时间，然后才能向法院起诉。这里的底线就是，欧盟委员会恢复了德国制定专利标准过程中的平衡。

20:39—21:49

In Japan, they had that Apple-Samsung again case and they looked carefully at the technology. It was actually quite an excellent case. In the long run, they didn't grant an injunction to Samsung because Apple was willing to try and negotiate a reasonable license. When the parties could not reach a reasonable license, the IP high courts set the damages probably too low. They were following U.S. court precedents at the time. They probably set, following the decisions in the U.S., the value of the technology too low. But again, if they continued to follow the U.S., they would probably improve.

日本也出现了类似苹果和三星的案例，他们非常仔细地核查了这项技术，这是一个非常完美的案例。从长远来看，日本不允许对三星签发禁令，因为苹果愿意尝试协商，获得一个合理许可。如果双方无法达成合理授权，知识产权高等法院也许过低地制定损害赔偿金。日本那时候正在效仿美国法院的先例，他们也许会效仿美国的判决，过分低估技术的价值。但是，如果他们继续效仿美国，他们也许会有进步。

21：49—24：42

China has been involved in standard setting. As we know in China, things do not happen only in the courts. There are also extensive administrative actions. In the first major action, the NDRC initiated an investigation against InterDigital for its use of its standard essential patents. Ultimately, InterDigital under pressure from NDRC agreed to offer a world license without requiring cross-licenses at a low rate. Once again, the Chinese NDRC was like other areas. They probably set the value of the technology too low. There are now policies in place from the State Council of Industry and Commerce that again require the use of a FRAND license by any technology company that includes its technology in standards. And here is a Huawei vs InterDigital cases. The court proceeding involving just the same licenses we just discussed involving NDRC. The Shenzhen Court set the rate probably again too low. But that was similar to the mistake made in other countries, including my own, the United States. The Guangdong Court affirmed in some... we see that this is a complex question. Courts struggled with it; administrative agencies struggled with it. The key, however, is to recognize that both standards and patents bring great value to our societies. Therefore, we need to ensure that there is balance in the way we evaluate technology as it's used in standards. 谢谢！

中国已经参与到标准制定中来了。我们都知道，在中国，法院不是解决问题的唯一途径。也有许多行政案件。在第一起主要的案件中，国家发改委发起了针对 InterDigital 无线电话通讯公司的调查，反对 InterDigital 使用它的标准必要专利。最终，InterDigital 迫于发改委的压力同意授予全球许可，放弃要求较低的使用费来提供互相授权。这也再次表明，中国发改委像其他地方一样，过度低估了技术的价值。国务院工商行政管理委员会现在发布了新政策，任何技术公司使用一个 FRAND 许可都包括标准中的技术。这是关于华为诉 InterDigital 公司案。诉讼程序涉及到同样的许可，我们刚刚讨论过的也涉及国家发改委。深圳法院过度低估了技术的价值。这个错误与其他国家相似，包括我的国家美国。广东法院维持原判，我们认为这个问题有点复杂，法院面临困难，行政机关也在奋力解决这个问题。然而关键在于意识到标准和专利都可以给我们的社会带来巨大的价值。因此，我们需要确保我们用平衡的方式来评估技术的价值，因为技术应用于标准。谢谢！

第十二单元 科学技术
Science and Technology

I. 实战练习一

1. 演讲背景

2013年，被誉为"大数据之父"的牛津大学教授Viktor Mayer Schonberger应邀到"美赛达汽车后市场新商业模式论坛"发表演讲。他在演讲中强调，决定汽车生产商能否取得成功的因素并不是电子产品，而是数据。他还提到了大数据的三大特征：更多、凌乱和相关性，以及如何应用大数据进行汽车销售、生产、改良。

2. 预习词汇

be dazzled by （使）目眩，眼花缭乱
gadget 小玩意/小配件/小装置
gigahertz 千兆赫
transistor 晶体管
high-resolution display 高清显示器
silicon chip 硅片
inventory 库存
focus group 焦点小组
correlation 相关性
aberration 偏差
data point 数据点
recommendation system 推荐系统
sunroof 天窗
configure 配置
flexible production 柔性生产
fingerprint 指纹
alarm 警报器
jet engine 喷射发动机
built-in sensor 内置传感器

parameter 参数
predictive maintenance 预测性维护
gigabyte 千兆字节
real-time 实时
route 路线
navigation system 导航系统
bottom line 盈亏总额
horse power 马力
hybrid vehicle 混合动力车
electric vehicle 电动车
deploy 部署
charging station 充电站
electric motor 电动马达
hook up 连接
battery 电池
self-driving car 自动驾驶汽车
outstrip 超过
computing capacity 计算能力
super computer 超级电脑
multi-modality 多模态
parking spot 车位

3. 演讲文本

00：00—00：08
Good afternoon.
下午好。

00：08—01：21
I am delighted to be here, delighted to speak to you this afternoon. I am going to speak about perhaps the most important development since the industrial revolution, the development called big data. And I am going to talk about what big data will do to the automobile industry. But to do that I need to ask you for a favor. All through this wonderful event here, you have been dazzled, dazzled by products, dazzled by gadgets, dazzled by one gigahertz speed, one billion transistors, graphics, processor units. You have been dazzled by Wi-Fi; you have been dazzled by high-resolution displays. In short, you have been dazzled by electronics.

第十二单元 科学技术 Science and Technology

我很高兴下午能在这儿发言。我将谈谈可能是自工业革命以来最重大的发展,我们称之为大数据。我将谈谈大数据对汽车产业会产生什么样的影响。但首先需要大家的配合。在这个大型的展览会上,大家惊叹于产品,惊叹于配件,惊叹于一千兆赫的速度、十亿晶体管、图表和处理器。大家惊叹于无线网络和高分辨率显示屏。总之,电子产品让大家感到惊叹不已。

01:21—02:29

I need to tell you a secret. And it is a very uncomfortable secret. Your future does not depend on electronic gadgets. Your future does not depend on whether the next generation of cars will have all these dazzling gadgets and there are not. This is like the surface. It is like a very thin cover of gold that comes off very quickly. And underneath it needs to be a foundation that can propel you to new successes and tremendous profits. But that foundation is not electronics. It is not silicon chips. It is data.

跟大家分享一个秘密,这个秘密让人非常不安。未来并不依赖于电子配件,不依赖于新一代汽车是否有这些让人眼花缭乱的配件。这些都只是表面而已,像是薄薄的黄金表层,很快就会褪去。表层之必须有是根基,有了根基才能创造新的成就和巨大的收益。但根基并不是电子产品,不是硅片,而是数据。

02:29—03:10

In my first part of my presentation, I'd like to talk about what big data will do to the selling and the production of cars. So let's start with something very straightforward. And as we go through step by step, what I will tell you about this, then we go through, I need you to come with me on this journey to think along rather than to remain in a mindset of gadgets.

在我演讲的第一部分,我想谈谈大数据对汽车销售和生产的影响。先从简单的开始讲,再一步一步讲大数据。请大家跟上我的演讲思路,不要再想电子装置了。

03:10—04:50

So let's (look about), look at the most important issue, selling cars. Normally, simplistically, selling cars is taking our customers, taking our (somebody has a microphone on; somebody has a microphone on and that is giving a hard time)... anyway, the first thing is selling cars. Normally, selling cars is all about telling the customers what cars are available and connecting them to their preferences. So most customers come in and want this car. But then, in the process of selling the car actually by this, because, they just cannot afford the Ferrari. More sophisticated place what selling cars is all about at its core is matching supply with demand. Here we have cars, there we have customers. How do we connect these two?

所以我们来看看最重要的问题——汽车销售。通常简单地说,销售汽车就是将顾客(有嘉宾的麦克风没关,所以产生了噪音)……第一件事就是销售汽车。通常,销售汽车就是告知顾客可选的车型有哪些,按照他们的喜好匹配车型。所以大多数顾客就选了某款车。但实际上,以这种方式来销售汽车的话,顾客其实是买不起法拉利,而且汽车销售的复杂之处就在于它的核心是供需匹配。这边是汽车,那边是顾客,如何将二者联系起来?

04:50—06:02

So here I have multiple cars and multiple shapes, 10 of them and I have 10 customers. Now how do we sell the ten cars? Well, in the traditional model, we would do a lot of sales and advertisement in order to attract these people, these ten people to buy the cars. And if we are lucky, at the end, a number of them in this case, seven out of the ten people buy seven cars. That is great! We've sold seven cars. But that is terrible, because we have only sold seven cars. There are three people whose demands, whose preferences have not met. And there are three cars that have not been sold. But that is standard, that is how traditional industrial production works.

这儿有不同型号的车,有不同的外观。10 款车,有 10 位顾客。如何销售这 10 款车呢?按传统的方式,我们会大力推销宣传,吸引这 10 位顾客购车。运气好的话,7 位顾客购车就已经很棒了!卖了 7 部车!但其实很糟,因为我们只卖了 7 部车。还有 3 位顾客的需求或者说喜好没有得到满足。还有 3 部车没有卖出去。但这是常态,传统工业生产就是如此。

06:02—07:14

You produce inventory and then you try to sell the products that you have produced. And you do it through advertisement, marketing and good sales techniques. But at the end, you always have cars that don't find buyers. And you always have buyers that don't find cars. Because there is a mismatch between the preferences of the buyers and what you have produced with the car manufacturers have produced and what you have available to sell. And so that can only be overcome in one way. That is to lower the price. Eventually, even the car that will not be liked at its ordinary price that eventually will find a buyer. But at such a low price that it doesn't give you any profit. That is how every manufacturing in retail sector works these days, everything, not just car manufacturing. And it is inefficient. It is wasteful. It is terrible.

生产库存,再售出。出售方式包括进行宣传、营销和使用高超的销售技巧。然而最终总有车没有买家要,总有买家买不到称心的车,因为存在不匹配的情况,买家的喜好、生产出的车辆、可卖的车辆之间不匹配。所以只能通过一种方式来解决，即降价。最终汽车的价格降到了市价以下也能卖得出去。但如此低价又没有任何利润空间可言。现在零售业的制造商都是如此，不仅仅是汽车制造业。这种情况效率低、浪费资源、危害大。

07：15—07：59

But there is no other way. Why? Because we have no data. We have no data at the time of production. What the people actually really want? Yes, we can go out and we can ask them beforehand. We can have focus groups; we can have surveys. But that is little data, small data, and that often is wrong data. As essentially we have no data. We fly blind. And then we hope to succeed.

但没有别的办法，为什么？因为我们没有数据。我们在生产汽车时没有数据。人们真正想要什么？我们可以提前询问，开展焦点小组，进行调查，但获得的数据很少，是小数据，通常是错误的数据。本质上说我们没有数据，我们盲目开展活动，却希望获得成功。

08：00—09：03

In the big data age, this will completely change. Why? Because in the big data age, we have all the information about all our customers. And so we, because we have the data about our customers, can not only match them best to the product that they need, but we can produce the cars that will actually be bought. We can produce the supplies, the elements that go into the car that are actually desired by people, so that at the end of the day, every car finds a customer. And every customer finds a car.

大数据时代则完全不同，为什么？因为在大数据时代，我们掌握了顾客的所有信息。因此我们不仅能匹配他们所需的最佳产品，而且能够生产适销对路的汽车。我们能制造产品，汽车里面加入一些元素使人们产生购买欲。最终，每辆车都有青睐的顾客，每位顾客都能买到心仪的车。

09：03—10：09

The core element to make this happen is data. Data flowing from the customer to the manufacturer, to the retailers, and data being available in plenitude. Until recently, there was no easy way for a data to flow from the customer to the manufacturer. But that is changing. That is changing because in the big data age, we can gather much more data, much more cost-effectively and use it. And that leads to our ability to do big data analysis with the data that we have. Big data analysis is very very different from small data analysis, from the kind of data analysis that we have done so far, from the focus groups, the surveys and so forth.

实现这一目标的核心在于数据。数据从客户反馈给制造商、零售商,而且要大量的数据。直到最近,数据从客户反馈给制造商仍非易事,但情况正在转变。这是因为在大数据时代,我们能获得更多的数据,成本更低,还能使用数据。这就使我们能够进行大数据分析。大数据分析非常不同于小数据分析,不同于我们目前已做过的数据分析,不同于焦点小组、调查等。

10:09—11:11

It is different in three ways. We call this more, messy and correlations. Let me step that through very quickly. More. More means that we can now collect much more data about the particular question that we have, that we want to answer. Will red cars sell next season, for example. With much more data about the particular question that we want to answer than ever before when we were limited to working with just a small sample. That way we can let the data speak; we can break it down into small details, understand not just big groups of customers, but understand small sub-groups of customers and address their needs precisely.

大数据的与众不同在于三方面。我们称之为"更多、凌乱和关联性"。我快速解释一下。"更多"意味着我们现在可以收集更多的数据,以了解想要解答的问题。例如红色的汽车下个季度会畅销吗?现在我们有更多的相关数据,但在以前我们只能局限于很小的样本数据。现在我们可以让数据说话,我们可以将数据分解,不仅可以了解大的顾客群,也了解小的顾客子群,精准地满足他们的需求。

11:11—12:09

Second is messy, the second quality of big data. It means that we don't have to go out and hire extremely expensive experts to collect a few data points for us about our customers' needs and desires. Pay them a lot of money. We can use less exact, more messy data. If we have only small amounts of data, we couldn't do that. A small aberration, a small inexactness in this data would have caused the result to be wrong. If you only have three data points, getting one wrong is dangerous. If you have three billion data points, getting three of them wrong, it doesn't matter.

第二个方面就是"凌乱",大数据的第二个特质。这意味着我们不需要请收费昂贵的专家收集几个数据点来了解顾客的需求和愿望。这样要付专家很多钱。我们可以使用相对粗糙、凌乱的数据,但如果只有少量的数据是无法达成目标,小偏差或不精确性都会造成错误的结果。如果只有三个数据点,错了一个就很危险;但如果有三十亿个数据点,错了三个,结果不会受影响。

12:09—13:45

More and Messy together lead us to the third one and that is correlations. Correlations mean that there are connections between two phenomena, between two things that tell us what is happening, but they don't tell us why. We don't know the causes of things through big data, but we know what is happening. And often times, that is good enough. With big data correlations, more stock is sold on the Internet through recommendation systems than ever before. You probably have already tried it when you buy something online, the system recommends you products. Amazon has a recommendation system based on big data correlations. That works so well that just this recommendation system is responsible for 30% of Amazon's sales. Big data correlations also drive a lot of services of other Internet companies like Google and so forth. They do not tell us why, but they tell us what.

"更多"和"凌乱"一起引出了第三个特质，即"关联性"。"关联性"意味着联系存在于两种现象、两个事物之间，告诉我们发生了什么，但不会告诉我们原因。我们无法通过大数据得知原因，但知道正发生什么。通常这就足够了。有了大数据的关联性，更多商品可以在网上通过推荐系统出售，数量超过以前。可能您在网购的时候已经体验过，系统会向您推荐产品。亚马逊有个推荐系统，就是基于大数据关联性建立的。这个系统运行良好，给亚马逊带来了30%的销售额。大数据关联性也推动了很多服务业务，包括谷歌等其他互联网公司的服务业务。数据关联不告诉我们原因，但告诉我们是什么。

13:45—14:55

Now, that is a fundamental difference from the past—knowing what customers want, not why. Remember your old days, current days, every good sales person would say, you need to know your customers. You need to understand, you need to know why they want a particular car. If they want a bigger car, you need to find out why. Have they started a family? The grandparents move in? Sales experts told you to go out for the why. That is old fashion. That is outdated. And the war of big data correlations, correlations will tell you what customers want, not why. But knowing what they want is good enough. And therefore, supply can meet demand.

这就是现在与以前的根本差别——知道顾客想要什么，不是为什么。回想以前甚至现在，好的销售都会说您要了解顾客，您要知道为什么他们想要某款车。如果顾客想要辆大点的车，您要知道原因。顾客是不是生孩子了？家里老人过来住了？销售精英告诉您去寻找原因。这是旧式做法，已经过时。现在大家都关注大数据关联性。关联性会告诉您顾客想要什么而不是为什么。但知道顾客想要什么已经足够了。这样供需可以匹配起来。

14:55—15:30

Now, already in many instances when you buy, when people buy cars, they can go online and select the various options, from the color of the interior, the color of the exterior, the wheels, the engine, of course, all the way to all this luxurious safety and security details of that car, fancy and make driving more comfortable.

现在很多情况下，人们买车都可以上网做各种选择，包括内饰颜色、外观颜色、轮胎、发动机、舒适安全性、车的安全细节。车辆精美、驾驶更舒适。

15:30—16:01

I just bought a car myself. And I was given this beautiful 80-question survey online. Do you want an automatic acceleration? Do you want a system that automatically and electrically moves your seat and remember seat position? Do you want a sunroof? So I can configure my car.

我自己刚买了一辆车。我收到一份有80个问题的在线调查问卷。您想要自动档吗？您想要电动记忆座椅吗？您想要天窗吗？因此，我就可以配置我自己的车。

16:01—17:02

But you know what? From most of these options, I have no idea what I wanted. Because I have preferences, I have needs that are not easily mapping onto the questions of whether I need the sunroof or not. The system isn't asking me, do you want a bigger space in your car? Do you want to see the stars? They just ask the sunroof. It does not tell me what the option is. And so these options are not meaningful to me. Yes, I have them, but I can not exercise them. I cannot do much with them. That's the small data age. We give people the options but they don't know what to choose. At the end, they are probably unhappy with the product.

但是，在诸多选择中，我不知道自己想要什么样的车。因为我的喜好、需求并不能很容易地通过一些问题反映出来，诸如我是否需要天窗之类的问题。调查并没有问我您是否想更大的汽车空间？您是否想看星星？调查只是问我天窗，调查并没有告诉我这个问题是什么，因此对我而言并没有意义。我是完成了调查，但并不起多大作用。这就是小数据时代。我们为人们提供问题，但他们不知道选什么。最终，他们可能对产品并不满意。

17:02—18:08

What we need to do is to understand truly what these people need and then to match millions of options to their needs, each and every customer individually. But we can only do that if we know the customer and what the customer wants, not why. This is what meaningful options is all about. It's not about options. Options, to create options is easy. To make them meaningful to your customers can only be achieved if you have the data available. That, of course, leads to something that is called flexible production, namely that we ask the customers what they want and only when we know what they want we produce the car that they want. Therefore, we never produce a single car that is not wanted and therefore, not being sold.

我们需要做的就是真正了解人们的需求,用数以百万计的选择去迎合顾客的需求,每位顾客都如此。前提是我们了解顾客,知道顾客想要什么,而不是为什么。这些才是有意义的选择。并不是光是提供选择。提供选择很容易,要使选择对顾客而言有意义就得有数据。这就谈到柔性生产,即询问顾客想要什么。了解了顾客的需求,我们才生产他们所需要的汽车。因此,我们从不生产没有需求、没有销路的车。

18: 08—19: 35

Flexible production with pioneer by IT companies, like Apple and Dell. A few years ago, Apple had an inventory of 160 days of sales, a computer inventory of 160 days of sales. Today, they have an inventory of 2 to 3 days of sales. There is no inventory for them, because they only produce when they already have a customer for the stuff that they produce. Now, I know that in the car manufacturing industry, to an extent, that already works, but it does not work down to the components. And therefore, flexible production can go much further than it does today. That's how selling cars will change. In the future, with big data, by knowing more about our customers and doing the big data analysis, we will be able to match supply and demand to achieve efficiency that we haven't achieved so far.

柔性生产由IT公司倡导,如苹果和戴尔公司。几年前,苹果公司有160天的库存。现在,他们只有两三天的库存。对他们而言没有库存,因为他们只生产已有顾客需求的产品。现在我知道在汽车制造业中,已经在一定程度上实现了柔性生产,但还没有用在零部件生产上。因此,柔性生产仍有进一步发展的空间。这就是汽车销售的变化趋势。未来有了大数据,对顾客有更多的了解,并做了大数据分析,我们就能够匹配供需,提高效率。

19: 35—21: 43

The second element is how to improve cars in the process. Now for decades, improving cars meant a bigger engine, a faster car, a car that uses less gasoline. In the future, improving car manufacturing, improving cars themselves will be tied to data. Some of those connections will be quite interesting and quite obvious. For example, researchers currently are working on a system, whereby, when you sit down, a system measures your seating position. Every person, it turns out, has a different back side. And when you measure the back side, it is like a fingerprint. So there are researchers out there who have now devised a system where you don't need a key anymore for your car. You just sit in a car seat. And the car recognizes it is you. If it does not recognize you, it will not start. It is an entire set of device. And it is built on a capacity to take the individual posture, the seating position of people and render that in the data form and then compare it. That is quite interesting. It's a big data application. And it will be used in the next generation of cars.

第二个要素就是如何改良汽车。数十年来,改良汽车意味着发动机更大、车速更快、更省油。未来改良汽车生产、改良汽车都依赖于数据。有些联系会很有趣、很明显。比如研究人员最近在研究一个系统,您坐下时,系统会测量您的坐姿。每个人都有不同的背影,测量背影就像在采集指纹。因此有研究人员现已设计出无钥匙启动系统。您只需坐在座位上,汽车就会识别出您。如果不能识别,车辆则无法启动。这是一整套装置,可以把人的坐姿拍摄下来,转化成数据形式进行比较,很有趣。这就是大数据应用,将应用于全新一代汽车。

21:43—22:19

But it can do more. Because through big data analysis, gathering these data and analyzing it, we can also understand that the seating position of most people changes before they fall asleep when they get tired on the wheel. And we can use this insight to set off an alarm in the car to wake them up, much better and much more precise than the current alarms that we already have in cars working today.

其作用远不止于此。通过大数据收集、分析,我们就知道大多数驾驶员坐姿发生改变时,他们可能驾驶疲劳,想睡觉。我们可以据此启动汽车警报器叫醒驾驶员,其效果和精确度远超目前已有的警报器。

22:19—23:15

But it's not just about data gadgets in the cars like the entire set device that I just mentioned that run on data. Our entire way of thinking about manufacturing will change. Here is a good example. It is an example from a company that you perhaps know called Rolls Royce. You may associate Rolls Royce with very expensive luxurious cars. But it turns out that Rolls Royce is also producing something else, namely jet engines. And in fact, Rolls Royce is the third largest jet engine company in the world.

不只是汽车配件,像我刚才提到的那套装置那样,应用了大数据,我们整个制造业思考方式都将改变。有个很好的例子,关于劳斯莱斯。您可能会将劳斯莱斯与昂贵的豪华汽车联系起来,但劳斯莱斯也生产喷射发动机。事实上劳斯莱斯是世界第三大喷射发动机公司。

23:15—24:31

Now, they are... Ten years ago, they were manufacturing jet engines. Today they are a big data company. Why? Because in every one of those jet engines, they have built-in sensors. The sensor measures pressure, temperature, vibration, sound and all of these diffcrent parameters continuously, and then sends these data back to Rolls Royce Central Headquarters. And then Rolls Royce does analysis. It is able to predict when a part in the jet engine will break before it breaks. Because parts don't break like that. Parts, before they break, give different sounds, different vibrations. Their signature, their sensor signature changes. And you can pick this up. And then Rolls Royce goes in and exchanges the part before it breaks.

十年前,他们在制造喷射发动机,今天他们是一家大数据公司。为什么呢?因为在每一个喷射发动机里都有内置传感器。传感器测量压力、温度、震动、声音及各种参数,持续不断检测,然后将这些数据传送回劳斯莱斯中心总部,然后劳斯莱斯进行数据分析,能预测何时喷射发动机部件会出故障。部件不会就那么出故障。部件在出故障之前会发出不同的声音、震动,传感器特征会发生改变,您能接收到故障信息,之后劳斯莱斯介入,提前更换零部件。

24:31—25:55

Now for jet engines, this is really good. Because if the engine breaks, well, the airlines, the airplane is in the air, you have a problem. That is one of the reasons why today we have so many airplanes not with four engines as they used to be, but just with two. Because the reliability of the engine has gone up. Why has the reliability gone up? Because they are able to exchange the parts before they break, so that they almost never break in flight. This is called predictive maintenance. And it works extremely well. It is a big data application. Every airplane, like the Airbus 380 that I show you, on each flight, collects gigabytes of data. These gigabytes of data are sent to Rolls Royce, analyzed and compared with all the other data that they have. And then Rolls Royce either knows that a part needs to be changed soon or not. Now you think this might be great for airplanes. But what does this have to do with you? It has to do a lot.

这对于喷射发动机是福音,因为如果发动机出故障,而飞机在飞行,麻烦就大了。这也是为什么现在很多飞机不像过去一样用四个发动机,而仅用两个,因为发动机可靠性提升了。为什么可靠性能提升?因为能够提前更换故障零部件,因此飞行中故障概率几乎为零,这就叫预测性维护,效果非常好。这就是大数据应用。每一架飞机，像我展示的空客 A380，都收集上千兆字节数据，然后将这些数据发送给劳斯莱斯，进行分析，与其他数据作比较，然后劳斯莱斯就知道某个部件是否需要马上更换。现在您会想：这对飞机而言很棒，但跟您有什么关系呢？关系很大。

25：58—26：52

UPS is arguably the world's largest package delivery and logistics company. They operate every single day 60,000 delivery vehicles around the world that deliver packages. Now UPS said, we can do predictive maintenance, too. They build sensors into the engines of their cars. They got all of the information where the car was, how fast it was driving and so forth, collect all the information real-time to big data analysis, in order to improve the delivery routes and the delivery routine system.

UPS 无疑是世界上最大的包裹派送和物流公司。每天都有 6 万辆快递车在世界各地派送包裹。现在 UPS 称其也可以做预测性维护。他们将传感器置于物流车发动机内部，就能获取信息，包括车辆位置、速度等。实时收集信息，做大数据分析，目的是改善包裹派送路线和包裹派送操作系统。

26：54—28：05

That way, for example, they found out that their navigation systems are all wrong. The navigation systems try to find the fastest, shortest way to the goal, to the target destination. But it turns out when you do the analysis, it is better, safer, more reliable and faster to make three right turns, rather than a left turn. Right turn, right turn, right turn and a right turn gets to the same point as one left turn. But because right turns don't have to cross the road, have taken less time, because you don't have to wait and have less tendency to cause accidents. And so they changed the delivery, the software for their delivery vehicles that navigates these vehicles.

比如他们发现导航系统都有问题。导航系统想通过最快最短的路线到达目的地，但经过大数据分析发现更好、更安全、更可靠、更快的路线是三个右转弯，而不是一个左转弯。四个右转弯和一个左转弯到达同一个地方，但因为右转弯不需要穿过马路，因此用时更短，因为不需要等，也不容易发生事故。因此他们改变了物流车的导航软件。

28：05—28：41

They also implement predictive maintenance exchanging parts before they break. Just last year, exchanging parts before they break saved UPS 50 million kilometers, 50 million kilometers. Think about what this means in terms of fuel being saved. It is good for the environment but it is also good for the bottom line, because you don't need to pay for that.

他们也进行预测性维护来提前更换零部件。去年，提前更换零部件为 UPS 节省了 5,000 万公里。想想这意味着节省了多少燃料。有利于环境，也有利于效益，因为节省了燃料的钱。

28：41—29：58

But there is more to it, because this data that is being generated, collected through these sensors for predictive maintenance, can be used to improve the car itself. If you know that the part is likely to break, you can exchange that part. But the next generation of this car will have a different part, a part that doesn't have this fault, this problem in it. So with big data, car manufacturers are dramatically improving the product, but only if they get the data. Keep in mind, Rolls Royce gets the data. In the case of UPS, the car manufacturers don't get the data. It is UPS that has the data. We'll get back to that in the second part of my speech.

益处远不止这些。因为通过传感器收集的数据在用于预测性维护之外，还能用于改良汽车本身。如果您知道某个部件可能出故障，就可以进行更换。而新一代同款车则会更新这个部件，不再存在这样的缺陷。因此有了大数据，汽车厂家极大地改良了产品，前提是他们获得相关的数据。记住是劳斯莱斯获得这些数据。就 UPS 例子而言，汽车厂家并没有数据，是 UPS 拥有大数据。我们在我演讲的第二部分会再次探讨这一问题。

29：58—31：24

So selling cars changes, improving cars changes to big data. But then there is a third element to it, an element that I would like to call enabling the dream, the dream the cars embody and come with. Cars used to be about horse power and pouch, the smell of oil and leather, the smooth sound of a mighty engine. But in the big data era, cars are more so than ever before, about something else, about finding elegant solutions to our complex and nomadic lives. A car is a beautiful thing. But for many people, what they are really interested in is that the car solve their mobility question. Their mobility desires and demand. For most people, therefore, the dream is mobility.

销售汽车、改进汽车都发生变化，原因是大数据的产生。但还有第三个要素，我称之为实现梦想——它体现在汽车上，也伴随汽车产生。汽车以前意味着马力、钱包、汽油和皮革的味道、大功率引擎的轰鸣声。而在大数据时代，汽车更是如此，也有新的内涵。汽车是让复杂、频频出行的生活更舒适。汽车很美好，而对于很多人来说，他们真正感兴趣的是汽车解决出行的问题。他们有出行的愿望和需求，因此对于大多数人来说，他们的梦想就是出行。

31: 24—33: 01

Now when we think about mobility, this kind of a dream requires big data at a level that we could never have thought would be necessary before. For once, we need to, with big data, understand the needs of mobility. What do people really want? You may have heard that BMW is in its big, big, big drive for the i serie, the i3 and the i8. The i8 we just reviewed yesterday. These are not cars. BMW has invested one billion USD into a mobility eco-system around these cars, because it turns out that these are hybrid cars and they may run out of electricity. What do you do for longer stretches? And so BMW came in and said, in these cases, we need to have another car available on demand for the owners of an electric car who want to go a long distance, just for a day or 2 or 3, that they need this special equipment.

我们的出行梦想对大数据的需求远超出想象。我们要用大数据了解出行的需求,人们真正想要什么?您可能听说过宝马大力推行i系列汽车,i3和i8。i8我们昨天刚研究过。这些都不是汽车。宝马投资了10亿美元发展i系列的出行生态系统,因为这些是混合动力车,可能有没电的情况。如果要开很长时间怎么办?宝马称在这种情况下,我们需要为电动车车主提供另一辆车,满足其长途旅行需求。旅途可能是一天、两天或者三天,他们需要这样的车。

33: 01—33: 57

We need to understand the needs of the people, their mobility needs, in order, for example, to deploy charging stations. Right now, our entire infrastructure of charging cars that is refilling them with gasoline is based on gasoline car. The density of gas stations is based on having a tank of 50, 60 and 70 liters. It is not based on electric cars that run out of a charge up to 100 or 150 or 200 kilometers or even less. So we need if we think about electric mobility, electric cars and mobility, have a different infrastructure of charging station.

我们需要了解人们的出行需求来部署充电站。加油站的基础设施是为使用汽油的汽车建设的。加油站的密度取决于油箱的容量,即50～70升,并不是取决于充一次电行驶的里程数,如100～200公里。因此考虑到如果是电动车出行,我们需要建立新的充电站基础设施。

33: 57—34: 49

We need to give the users and the cars a better sense of how far they can go with the charge, not in terms of kilometers, but in terms of will this charge fulfill your needs for the day. Will it get you to work and back? Will it be able to bring the kids to the piano lessons and back? For that, we need data. Where is the place for charging stations? For that, we need data. How many charging stations do we need? For that, we need data. How many alternative vehicles do we need? For that, we need data. We need to understand the mobility needs. And for that, we need data. We need to plan the mobility infrastructure and for that, we need data. And we need to allocate the mobility elements for these needs. And for that, we need data.

我们要让用户更清楚车的电量能行驶多远,不是以公里数计算,而是以能否支撑当天的行程计算。这些电量够不够上下班？够不够接送孩子上钢琴课？这需要数据。充电站建在哪里？这需要数据。需要建多少个充电站？这需要数据。需要多少辆备用车？这需要数据。我们要了解出行需求,这需要数据。我们需要规划交通基础设施,这也需要数据。我们需要分配这些出行要素来满足需求,这也需要数据。

34:49—35:50

I talked already about electric and hybrid cars, which require us to understand mobility and this hybrid mobility very differently. And without data, massive amount of data about how people use the cars, what kind of mobility they want to achieve, we will not succeed. That is where the really smart car manufacturers are investing their money right now. Everybody can put an electric motor in a car. Everybody can hook up a battery to it. That is easy-peasy. What is not easy-peasy is to understand the mobility infrastructure for these new cars to work and to be successful, to be appreciated and embraced by the customers.

我已经讲了电动车和混合动力车,我们要明白出行和混合动力车出行有很大区别。没有海量的数据,无法了解人们如何用车,如何出行,我们是无法成功的。这就是真正聪明的汽车厂家目前的投资点。任何人都可以在汽车里装电动马达,都可以连电池,这简单得很。难的是了解混合动力车出行的基础设施,有了这些设施,混合动力车才能使用,才能得到重视,受到欢迎。

35:50—37:11

Or think of self-driving cars. Every car manufacturer is now announcing self-driving cars. Google has a self-driving car. And that Google's self-driving car can not drive through cities, at speeds of 50 or 60 kilometers an hour. Do you know how many data points this self-driving car from Google collects and evaluates every second? One billion data points! One billion data points! That's what is required to have a self-driving car. It far outstrips the computing capacity of the super computer just a few years ago. But the self-driving car itself will be dead if it is not part of an eco-system, part of an infrastructure in which it works, where its maps are continuously updated, where the road conditions are measured and then digitized and transferred to the cars on the road, etc, etc.

想想无人驾驶汽车。每个汽车厂家都在宣传无人驾驶汽车。谷歌有无人驾驶汽车,谷歌的无人驾驶汽车无法以50或60公里每小时的速度在城市里行驶。您知道谷歌无人驾驶车每秒需要收集和评估多少数据点吗?10亿个数据点!这远远超过了仅仅几年前的超级计算机的运算能力。但无人驾驶车要生存,就需要有生态系统,有配套基础设施,地图要不断更新,路况要进行测量、数字化,再传输给汽车。

37:11—38:20

Or think of parking in multi-modality, very important in cities that have traffic problems. Many large cities have traffic problems. Many large cities have parking problems. One of the biggest hottest items in the world, in the West right now, are Parking Application. That is smart phone applications that tell you where there is a parking spot available, so that you can find one quickly. That is fulfilling a very important need. And that cannot be done by the car itself. The car does not know. Somebody else needs to know about what is behind the line of sight around the corner if there maybe an empty spot. That is the kind of infrastructure that is based on data. That will be crucial in the success of the next generation of cars.

想想多模态停车,这对存在交通问题的城市非常重要。很多大城市都存在交通问题,很多大城市都有停车问题。目前最热门的一款应用,不论是在全世界还是在西方国家,就是停车APP,这个智能手机APP能告知您哪里有空的停车位,这样您很快就能找到位置,这样就解决了一个重大问题。靠汽车本身是不行的,汽车不知道有没有车位,需要有其他人知道我们视线看不到的地方是否有空余的位置——这就是基于数据的基础设施。这是新一代汽车能否成功的关键。

38:20—39:55

Our lives, ladies and gentlemen, our lives are complex and getting more complex every single day. What we want our cars to do in the future is not to give us a gazillion of options, is not to have 10 new gadgets that come with a manual that thick that I am not reading. I want my car to make my life simple again. I want my car to de-complexify my already complex life, to make life simpler for us individually and for us as a society. And doing so requires much more than what just a car can do. It requires, like selling cars and improving cars and enabling the dream, requires big data, the ability to collect data at vastly greater scale than we knew, the ability to analyze and the ability to make sense of it. Doing so will radically change how we sell cars, how we build and improve them, and most importantly, are we enabled to dream. Thanks very much!

女士们、先生们,我们的生活日益复杂。我们并不需要汽车给我们无数选择,不需要10个新部件，我们并不会去看这些部件的厚厚的说明书。我希望我的车能简化我的生活，无论对于个人还是群体都是如此。我们需要的远远不止汽车能给我们提供的。就像销售汽车、改良汽车和实现梦想一样，需要大数据，需要能以更大的规模收集数据、分析数据、理解数据。大数据将彻底改变我们如何卖车，如何造车，如何改进车，甚至改变我们实现梦想的方式。谢谢大家！

II. 实战练习二

1. 演讲背景

被誉为"物联网之父"的 Kevin Ashton 应邀在"2015年腾讯智慧峰会"上做主旨发言，解释了什么叫做"物联网"，纠正了普通公众对物联网的误解，并指出物联网具有三大要素：自动采集数据的传感器，帮助人类做出决定的数据，改变生活、改变世界的决定。三者循环往复。他还列举了几个物联网的例子，包括数码相机、GPS、RFID、无人驾驶汽车等。

2. 预习词汇

Internet of Things/IoTs 物联网
high definition 高清
facial recognition algorithm 人脸识别算法
shipping route 航运路线
molecule 分子
atom 原子
supply chain 供应链
fuel 燃料
mobile device 移动装置
shaver 剃须刀
frivolous 无聊的
gimmick 花招
shipping container 集装箱
keyboard 键盘
sensor platform 传感器平台
atmospheric pressure 气压
altitude 海拔
fingerprint 指纹
heartbeat 心跳

interface 接口
deployment 部署
navigation 导航
Uber 优步
chip 芯片
antenna 天线
radio wave 无线电波
Four Seasons 四季酒店
room key 房卡
tag 标签
windshield 挡风玻璃
self-driving car 无人驾驶汽车
Foxconn 富士康
economics 经济学
feedback loop 反馈圈
bauxite 铝土矿
aluminum 铝

3. 演讲文本

00：00—00：43

Thank you. So I just did something that, maybe five years ago, would have seemed amazing. I took this tiny device from my pocket. I just took a high-definition movie of everybody here in Guangzhou and it is now available on the Internet. People all over the world are looking at you right now. I also run a facial recognition algorithm to see who was waving and who wasn't waving. I will be complaining to some of you later.

谢谢大家！我刚才做的事情可能在五年前还是不可能的。我从口袋里拿出手机，拍下了一段高清视频，在座各位都在视频中，现在这段视频已经放上网了。全世界的人都在看这段视频。我还可以运用人脸识别算法看看谁挥手了，谁没挥手。我待会要和没挥手的人谈谈。

00：43—01：49

The world changes incredibly quickly. So what would have been a miracle five or ten years ago is ordinary today. The most important thing to understand about the future is that the future is easy to predict, but it is hard to believe. So as we talk this morning about the Internet of Things, I can show you the future. That is the easy part. The hard part is believing it just as five years ago it would have been hard to believe that somebody could take a movie using a device from their pocket and broadcast it instantly to the world.

世界瞬息万变，五年或十年前认为不可能的事情，如今已是再平常不过了。最重要的是，对于未来，做出预测很容易，难的是相信这些预测。今天早上我们的会议主题是物联网，我可以给你们预测一下未来，这很容易。难的是让你们相信我的预测，就像五年前人们很难相信可以这样拍一个视频，就是用手机拍一个视频，还能即时发布，让全世界看到。

01: 49—02: 32
We understand that the world we live in is connected. But it is important to remember that it's actually been connected for a very long time. What you see here is a network, a very important network. This is air travel around the world. What is travelling around the world is not information on airplanes. It is people. It is packages. It is luggage. It is things.

我们已经知道世界是互联互通的。但重要的是要知道其实世界互联互通已经很长时间了。你们现在看到的是一个网络，一个非常重要的网络，它其实是全球的飞机航线图。全世界飞的不是飞机上的信息，而是里面的人、包裹、行李，各种物品。

01: 49—03: 38
Here is another network. These are shipping routes. These are ships moving around the planet. I could show you a map from the 1800s, and it would look a lot like this. This is a very old and important network. What is travelling on these ships is not ones and zeros. It is things, finished goods, raw materials, food, things the world depends on everyday. This is energy. This is oil and natural gas, moving through pipelines, or on ships, again, not ones and zeros. Molecules, atoms, things.

这是另一个网络。这是航运路线。这是在全球航行的轮船19世纪的航海图，是这样子的。这是一个古老但重要的网络。轮船上装的不是信息，是物品，各种成品、原材料、食物，人类赖以生存的各种物品。能源、石油和天然气，通过管道，或轮船运输，再次强调，船上装载的不是信息或数据，是分子、原子、物品。

03: 38—04: 56
You could turn off the Internet right now, and it would be very inconvenient, but we would survive. If you turn off the global supply chain, all these other networks, these networks of things, networks of atoms, civilization would collapse probably in 48 hours. To survive, we depend first and most on things, not on information. Why?

Because we are physical. We are in a way things. You can't eat ones and zeros. Ones and zeros would not keep you warm. Ones and zeros would not make your car go, or light your house at night. All those needs are physical because we are physical. So these networks are profoundly important. Then this is the network we think about when we think about networks.

如果您现在关掉互联网，虽然会非常不方便，但还可以生存下去。但如果您暂停全球供应链，包括刚才那些网络，那些物品网络，原子网络，人类文明可能在48小时内消失。要生存，最重要的是物品，而非信息。为什么呢？因为我们是肉体，在一定程度上是物品。数据不是食物，不能解决温饱，不能驱动汽车，不能在夜晚点亮房间。我们需要物质，因为我们就是物质。所以上述网络都十分重要。我们想到这些网络的时候会想到另一个网络。

04：56—05：28

This is the Internet. This is data moving around the world. This is the most recent of our networks. When we talk about the Internet of Things, our vision is to integrate this network, this network of information, this network of bits, of ones and zeros, with all those other networks, with all the things that we depend on for our survival.

那就是互联网。这是在全球流动的数据。这是各个网络的最新状况。说到物联网，我们希望能整合这个网络，这个信息的网络、计算机网络、数据网络，把它与其他网络进行整合，与我们赖以生存的物品整合。

05：28—06：43

Before I go on, I want to talk about what the Internet of Things is not. Because when I say things, we can take stuffs like water, and fuel, and food, and clothing so much for granted that we forget they are things. So when I say things, a lot of people think about gadgets or devices, stuffs you can plug in, rice cookers or refrigerators. Then when they think about the Internet, they think about these things, these mobile devices that we call smart phones. They assume that somehow the Internet of Things means the rice cooker that talks to the APP. That is not the Internet of Things. There are hundreds of truly terrible ideas that fall into this category of it is the thing that you plug into the wall that talks to an APP.

在继续往下讲之前，我想澄清一下大家对物联网的误解。我所说的物品，指的是水、燃料、食物、衣服，这些随手可得的容易被我们忽略的物品。所以当我说到物品，大多数人会想到装置和设备，需要用电的东西，比如电饭锅和冰箱。想起互联网，人们会想到的物品是移动装置或手机。他们认为物联网就是与APP连接的电饭煲。这不是物联网。很多错误糟糕的想法认为这些插电的东西，连接APP的东西就是物联网中的物品。

06:43—07:32

This is real. I didn't make them up. This is a smart wine bottle. I guess it tells you how drunk you are and are none. A smart bikini tells you whether or not you are getting sunburn or give you a clue. If you are getting sunburn, it hurts. You don't need to look at the map. Smart water bottle tells you whether or not you are thirsty you probably already know. This is the very recent entry, the smart shaver. I guess it tells you whether or not you shave today. If you don't know whether or not you shave today, you probably have problems that this device cannot solve. I know that I didn't shave today.

事实就是如此。我没有乱说。这是一个智能酒瓶,我想它可以告诉您醉酒程度。一件智能比基尼可以提醒您是否晒伤,但其实晒伤的话,皮肤自然会痛,您没有必要去看量表。智能水瓶可以告诉您您是否口渴,但您自己可能已经感觉到渴了。还有最新的智能剃须刀,可以告诉您今天有没有刮胡子。但如果您不清楚自己今天是否刮了胡子,那么可能您的问题就是这些设备无法解决的。我知道我今天没刮胡子。

07:32—07:54

So this is not the Internet of Things. These ideas are somewhat frivolous, a little bit like gimmicks and not terribly interesting. So when you think about the Internet of Things, try not to think about gadgets you plug into the walls that talk to your phone.

这不是物联网。这些都是无聊的想法,有点像噱头,但是无趣的噱头。所以,当您想到物联网的时候,试着忘掉那些插电的连接手机 APP 的设备。

07:54—08:48

So what is the Internet of Things? What do we mean? Let me show you one of the very best definitions of the Internet of Things that I have ever seen. Wen Jiabao, 2009, gave a speech in which he said, "Here is what I understand about the Internet of Things. The Internet of Things is the wisdom of the earth." This is a beautiful, a beautiful insight into what we are actually talking about when we talk about the Internet of Things.

那么到底什么是物联网?指的是什么?让我分享一个特别好的定义,这是我见过的有关物联网最好的定义。温家宝在 2009 年的一个演讲中说到:"以我的理解,物联网是地球的智慧"。这是一个非常独到的见解,解释了究竟什么是物联网。

08:48—09:33

If you think about all those networks that I just showed you, if you think about this room that we are in right now, how much information is around us? I don't mean how much information has been captured, how much information is there on your phone right now. I mean how much information is there altogether. How many bottles of water, how many people; what is the temperature? How noisy is it? How much air is there? How clean is the air? What kind of carpet is on the floor? There is so much information. It is almost impossible to conceive just in this room now.

想想我刚才所展示的网络，想想在这个会场里，我们身边有多少信息？我不是指被采集的信息，也不是您手机上有多少信息，我指的是一共有多少信息。多少瓶水？多少人？温度是多少？噪音有多大？空气浓度是多少？空气洁净度是多少？用的是哪种地毯？我们周围有这么多的信息，弄清这个会场里有多少信息几乎不可能。

09：33—10：37

Expand that to the world for those shipping containers moving around and so on. What you see is that not only do we live in this world that is brimful of billions and billions and billions of terabytes of information being created every single second, but we now have captured hardly any of it today. Why? Because the data capture technology of the 20th century was the keyboard, maybe the bar code. Everything was very manual, with these very sophisticated machines for processing information, for storing information, for sending and sharing information, but our technology for capturing the information was us typing. So all of the information in the world was not getting captured.

再扩展到全球的集装箱等等。我们生活的世界中有海量的信息，每秒钟都产生海量的信息，但是我们今天几乎采集不到。为什么？因为20世纪的数据采集技术工具是键盘，或许是条形码。所有工具都是手动的，使用非常复杂的机器来处理信息、存储信息、发送和分享信息，但我们采集信息的技术就是打字，因此我们无法采集到世界上所有信息。

10：37—11：14

Now move to the 21st century, move to now, things have changed. They will continue to change. The Internet of Things is not this year; the Internet of Things is this century. We are 15 years in to a revolution that would take 100 years. What is happening is we are starting to gather this data about the world that we could not gather before. We are doing it automatically. We are doing it using sensors.

到了21世纪，到了今时今日，情况发生了变化。而且会继续变化下去。物联网不是今年的话题，而是这个世纪的话题。这场变革已经15年了，完成变革一共需要100年。我们正在收集全球数据，那些之前无法收集的数据。收集过程是全自动的，由传感器完成。

11：14—11：53

Let me ask you a question about this device. What is this? I know we call it a phone. But is it really a phone? How many hours do you spend each day using a device like this? How many of those hours are for phone calls? Phone is just one APP on this portable device. It is possibly not the APP you use most frequently.

我想问大家一个关于这个设备的问题，这是什么？我知道大家称之为电话。但它真的是一部电话吗？您每天有多少时间花在这个设备上？又有多少时间是用来打电话的？电话只是这个便携装置的其中一个应用，而且很可能不是您最常用的应用。

11：53—13：19

Here is something else about this. This contains about ten sensors. It is not even a portable computer. It is really a portable sensor platform. It is automatically gathering information about the world right now. What sensors are in this device? GPS. It knows where it is automatically. It is gathering location information automatically. It has a camera. I just used that. It can sense the room and we can analyze that image and get data from it automatically if we want to. It senses atmospheric pressure. It senses motion. It knows how many steps I've taken and it knows what altitude I am at. It knows all these things automatically. It can detect my fingerprints, my heartbeat. It can listen. It has more senses than we do. So although we call it a phone, don't be confused. It is not a phone. It is a mobile sensor platform, with an interface that is part of the Internet of Things.

电话还有其他的应用，它有大约10个传感器。电话不算是便携式电脑，其实是便携式传感器平台。能自动实时收集世界各地的信息。其中有哪些传感器？有GPS，GPS能自动定位，自动收集方位信息。还有相机，我刚刚才拍照。它可以感知这个会场，我们可以通过分析照片自动得到照片中的数据。它可以感应气压，感应动作，知道我走了多少步，知道我所处的海拔高度，它能自动地知道所有这些信息。还可以识别我的指纹，读取我的心跳，听到我的声音。它比我们拥有更多的感官。所以，尽管我们称之为电话，但是不要被名字迷惑了。它不是电话，而是一个移动的传感器平台，有连接物联网的接口。

13：19—14：40

So we gather more and more data about the world automatically. That is not the wisdom of the earth. Right? That is data about the earth. How do we convert that data into wisdom? Well, this is partly why the Internet, part of the Internet of Things, is so important. Because by streaming all this data from all of these different sources into the Internet, we can then process them, using software, using automatic analysis tools, artificial intelligence, machine learning, we can turn the data into some kind of decision. That might be a decision that tells me to do something. It might be simply tell me to walk or I am not getting enough exercise, but it can also be a decision that is sent to an automatic system, a robot, some device. But as this action taken because of the decision, that changes the world. Something changes in the world and then we got all the way back to the beginning. We have new data to capture. We can make a new decision. Perhaps it can improve the decision we've already made. We change the world all a little bit more.

因此，我们自动收集到全球越来越多的数据。但这不是地球的智慧。对吧？这只是地球的数据。我们如何把数据转化为智慧呢？这就是为什么互联网，也就是物联网的一部分如此重要。因为通过把各种来源的数据输入到互联网，我们就可以进行处理，通过软件、自动分析工具、人工智能和机器学习，我们就可以用数据做出决定。比如告诉我们去做某件事。可能就是简单地告诉我需要多走路或者运动量不足，这个决定也可以发送至一个自动系统，机器人，或某种设备。因此而采取的行动能改变世界。世界发生了改变，接着我们又重头再来。我们可以采集新的数据，做新的决定，或者还可以改进之前的决定。我们一点一点改变世界。

14：40—15：07

So when we talk about the Internet of Things changing the world, yes, that is a big visionary statement, but it is also literally true. So that is what the Internet of Things. It is an amazing network of automatic sensors that leads to automatic decisions that changes the world and then back again. That is the Internet of Things.

我们在谈论物联网改变世界，是的，这是很有远见，但也千真万确。这就是物联网的本质。它是一个由自动传感器组成的神奇网络，能自动做出决定，改变世界，循环往复，这就是物联网。

15：07—15：24

Now, one of the funniest questions you can ask about the Internet of Things is when will the Internet of Things begin. When is the Internet of Things going to happen? I have been hearing about this for a while. But when will it take off? It is already here.

人们问过的关于物联网最有趣的问题是物联网将在什么时候开始？物联网会在什么时候开始呢？我听到这个问题有一段时间了。什么时候开始呢？其实物联网现

第十二单元 科学技术 Science and Technology

在已经存在。

15:24—17:14

Let's talk about the deployment of network sensors during the 21st century that has already happened. One of the most basic sensors, one of the easiest ones to talk about, because we are so familiar with it, is the digital camera. Now, here is a nice example of digital photography because that photograph of me was taken five minutes ago. I know 'cause I only wore this tie here, OK. We couldn't have done that in the 1900s, not very easily. In the year 2000 right down here, there weren't pretty much know digital cameras. There were a few and they were very unusual and they weren't networked. So it's only 15 years ago. Gradually, year on year, the number of digital cameras shipped in the world has grown and grown. Those cameras have become more and more networked until about two years ago we reached a point where more than a billion digital cameras were sold in a year. That was about 2013. So it went from none, 13 years later, one billion today, that number is probably more like three billion a year. Of course, the old digital cameras are still around. So there is lots and lots digital cameras in the world. They are taking more and more photographs than ever before. There are probably more photographs taken this year than they have ever been taken in the rest of human history put together because of this technology.

我们来谈谈网络传感器部署,21 世纪的部署已经开始了。其中一种最基本的传感器,最常讨论的传感器,大家都很熟悉,就是数码相机。关于数码摄影有一个很典型的例子,因为我刚拍了一张数码照片,就在 5 分钟前。我认出这张照片是因为我打了这条领带。这在 20 世纪是做不到的,起码很难做到。2000 年的时候,很多人不知道数码相机。数码相机很少,很罕见,不能联网。这就是 15 年前的情况。慢慢地,年复一年,数码相机越来越多,逐渐能联网。2 年前,数码相机的年销售量超过了 10 亿台,也就是 2013 年。13 年前,从零开始,到如今年销售 10 亿台,之后可能每年会销售 30 亿台。当然,旧式的数码相机仍然存在。因此,世界上有大量的数码相机,它们拍摄的照片也越来越多。今年拍的照片很多,可能比之前人类历史上拍的所有照片还多,这都有赖于数码相机技术的发展。

17:14—18:20

Now, how automatic is this? right? If you take a digital photograph, most of the time today, you hold up your phone, typically, or your camera, you push a button. That is fairly manual. But think about what is happening once we put that in each on the network. You can stop like this. This is how facial recognition technology works. Facial recognition technology is becoming much more sophisticated now. We have tools that

205

can identify whether someone is a male or a female, how old they are. Are they smiling? We can process group photographs, not just individual faces. We can process motion. You can put security cameras in cities and see if somebody is being attacked. You can identify suspicious behavior all automatically. So digital photography is part of the first wave of network sensors gathering the wisdom of the earth.

这种技术的自动化程度有多高呢?如果拍摄一张数码照片,现在您会举起手机,准确的说是您的相机,按一个键,这完全是手动的。但想想我们把它放到网上的时候会发生什么?您可以这样,人脸识别技术就会工作。人脸识别技术越来越成熟。我们有工具识别性别、年龄、甚至表情。我们可以处理整组照片,而不[只]是个人的脸部,我们可以处理动作,我们可以在城市各处安装监控摄像头,查看是否有人被攻击,还可以自动识别可疑行为。因此,数码摄影是网络传感器的第一波,凝聚了全人类的智慧。

18:20—19:23

Here is another ubiquitous sensor technology that we don't even think about anymore. So if we go all right back to like 2005, 2000, GPS was a military technology that was just not available to regular people like us. It was only around the mid-2000s that it became a consumer product, a tool. So in 2008, there were maybe a few hundred million GPS devices sold. Again, as we progress from then to now, the number keeps creeping up and up and up. More and more GPS until again around 2013, we crossed the one billion unit mark. Where would we be without GPS today? How did we get around before 2008? I don't remember.

还有另一个常见的传感器技术,我们很少留意到。如果回到2000年,GPS还是军用技术,普通人是不能用的。到了2005年左右,GPS就变成了消费品,变成了一个工具。到了2008年,几亿个GPS装置售出。从那时到现在,售出的数量快速增长。直到2013年,销量突破了10亿大关。如果没有GPS我们现在的生活会怎样呢?我们在2008年之前是如何出行的?我已经不记得了。

19:23—20:20

The other thing is, partly because of the networking, if you integrate the sensor data, if you add the GPS data to the camera data, you can do even more powerful things. GPS is not just for navigation. It used to be about maps, OK? But think about, for example, there is an application here in China call Didi or in the US it is Uber, like taxi ride sharing that is GPS enabled. But there are two pieces of GPS information that APP needs. One is where you are. One is where is the nearest driver. But putting both pieces of information on the Internet and connecting them, you find the car close to you

第十二单元 科学技术 Science and Technology

quickly. So GPS is not just about maps, but other stuff as well.

而且,在一定程度上,因为网络,如果您整合传感数据,把 GPS 数据加入相机数据,您可以做更厉害的事。GPS 不仅用于导航。它以前是移动地图,对吧?比如中国的滴滴打车,在美国就是优步,其拼车功能是以 GPS 为基础的。但其中有两部分的 GPS 信息是 APP 所需要的,一是您的位置,二是最近的司机的位置。把两样信息放入互联网,将其连接起来,就能快速找到最近的司机。所以 GPS 不仅是地图,还有很多用处。

20:20—21:15

So there is another ubiquitous sensor that has emerged in the last few years and is networked. It is important that this is networked. Now, you could say, oh, hang on a minute. That is not the Internet of Things. That is smart phones. 'Cause most of these digital cameras are in smart phones. Most of those GPS devices are in smart phones. So what we are really saying is smart phones are becoming popular. That is true. In the last few years, we've seen about three billion smart phones a year shipped. So now, there are lots of smart phones in the world. So why don't we look at an Internet of Things technology that is not in the smart phone and see how that is doing, because maybe it is not the Internet of Things. Right? Maybe it is just smart phones.

还有另外一个无处不在的传感器在几年前就出现了,现在已经联网。联网很重要。但是,可能您会说,等一等,这不是物联网,这是智能手机。因为大多数数码相机安装在智能手机内,大多数 GPS 设备也安装在智能手机内。所以应该说智能手机越来越受欢迎。这话不错。在过去几年里,每年智能手机的销量高达 30 亿。所以,现在全球有很多智能手机。那么我们为什么不找一种没有应用在智能手机上物联网技术,看看会有什么效果呢?因为或许这并不是物联网,是吧?或许这只是智能手机。

21:15—23:08

The most fundamental Internet of Things technology is probably a technology called RFID that stands for Radio Frequency Identification. The most simple wireless network computer that you have ever seen is just a chip with a little antenna that allows you to discover the identity of something using radio waves over a range of, you know, maybe 10 or 20 feet. I've got one right here. If you are staying in the Four Seasons, you have an RFID-enabled room key. You cannot even see it 'cause it is just like a piece of plastic. But inside here, there is a chip with an antenna. So how many RFID tags are we shipping each year compared to cellphones? Perhaps everybody would agree smart phones are everywhere. So how is RFID compared? Well, for the last few years, we have

207

shipped one billion more RFID tags every year than smart phones. So if you think smart phones are everywhere, let me tell you something. RFID is even more everywhere. But you can't see it. It is invisible. It is in room keys. It is in tickets for buses and sporting events. It is at the back of the supply chain. It is in car windshields to get you through toll roads more quickly. It is disposable, which is one of the reasons we shipped a lot of it. Here is another Internet of Things technology that is becoming truly ubiquitous. It will continue to grow.

物联网最根本的技术大概就是RFID无线射频识别技术。最简单的无线网络计算机就是一个芯片加一条小天线，这样就可以让您发现和识别物体，方法是利用无线电波，10—20英尺的无线电波识别。我这里就有一个这样的装置。如果您住在四季酒店，会得到一把RFID房卡。但是您看不到RFID，因为钥匙就是一片塑料。但其内部有一块芯片和一条天线。RFID标签每年的销量与手机相比如何呢？大概所有人都会认为智能手机无处不在。那么RFID呢？过去几年里，RFID标签的销量比智能手机每年多10亿件。所以如果您认为智能手机无处不在，那么我要告诉您，RFID更加无处不在。但是您看不见它，它是无形的，藏在房卡里面，藏在公车卡或体育比赛门票里面，它在供应链的背后，它在汽车的挡风玻璃里，让您更快通过收费站。RFID是一次性产品，这也是它需求量大的原因之一。这是另外一种物联网技术，越来越常见。它将会不断发展。

23：08—23：56

So Internet of Things is already all around us. Who is leading? Who is leading the world in the Internet of Things in this incredible historic technology transformation going on in the world? In the 1980s and 1990s, I guess we could call that the Personal Computing Era. That was the world of personal computer. But if we look at high tech exports during that period, the clear leader, this line here, is the United States. Then we have sort of Germany, South Korea. This red line is China. China is a fairly typical high tech exporter in the 1980s and the 1990s.

所以，物联网就在我们身边。那么谁是先锋呢？在重大的技术变革席卷全球时，谁在引领世界物联网？20世纪八九十年代，我想大家可以称之为个人电脑时代，那是个人电脑的黄金时期。看看那时候的高科技出口，明显领先的国家，如这条线所示，就是美国，之后是德国和韩国。红线代表中国，中国也是典型的高科技出口国，就在那个时期。

23：56—25：36

Then around the year 2000, the Internet of Things Era begins. I coined the term the Internet of Things right here in 1999. Something starts to happen. China's high tech exports start to increase. China surpassed South Korea very quickly and it surpassed Germany, and then around 2004, 2005, surpassed the United States to become the biggest high tech exporter in the world. It continues to grow. Here is Wen Jiabao. When he starts talking about the Internet of Things publicly, the first head of state in the world in history, to the best of my knowledge, to ever say the word Internet of Things in public. Others did it later, but he was the first. China's exports continue to grow. The U. S. declines. Germany becomes the second largest high tech exporter in the world. Probably by now, South Korea which is also pretty substantial in the Internet of Things, is about to take over the United States. But this is the country that is leading the Internet of Things revolution. This is the country that will continue to lead the Internet of Things revolution. This is where the action is right now and the defining technology of the 21st century.

2000年左右，物联网时代开始了。我发明了"物联网"这个词，就是在1999年。开始发生重大变化。中国的高科技出口开始增长，很快超过韩国，接着超过德国，在2004年、2005年左右，中国超过美国，成为了全球最大的高科技出口国，规模不断扩大。温家宝在公开场合谈到物联网，他是全球首位国家领导人，如果我没记错的话，首位公开谈及物联网的国家领导人。之后也有别人谈及物联网，但他是第一位。中国的出口持续增长，美国的在下降，德国成为了全球第二大高科技出口国。可能在目前来看，韩国的物联网已经非常强大，将要取代美国的地位。但中国在引领着物联网变革，将继续引领物联网变革。中国现在的行动将深刻影响着21世纪的技术。

25:36—27:08

Give you some real examples before we finish. One very cool, very exciting, very fast moving Internet of Things technology is the self-driving car. This is a sensor platform on wheels. It shares the information over the Internet. It gets the information over the Internet. Because it does such things, it can drive itself. One of the funniest questions that I've got asked about the self-driving car is "Is it safe"? That is the wrong question. The right question is "Are human-driven cars safe?". The answer is no. How many people are killed by human beings driving cars every day? Three thousand. Three thousand people a day. What percentage of those deaths are caused by human error? Not really error, but just human that not being able to drive? About 95% of them. How many accidents of self-driving cars had? A few. How many of those are caused by self-driving cars? Zero. There are many reasons to embrace self-driving cars. Safety is the first one. They are also used fuel more efficiently. They use the lamps more efficiently. They are much better.

结束前，我给大家举些真实的例子。有一项非常激动人心、快速发展的物联网技术，那就是无人驾驶汽车。这是一个移动的传感器平台，可以把信息分享到互联网上，也可以从网上获取信息，因为有这样的能力，所以能进行自动驾驶。我听过的最有趣的问题，有关于无人驾驶汽车最有趣的问题是"它是否安全"？这个问题本身就是错误的。正确的问题应该是人驾驶的汽车是否安全？答案是不安全。每天有多少人死于车祸？3000人。每天3000人。其中多少事故是人为过失？也不能说是过失，应该说是人没有开好车？答案是95%。无人驾驶汽车导致的事故呢？很少。刚才所说的事故多少是无人驾驶汽车造成的呢？零。支持无人驾驶汽车的理由很多。安全是第一条，而且能高效节能、节约用电。无人驾驶汽车更好。

27：08—28：21

They are coming. But where are they coming from? Well, interestingly, the countries leading the self-driving car revolution are the first two on that last chart. Germany is providing the car technology, the BMW ConnectedDrive. China is providing the self-driving technology, the Internet of Things technology. In fact, one of the leading companies in China, in self-driving cars, is Tencent. They have a partnership with Foxconn and another one with BMW. They are not just WeChat anymore. Maybe that is already obvious, but in case. OK? This is the company that is driving—no pun intended—driving forward into the self-driving era. This is Yutong, another Chinese company. They make buses. They have already tested a self-driving bus in China, buses that drive themselves.

无人驾驶汽车来了。但是来自何方？有趣的是，引领无人驾驶汽车变革的国家就是最后一张图中的头两个，德国提供汽车技术，就是宝马Connected Drive；中国提供无人驾驶技术，物联网技术。实际上，其中一家领军企业在中国，引领无人驾驶汽车发展的企业就是腾讯。腾讯和富士康、宝马合作。腾讯不仅仅有微信，可能大家都知道，但我还想多说一句，好吧？腾讯确实正在引领无人驾驶的时代。宇通，另一家中国企业，是大巴制造商。他们已经测试了一款无人驾驶公交车，就在中国。

28：21—29：24

What is the overall point of all those stuffs? What is the economic benefits of the Internet of Things? It is really very simple. Think about what the word economics means or economy means. It is how much can you do with a certain amount of input, how much can you output with a certain amount of input. That is economics. That is what economics is. The problem we face in the human race is that our population is going incredibly quickly. It is not just growing. People are living longer. They are expecting a higher standard of living. There are seven billion on earth right now. There will be ten billion on earth right now by about 2090. People used to live to be about 40 and now we live to be about 80. Lots of more people living much longer, running a much better life.

上面这些意义何在？物联网能带来怎样的经济利益？答案很简单。想想词语"经济学"或"经济"是什么意思，意思就是您投入后能得到多少产出，这就是经济学，这就是经济学的意思。人类面临的问题是人口迅速增长。不仅人口数量在增长，寿命也越来越长。人们期望更高的生活质量。现在全球有70亿人，还将增至100亿人，时间就在2090年前后。以前平均寿命为40岁，现在是80岁。寿命越来越长，生活也越来越好。

29:24—30:44

How do we sustain that? What is the economic problem? It is about doing things with things. We are back to things again, you see. What the Internet of Things does is by giving us this automatic information about the world and in creating this feedback loop where we learn about the world and change the world, learn about the world more and continue. We are becoming able to do more with less, to get greater outputs from fewer inputs. That is already happening. So compared to the year 1990 or so on, we are already producing more with fewer inputs. What we are going to see over the next few decades is the amount we use going down and the amount we produce going up. The secret of all these is good information. Good information is automatic information. Good information is automatic networked information. Good information comes from the Internet of Things. So the key to scaling the human race up to sustaining our ever growing population without destroying the planet in the process is the Internet of Things. The home of the Internet of Things is right here, right here in China.

如何才能维持呢？有什么经济问题？我们要用物品来解决这些问题。看，我们又回到了物品的话题。物联网为我们提供全球自动获取的信息，打造了反馈圈，让我们可以了解世界，改变世界，更多地认识世界，如此往复。我们可以事半功倍，以较少的投入得到更多的产出。这已经实现了。与1990年前后相比，我们现在的确可以事半功倍。在未来几十年，投入将继续减少，产出将继续增加。其中的秘密就是优质信息。优质信息是自动获取的信息，是自动联网的信息，是来自物联网的信息。适应人口增长、使人类可持续发展的秘诀，而且能做到不破坏地球的方法就是物联网。物联网的发源地就在这里，在中国。

30:44—32:21

So just to bring it all back down to earth. The largest fleet of self-driving vehicles in the world right now is not what you think it might be. It is this eight-meter-high truck made by a Japanese company called Komatsu. There are hundreds of these trucks right now driving themselves around Western Australia. What they are doing is strip mining. This is an aerial photograph, looked from above, strip mining a raw material called bauxite. The part of Western Australia where the bauxite is is not a place anybody wants to live. So it is very hard to get truck drivers. So it is very helpful to have self-driving trucks. More outputs, fewer inputs. The bauxite is separated into a waste material called red mud, a useful element called aluminum. The aluminum is turned into soda cans. The point is, if you want to see the Internet of Things, it is right there in your next can of soda, which contains aluminum, which was probably mined by a self-driving truck in Western Australia, a self-driving truck that could not operate if it didn't have a platform of network sensors that is part of the Internet of Things. The revolution is here and now. But we have a long way to go. It is going to be a very exciting journey.

回到现实情况。目前全球最大的无人驾驶汽车队可能和您想象有出入。它是一辆8米高的卡车，由一家叫做小松的日本公司生产。数百辆这样的卡车正穿梭于西澳大利亚州，被用于露天采矿。这是一张航拍照片，展示了露天开采一种名为铝土矿的原材料。西澳盛产铝土矿，但没人愿意居住在这里，所以很难找到卡车司机。无人驾驶卡车帮了大忙，事半功倍。铝土矿被离析为一种名为红土的废弃材料和一种有用的元素铝，铝可以制成易拉罐。重点是如果您想看看物联网，您身边的易拉罐就是物联网，因为它是铝做成的，这些铝很可能是由西澳的无人驾驶卡车开采的。无人驾驶卡车的运作取决于网络传感器平台，那就是物联网的一部分。物联网的变革就在身边，但是前方的路还很长，这将是一段令人激动的旅程。

32:21—32:36

If you like to know more, you can find me on Twitter. This is also my WeChat ID. So say hi to me on WeChat. We can continue the conversation. *Xiexie*!

如果大家想了解更多，可以关注我的推特。这里是我的微信号，也可以加我微信，我们可以继续交流。谢谢！